Falkirk

Falkirk

A History

Ian Scott

BIRLINN

This edition published in 2006 by
Birlinn Limited
West Newington House
10 Newington Road
Edinburgh
EH9 1QS

www.birlinn.co.uk

First published in 1994 as *The Life and Times of Falkirk* by
John Donald Ltd, Edinburgh

ISBN 10: 1 84158 469 X
ISBN 13: 978 1 84158 469 0

British Library Cataloguing-in-Publication Data
A catalogue record for this book is available from the British Library

Typeset by Iolaire Typesetting, Newtonmore
Printed and bound by GraphyCems, Spain

Contents

List of Illustrations   vii
Acknowledgements   xi
Preface   xiii

1   The Legions of Rome   1
2   Christian Missionaries and Feudal Barons   18
3   Wallace and the Battle of Falkirk, 1298   29
4   The Livingstons of Callendar   36
5   Kirk Session and Baron Court   50
6   Cattle Trysts and Highland Armies   70
7   A New Iron Age   90
8   The Transport Revolution   103
9   Stentmasters and Feuars   115
10 Church and School in Victorian Falkirk   128
11 Building a New Town   146
12 Falkirk at War   173
13 All Change   194
14 The Towns   206
15 The Villages   242
16 Today and Tomorrow   298

References and Further Reading   311
Index   315

List of Illustrations

1. An impression of the Antonine Wall — 5
2. The surviving ditch at Watling Lodge in Camelon — 6
3. The sculpted panels on the Bridgeness Slab — 7
4. Geoff Bailey during the excavation of the Falkirk Fort — 11
5. The Callendar Riggs coin hoard — 13
6. Arthur's O'on — 14
7. The Blaeu map of Stirlingshire, 1654 — 21
8. Old Parish Church 'Foundation Stone' — 22
9. An impression of the 'Thanes's hall' — 25
10. The land divisions in Falkirk area around 1300 — 27
11. Plan of the Battle of Falkirk, 22 July 1298 — 31
12. The tomb of Sir John de Graeme and grave of Sir John Stewart — 34
13. The pre-Reformation church of Falkirk and the Livingston roof boss — 38
14. The Livingston effigies from the old Parish Church — 38
15. The embroidered panel from Callendar House — 43
16. James Livingston of Almond, Ist Earl of Callendar — 56
17. The original Cross Well from 1681 with its 1817 replacement — 67
18. The steeple and tollbooth erected in 1697 — 72
19. Plan of the Battle of Falkirk Muir, 17 January 1746 — 76
20. The stained glass windows from the Howgate Centre — 78
21. The Battle of Falkirk monument erected in 1927 — 80
22. William Boyd, Earl of Kilmarnock, executed in 1746 — 82
23. The first William Forbes of Callendar — 86

24. Callendar House in 1789   88
25. *Copperbottom's Retreat* by John Kay, published in 1837   89
26. Charles Gascoigne of Carron Company   93
27. A naval carronade in action   94
28. The yard at Carron Works in the mid nineteenth
    century   96
29. The bascule bridge on the Forth and Clyde Canal
    at Camelon   105
30. William Symington's *Charlotte Dundas*   108
31. The mouth of the Union Canal tunnel at Bantaskine   110
32. The Union Inn and Lock 16, Camelon   112
33. The Cross of Falkirk around 1820   117
34. A view of Falkirk from the south in 1824   119
35. The Silver Row building of the original Erskine
    Church, later the Roxy Theatre   129
36. The Parish Church built in 1811   131
37. The Tattie Kirk   133
38. The Grammar School of Falkirk in Park Street   140
39. Silver Row from the Callendar Riggs showing
    St Francis School   142
40. Comely Park School   144
41. The 1880 office building of Carron Company   147
42. The new building of James Aitken's brewery opened
    in 1900   148
43. The Glasgow Buildings in Williamson Street   150
44. The Sheriff Court building opened in 1868   151
45. The Town Hall in Newmarket Street opened
    in 1879   152
46. Silver Row in the early years of the twentieth
    century   154
47. The first Matron, Miss Joss, and her staff at
    the new Cottage Hospital in 1895   162
48. Falkirk Infirmary in Thornhill Road before
    the First World War   163
49. One of the first trams passing the Burgh
    buildings in 1906   167
50. Newmarket Street around 1900, looking east   169
51. The west end of Falkirk around 1910   169

52. Falkirk High Street, looking east, around 1910   170
53. Brodie's butcher's shop at the bottom of the steeple   171
54. Women at work making munitions for Falkirk Iron Company   177
55. The First World War Certificate of Honour presented to Private James Morton   178
56. The Dollar Park War Memorial   179
57. The moulding shop at Carron Works in the early years of the century   180
58. Three of the art deco buildings from the 1930s   184
59. Digging a shelter in Falkirk town centre   190
60. The Shieldhill Home Guard   191
61. Falkirk Football Club: Scottish Cup Winners, 1957   195
62. The new Falkirk Technical College, opened 1961   198
63. The pedestrianised High Street after the restoration project   201
64. The old Howgate, lost beneath the new shopping centre   202
65. The Callendar Square shopping centre   203
66. Canal Street, Grangemouth   207
67. Postcard view of Grangemouth Old Town   208
68. Charing Cross, Grangemouth   209
69. Charing Cross looking east   211
70. Zetland Park with the Grange School in the centre   212
71. Grangemouth Airport with the terminal building and hangars in 1939   216
72. Kinneil House, Bo'ness   220
73. Old Bo'ness, with the clock tower of the original Town Hall   225
74. Corbiehall with the original Parish Church   228
75. Kinneil Colliery   230
76. The Hills of Dunipace, graveyard   232
77. Denny Cross and Parish Church around 1900   234
78. Denny Town House   239
79. Union Canal locks at King's Bridge   243
80. Camelon Main Street at Rosebank Distillery   246
81. Industrial Bonnybridge around 1908   251
82. The ill-fated Bonnybridge Public Hall   254

83. Stenhouse mansion, home of the Bruce family   258
84. Larbert Old Parish Church   262
85. Airth Castle from a nineteenth century engraving   269
86. The new Airth Mercat Cross in the High Street   271
87. The Dunmore Pineapple   276
88. Polmont's first church   278
89. Millfield House, Polmont   279
90. The dedication of the Laurieston War Memorial
    in 1920   283
91. Westquarter School: the 'jewel in the crown' of the
    model village   289
92. The main street in Slamannan with the Boer War
    memorial   296
93. The Falkirk Wheel   300
94. The new Falkirk Stadium at Westfield   306
95. Model of the new Forth Valley Infirmary, due to
    open in 2009   307

Acknowledgements

The photograph of the Roman coin hoard on page 13 is used by permission of the National Museums of Scotland.

The portrait of the Earl of Kilmarnock on page 82 is from the collection in the Dick Institute in Kilmarnock and is used by permission of East Ayrshire Council Arts and Museums.

The portrait of William Forbes of Callendar by Sir Henry Raeburn on page 86 is from a private collection on loan to the Scottish National Portrait Gallery and is used by permission.

The photograph of the planned new Forth Valley Hospital on page 307 used by permission of the Forth Valley Health Board and *The Falkirk Herald*.

Preface

When *The Life and Times of Falkirk* was published back in 1994 a number of people asked why I had not included their particular part of the district. Irate Bo'nessians and loyal sons of Airth or Denny felt that the history of their communities was as interesting and important as the 'big town' and, of course, they were quite correct. A dozen years later I have been given the chance to put this right and at the same time to extend the coverage of a number of topics, and to bring the story up to date. The result is a much bigger and, I hope, better balanced and more comprehensive history of 'Falkirk' in its widest sense. Interest in history and heritage has continued to grow in the intervening years and a great deal of new research has improved our understanding of the past from the earliest times to the modern era. Much of this work has been published in *Calatria*, the journal of Falkirk Local History Society, which I have edited since 1991, and much of the original research there is the work of Falkirk's two leading historians, Geoff Bailey and John Reid. It would be difficult to exaggerate the amount of help they have given me in compiling this account – indeed without them the work would have been impossible. Brian Watters, the historian of Carron Company and, more recently of Larbert and Stenhousemuir, is another whose vast knowledge was freely available to me, and I thank him along with Geoff and John for their generosity over many years. Despite such guidance there will no doubt be some errors and omissions and for these I take full responsibility.

I would also like to thank Ronnie Blackadder for a number of excellent photographs and Geoff and John (again) for several photos, maps and drawings. I am grateful to Hugh Andrew and his colleagues at Birlinn for suggesting this new edition of the history and then for patiently 'managing' me through the process. Finally I thank my wife and family for putting up with my obsession for so many years. This book is for them and, especially for Christopher, Jennifer, Matthew and Blair Lenathen, my four beautiful grandchildren. The past belongs to them just as surely as the future.

Ian Scott
Falkirk 2006

CHAPTER I

The Legions of Rome

The town of Falkirk stands in the very heart of central Scotland at the point where the southern uplands slope gently down to the valley of the River Forth. Today it is the administrative centre of a huge district which stretches 20 miles from the castle town of Blackness in the east to Banknock in the west and from the Forth southwards to the Slamannan plateau 8 miles away and 500 feet above sea level. As well as almost 15 miles of the Forth it includes the Rivers Carron and Avon and several large towns and many villages each with a different story to tell. Although the flat and fertile carse lands to the north and east, and the pasturage and mineral wealth of the higher ground to the south, brought relative prosperity to the area over the centuries, it was Falkirk's position which ensured its central role in Scotland's story from the very earliest times. For centuries the Forth proved a formidable barrier to movement and all the major land routes from south to north, or east to west between the castle towns of Edinburgh and Stirling, crossed the district. And it was to the river estuary that the first people came to live and work in the centuries after the ice disappeared over ten thousand years ago.

Who they were, where they came from or exactly when, remain as yet unknown, and only tantalising fragments of their story, accidentally uncovered over the last century or so, confirm their existence in this part of central Scotland. Earliest and most spectacular of all are the great 'middens' – mountains of shells discarded by a people who hugged the beaches of the firth for centuries before the art of tillage and husbandry freed them from their dependence on the sea. At Nether Kinneil, in

1978, archaeologists discovered one such enormous Stone Age deposit – fifteen tons of oyster shells – discarded at various dates ranging from 2500 to 4000 BC. Elsewhere, at nearby Polmonthill and Inveravon, on beaches once at sea level and now many feet above the river, similar mounds speak of Neolithic man spreading along the Forth, using bone and stone implements to hunt and fish and finally to practise rudimentary agriculture on fertile clearings in the forests which cloaked much of the land area here for tens of centuries.

A thousand years after the shell middens were abandoned another scattering of relics confirms the existence of men of the Bronze Age. At Camelon, stone kist burials containing food vessels from 1500 BC or thereabouts, along with cremated remains and flint tools; at Stenhousemuir, in the Goshen sands, a bronze spear head close to another kist; and most amazing of all, at Denny a longbow made of oak dated at 1200 BC, one of only five such weapons found in Britain and the only one made of this material found in Europe. Inflexible oak certainly seems an unlikely choice for a longbow even in Denny, and one is left to speculate on how long the bow-maker remained in this particular business before moving on to a more profitable enterprise. In other parts of the district settlements from a century or so later have been found, with evidence of defensive palisades protecting houses with cooking pits – the homes of farmers of the late Bronze and early Iron Age – around 500–100 BC.

Fascinating as these discoveries are, they represent no more than a handful of pieces in a puzzle of almost infinite size. There is very little continuity in the snapshot pictures they provide of peoples separated by many centuries from each other and from us, and much more awaits discovery. More systematic excavation is required, but little is happening at present and the task of completing the picture must remain for future generations.

We can be fairly sure however that over many centuries, several waves of settlers found their way from the Continent to this part of the country, eventually merging with or superseding earlier arrivals and ultimately living in loose tribal groupings with similar language and traditions. They were the ancestors of those whom later generations would call the Picts and who were the first to encounter the formidable legions of the Roman Emperor towards the end of the first century AD. And it is only with the arrival of the Romans in Scotland that we can talk with any certainty about the early history of Falkirk district and even begin to speculate on the origins of the settlement itself.

In the year AD 80 the Governor of Britain, Julius Agricola, pushed northwards in an attempt to secure the southern territories of Britannia by subduing the hostile tribes. Possession of the central valley was obviously crucial to such an undertaking and a number of small fortlets were built across the country as well as roads both north and south of the line. At Camelon a heavily garrisoned fort guarded the vital crossing point of the River Carron, and from this base Agricola conducted a number of punitive campaigns against the northern tribes, culminating in the great Roman victory of Mons Graupius in the north-east. Despite this success, opposition to the Roman presence continued to grow, and after more than a decade of sustained pressure the Legions began a gradual withdrawal from central Scotland. By AD 100 they were once again on the line of Solway and Tyne.

It was forty years before the Romans returned to the district and it may have been during this absence that local tribesmen, of whom we know very little, constructed the formidable defensive position at Torwood, a mile or so north of the Carron crossing. This mighty circular stone broch of Tappoch stood on high ground overlooking Agricola's road north and may well have been over 20 feet high with walls of the same thickness enclosing a courtyard area over 30 feet in diameter. The walls contained rooms, passages and stairs and the whole was probably designed as an occasional safe retreat for the leading families and their supporters in times of difficulty. The existence of such a defensive structure in this part of Scotland, far from the traditional broch area of the north-west, has exercised the minds of scholars over the years, with some suggesting the existence of itinerant broch builders selling their skills well beyond their normal domain, while others see Tappoch as the work of immigrants drawn south in the era after Agricola's departure. More recently it has been argued that many similar structures may have been in use during the early Iron Age but that they have been lost or wrongly identified in succeeding ages. Excavations have revealed only insignificant Roman finds which might suggest a date of construction after the occupation of the Falkirk area, but it is difficult to be sure. Whatever its origin the broch remains an amazing structure despite the deterioration wrought by our own careless age and it can still be seen by visitors to the Torwood area. From the vantage point afforded by the high stone rampart the inhabitants might well have have watched in dismay as the feared legionary eagles signalled the return of the formidable Roman fighting machine to the district around AD 139.

Despite the construction of the mighty Hadrian's Wall in northern England between AD 122 and 128 the Romans came north once again in what must have been another attempt to subdue their troublesome neighbours. It is with this advance under Lollius Urbicus that the real story of Roman Falkirk begins. In AD 142 Agricola's abandoned posts were replaced by the great 38-mile wall from Forth to Clyde everywhere dedicated to the Roman Emperor Antoninus Pius and known to our age as the Antonine Wall. Fifteen miles of this incredible work of engineering lie in Falkirk district, from the starting point on the Forth at Carriden near Bo'ness, through Kinneil, Inveravon and Laurieston, then across the very centre of Falkirk itself and on past Camelon, Bonnybridge and Castlecary to the west. Though not so long, high, or permanent as the stone barrier of Hadrian, it was by any standard an amazing achievement involving the combined energies of detachments from at least four legions, perhaps 10,000 men in all, over a period of nearly two years.

The builders began by laying a six- to nine-inch thick base of stone some fifteen feet wide with squared or 'dressed' stones along the outside edges and unshaped stone rubble in the middle. At intervals along the length of this base they left stone-lined drainage culverts. Upon this solid bed stood the great rampart of the wall itself, rising ten feet and tapering from fourteen to six feet in width at the top where a wooden palisade

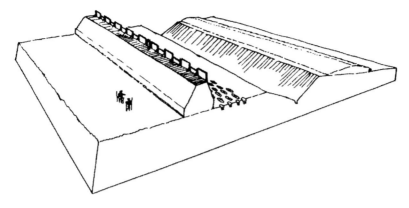

1. An impression of the Antonine Wall showing the turf rampart, the defensive ditch and the lillia in between the two (*Drawing by Geoff Bailey*)

or breast-work may have increased the height by another four or five feet. The wall was built according to a familiar Roman pattern, using blocks of turf rather than stone and, in an apparent attempt to compensate for its relative fragility, the Roman engineers placed an even bigger ditch to the north than had been the case at Hadrian's. Varying between 30 and 40 feet wide in places and up to 15 feet deep, this great V-shaped barrier lay some 20 or 30 feet from the base of the wall and, though it was never planned as a moat, the drainage culverts, Caledonian weather and sewage from the forts where up to 20,000 men were eventually garrisoned ensured that it was seldom empty in the winter months! In front of the ditch the excavated earth was, in most places, thrown up to create yet another obstacle, helping to complete what must have seemed to the watching tribesmen in their hill forts and brochs an impregnable barrier, towering above the flat lands of the river valley and stretching in a continuous line both east and west as far as the eye could see.

It was a silent but constant reminder of the sheer power of the Roman invaders, intended to impress and overawe the local tribes. But, as has often happened before and since, mighty power goes down in the dust of the centuries. Hardly a trace of the rampart now remains anywhere, though the great ditch can be identified here and there either from surface markings or as a genuine depression often up to 15 feet deep. In Callendar Park for example, a fine stretch is quite evident, and at Watling Lodge in Camelon, visitors can come closest to experiencing the ditch as it was 1,800 years ago. Forty feet wide and 15 feet deep, it is the best preserved example on the whole length of the wall. Between these two points to the east and west of the town, the line of ditch and wall has been plotted with as much accuracy as occasional excavation will allow. From Callendar Park it ran across modern Kemper Avenue towards the Pleasance, across Cockburn Street, Arnothill and Maggie Woods Loan to Frobisher Avenue, Blinkbonny Road and on towards Watling Lodge. Approximately twenty feet behind the wall to the south ran the continuous line of the military way, a substantial service road designed to allow rapid movement of troops to reinforce any part of the wall. The whole mighty work and the construction of the roads, forts and fortlets which completed the defensive system was accomplished by professional soldiers from Rome and auxiliary troops recruited in various parts of the Emperor's huge domains. Detachments or 'vexillations' of four

2. The surviving ditch at Watling Lodge in Camelon

legions were involved – the second (Augusta), Sixth (Victrix), Twentieth (Valeria Victrix) and Twenty-second (Primagenia). Within their ranks were skilled surveyors and masons, wood-cutters and road engineers, and they were probably assisted by the pressed, paid or voluntary labour of the local inhabitants. Over the years twenty magnificent distance slabs have been discovered on the whole length of the wall, which identify the builders and their particular contributions. Unfortunately only one of these refers to the Falkirk end of the wall but the compensation is that it is the most magnificent. This 'Bridge-ness' slab, discovered in 1868 near Bo'ness, shows sculpted Roman figures on horseback with defeated tribesmen falling beneath flying hooves on one side, and on the other a ceremo-nial sacrifice seeking divine blessing on some great activity – a campaign perhaps or a mighty undertaking like the wall itself. The legend tells us that: 'For the Emperor Titus Aelius Ha-drianus Antoninus Pius, father of his country, the Second Augustan Legion completed the work for 4652 paces'. Many more such slabs await discovery, hidden where the Romans buried them before the wall was finally abandoned.

As well as the great rampart and the military way, the legionnaries also built a series of forts and fortlets along the length of the wall to house the garrisons which would even-tually hold the new frontier. Forts at Carriden near Bo'ness,

3. The sculpted panels on the Bridgeness Slab, discovered near Bo'ness in 1868

Inveravon, Mumrills in Laurieston, Rough Castle and Castlecary have been identified and most excavated, and the pro-
jected town centre fort in Falkirk was confirmed by excavation
in the Pleasance area in the late summer of 1991. Only Seabegs
remains unlocated at the time of writing. In addition, small
fortlets have been identified and excavated at Kinneil, Laurieston, near Seabegs and, most importantly, at Watling Lodge
in Camelon where the Roman road north crossed the wall.

A mile north of Watling Lodge the Romans built what must
have been one of the most important forts in Scotland, at
Carmuirs in Camelon. Its position was critical. To the east, the
Forth itself provided a major barrier to movement towards the
wall from the north. If an attack was to come it would most
likely funnel down through the natural gap between the Ochil
and Lennox Hills in the valleys of the Forth and the Carron.
The new Antonine fort at Camelon stood guard over this route
and especially over the military road from the wall to the
Carron and beyond, as had the original fort of Agricola sixty
years earlier. Excavations in 1898 identified a complex maze of
defensive ditches and building foundations which suggest several camps and forts of different periods and occupations. The
Antonine fort alone occupied six acres of what is now Falkirk
Golf Course and contained many substantial stone buildings
capable of serving the needs of a very large garrison of soldiers.

Important as the site undoubtedly was it does seem a little
over cautious to make such extensive provision for defence
when the great wall half a mile south would provide even
greater security, and this raises an interesting problem. It has
always been the view of scholars that construction of the wall
began near Bo'ness and proceeded by degrees across the
country to the Clyde. But a glance at the map of Scotland
shows that the stretch from Bo'ness to Camelon is something of
a luxury, since the Firth of Forth itself was surely barrier
enough at the eastern end. And that stretch of wall is quite
different in composition from the rest, being built of clay and
not turf blocks. Why should this be? Not because of a shortage
of turf surely, for the eastern fortlet at Kinneil had turf
ramparts. Could it be that the wall from Bo'ness to Falkirk

was an afterthought, built when the Antonine frontier was complete? According to this theory, proposed by archaeologist Geoff Bailey in 1991, the main work began not at Bo'ness but at Camelon with the fortlet of Watling Lodge and proceeded west using turf for the rampart. The gap between Watling Lodge and the River Forth, that is the eastern flank of the wall, was protected by the substantial fort at Camelon which would explain its size and importance. Later on, perhaps a year later, and for reasons that are not yet apparent, the additional section from Camelon to Bo'ness was completed, this time using clay. It is an intriguing thought and one that will no doubt fuel the never-ending debate on this fascinating period in the history of the district.

The two forts on the wall nearest Falkirk offer a very interesting contrast of both size and function. The east end of Laurieston village, two miles from the town, shows no evidence today of its former glory, but where Sandyloan leaves the main street and bends round to Grahamsdyke Road, stood Mumrills, the biggest fort on the entire length of the wall, covering some six and a half acres. What a contrast the tranquillity of today's scene makes with the bustling garrison of Tungrian cavalrymen from the Rhine and Thracian infantry from Bulgaria, perhaps 1,000 in all, who occupied the substantial buildings that once stood here, protected on all sides by ramparts and ditches on the same scale as the wall itself. And what a contrast with the 1920s when the legendary Sir George Macdonald and his team conducted extensive excavations over the whole site and established most of what we know today about Mumrills in AD 142.

Macdonald identified seven stone buildings including the headquarters or 'principia' and a commanding officer's house or 'praetorium' with its own bathing area along with two granaries for storing the garrison food supply, and a bath house for the soldiers. Evidence of timber-framed barrack buildings was also found and, along with many coins and pieces of pottery, two inscribed stones have been recovered in the locality, telling something of the story of life and death among the Roman soldiers of the Mumrills garrison. One discovered near Brightons was an altar, 'Sacred to Hercules Magusanus. Valerius Negrinus, Duplicarius of the Tungrian Cavalry Regiment was the dedicator', and another, a tomb-stone dedicated to 'The spirits of the departed. Nectovelus, son of Vindex, aged thirty, a Brigantian by tribe, he served for nine years the Second Cohort of Thracians'.

The fort at Rough Castle, two miles west of Falkirk, was by contrast the second-smallest on the wall and, unlike Mumrills, is one of the best preserved and presented. Again early excavation proved the existence of the principia, praetoriam, granary and barracks, although the whole fort occupied just one acre. Like Mumrills there was an annexe, this time to the east of the fort, and here the foundations of a bathhouse have been identified. An inscribed tablet was discovered in the foundation of the headquarters building in 1903, identifying the builders of Rough Castle as 'the sixth Cohert of the Nervii' who 'erected the principia for the Emperor Caesar Titus Aelius Hadrianus Antoninus Pius, Father of his Country'. The Nervii, who like the Tungrians, were recruited by the Romans among the conquered peoples of the Rhine, were auxiliary troops who served alongside the legion, Valeria Victrix, which appears to have constructed this particular section of the wall with its forts and fortlets. The most interesting refinements added to the wall's defences here are the amazing ten rows of oval defensive pits once filled with sharp stakes camouflaged to resemble the surrounding land and called, with black Roman humour, the 'lillia' or lillies. It is common enough among observers these days to play down the Antonine Wall's role as a defensive position and suggest instead that it was no more than a frontier or even a customs barrier. It may, of course, have served as both, but the lillies are a stark reminder that to the north of the wall lay an unknown number of 'Caledonian' tribesmen who had already spent more than half a century fighting the invaders and would continue to do so with increasing vigour until the occupation of their territory was ended.

And what of the once elusive fort of Falkirk itself? Midway between Mumrills and Rough Castle, the town centre had long been thought of as the likely site. Taking into account the

4. Falkirk archaeologist Geoff Bailey pictured during the excavation of the Falkirk Fort at Rosehall in the Pleasance area

established line of the wall and ditch in Callendar Park and at several other points in the town, the area of the Pleasance – St Andrews Square and Booth Place – seemed the most likely place. Certainly the area had yielded a host of small finds over the years including coins, pottery, dressed and decorated stones, all of which fit the period of the wall's occupation. Much of the area has been built over several times as the town expanded in the intervening centuries and the chances of locating the fort seemed to be diminishing with each passing generation. And yet, fresh discoveries are made from time to time, even in these days when mechanical power moves mountains and fills valleys with consummate ease and wipes out the traces of a hundred generations in one quiet afternoon. In the late summer of 1991 Geoff Bailey was able to confirm the Pleasance location when he excavated on the Rosehall site to the north of the old Scout Hall and discovered the fort's defensive ditching along with Roman pottery of the Antonine period. In addition there was evidence of an industrial annexe with iron-working of a rudimentary kind. This final confirmation of the fort's location followed another intriguing discovery in 1980 in a new car park in Kemper Avenue in the old 'Cleddens' area of the town. Excavation identified the base of the wall and the foundation of an oblong building with a Roman hypocaust system – that is, central heating channels. It seems to have been a Roman bath-house and, though some distance from the probable fort, the crude nature of its construction suggests the possibility of local civilian use after the Roman period or perhaps an early entrepreneurial Falkirk 'bairn' providing a service for the soldiers of the garrison.

This suggests that there were local people settled in or near the forts. We know that at Carriden there is clear evidence of a 'vicus' or official civilian settlement and there are many examples in Roman occupied territories of tribes working with and for the legionnaires, and enjoying the fruits of the protection and relatively peaceful trading and working conditions offered by this local 'pax Romana'. So it is neither far-fetched nor over romantic to see in such a 'vicus', in or near the Falkirk fort, the first people of the town. We do not know who they were or what they did or what they called their settlement, but when the Romans left they may well have remained in place to begin the Falkirk story. In 1933 an amazing hoard of Roman coins was discovered during the excavation of the Callendar Riggs area, nearly 2,000 in all, covering several Imperial reigns. Such a collection, placed as it was some distance in front of the wall and fort on the hostile northern side, suggests hidden treasure probably accumulated from Roman bribes by some tribal chief in return for securing local support. Inside the earthenware pot which held the coins was a small piece of brown and yellow checked crosswoven cloth. It is now a museum piece of course, but it is still known as the 'Falkirk tartan' thought to be earliest known example of the national weave in existence.

But before leaving Roman Falkirk one story remains to be told. No aspect of the local occupation – walls, forts, ditches,

5. The Callendar Riggs coin hoard (National Museums of Scotland)

tablets, coins or weapons – has received quite so much attention over the centuries as the incredible beehive-shaped stone building which for 1,600 years stood on the north bank of the River Carron some miles north of the wall. The story of this unique building runs like a continuous thread through the many centuries of its existence, from its construction during the Roman occupation, through the Dark Ages with its dubious links to the shadowy legends of King Arthur, to the time of its wanton destruction in 1743. Arthur's O'on or Oven, as it was and still is known, stood over twenty feet high and had a similar base diameter. The four-foot thick walls of dressed freestone narrowed towards the top which was open when detailed architectural drawings were prepared in 1726. Described then as 'The Roman Sacellum of Mars Signifier, vulgarly called Arthur's Oon' it was thought to be some kind of temple or shrine – a brass finger from a long lost statue found lodged inside the building seemed to confirm this view. From its

position out in the open, well in front of the wall, some observers
have argued that the O'on was a triumphal monument set up
further to remind the Caledonians and other tribes of their
defeat and subjugation to the might of Rome. How it came to
acquire the Arthurian association is unclear, though there is a
suggestion that when the formidable Edward I of England was
tightening his grip on Scotland following his victory over
Wallace at Falkirk in 1298 he was persuaded not to destroy
the O'on because local intelligence said it was linked to King
Arthur. Edward's admiration for the legendary Briton was, of
course, not merely a personal enthusiasm but part of his
conviction that the two kingdoms were united in the Dark
Age period and that he was the inheritor of Arthur's mantle as
their rightful king. We do know that Edward was indeed in the
Falkirk area in 1302 and that he chose the occasion to re-
institute the knightly order of the Round Table. This has led a
few modern myth-makers to claim Arthur's O'on as the fabled
'table' itself, with its circle of stone seats creating a kind of

6. An early drawing of Arthur's O'on which stood near the Stenhouse
mansion of Sir Michael Bruce. He demolished it in 1743

council chamber! Whatever the legend we can be sure that by the sixteenth century it was acknowledged by Scottish scholars, including the formidable George Buchanan, as a Roman monument of considerable importance. However, this recognition, and the justifiable fame which the O'on enjoyed, did not preserve the triumphal monument, perhaps the only one of its kind in Roman Britain, from the fate which awaited it at the hand of Sir Michael Bruce. The impoverished Laird of Stenhouse, whose estate took its name from the great 'stone house', had a large family to feed and in 1743 he had the building dismantled to provide a cheap supply of dressed stones for a new weir on the River Carron. But the gods of archaeology had the last word when a spate swept the ancient stones away not long after the weir was built. When the scholars of the day discovered this act of vandalism they did not spare Sir Michael but prayed that 'if there is a pit deeper than ordinary destined for the reception of such villains and sordid rascals, condemn him to the bottom of it!' Another had an even more painful fate in mind for Laird of Stenhouse:

In order to make his name execrable to all posterity, he should have an iron collar put about his neck like a yoke. At each extremity a stone of Arthur's Oon to be suspended . . . Thus accoutered let him wander on the banks of the Styx, perpetually agitated by angry demons with ox goads, 'Sir Michael Bruce' wrote on his back in large letters of burning phosphorus.

The passage of two and a half centuries has not modified the verdict or in any way rehabilitated the villain, whose act deprived future generations of such a special relic of the past, and one which would surely have delighted local people and drawn visitors from far and near. But though it is gone it is far from forgotten. Every year or so, as we have seen, a new theory, as unlikely as its predecessor, seeks to place the O'on in a scheme linking various sites in Scotland with the Dark Age King Arthur and his famous knights. But these fanciful ideas vanish just as quickly as they appear, only to return once again in a year or so. A more interesting development came in the late 1980s when an American researcher, Robert Mitchell, claimed that the stones of the O'on were not scattered beneath the Carron waters at all but lay under a dismantled blast furnace where they were deposited when the river changed its course. He thus held up the possibility of recovery and reconstruction in the future, but so far there has been no confirmation of the find and no response to the proposal. Indeed the whole notion of the Carron having changed course at this point has been dismissed by other researchers. John Reid of Falkirk, who sees patterns in land forms that most other observers miss, has speculated that the O'on's position in relation to various key points on the Antonine Wall, as well as other prominent geographical features, suggests that it may have marked a fulcrum point in the mathematical calculations used by the Roman land surveyors to plan the construction of the whole barrier. A fascinating idea with plenty of persuasive geometrical evidence to support it, though not one taken up as yet by the 'official' wall watchers. As for the lost building itself, the interested observer can see a replica in East Lothian. So annoyed was the occupant of Penicuik House, Sir John Clerk, that he had his own O'on built in 1766, using the early drawings. It was used for many years as a doocot, perhaps the most unusual example in central Scotland. The site of the real O'on is now a housing estate, and no sign or mark tells a passer-by, or even the people who live there, of the former glory that lies beneath their feet. A sad finale indeed.

Despite such a triumphal monument and the seemingly impenetrable barrier behind it, the Roman stay in the district was remarkably short. The picture is very confused but it seems likely that the legions withdrew from the wall about 25 years after starting the building work and retired to the Hadrianic frontier. Sixty years later the aggressive campaigning of Septimus Severus brought the Romans back to Falkirk, but it was a short-lived occupation and by AD 210 the mighty wall with its network of roads and forts was finally abandoned and given over to the very tribes it was meant to subdue. What they did with the legacy is impossible to say, but the sheer scale of the barrier ensured that it loomed large in the lives of successive generations. They may have found that the road network offered a rapid east–west line of communication linking them with distant tribal groups. Alternatively, the great wall and ditch may have restricted communications, separating peoples and defining territories for many centuries after the last Roman soldier departed for more hospitable climes.

CHAPTER 2

Christian Missionaries and Feudal Barons

The eight centuries which follow the departure of the Romans from the Falkirk district present historians with an almost impossible task. Having dined on a rich harvest of archaeological evidence for the Roman occupation, they must now return to living off scraps carefully teased from a scattering of sources. Chronicles and annals, often recorded many centuries after the events, provide part of the story, but a careful analysis of place-name evidence tells even more about the ebb and flow of competing cultures which struggled for supremacy in what was surely the birth crucible of the Scottish nation. Here the Pictish people beyond the Forth and Irish Scots from Argyll coalesced over the centuries with the Welsh-speaking Britons of Strathclyde and the Germanic Angles pushing north through the Lothians.

Sometimes the conflicts which arose were resolved by clash of armies, and we are told by the chroniclers of great battles in Strathcarron or in the valley of the Forth between Pict and Angle, Scot and Briton by turns. The rivers ran red with blood so ferocious were the encounters, and great destruction was wrought on both land and people. At such times the local population was no doubt elbowed aside and temporarily displaced by whatever invading army was active, but for the most part, the evidence, such as it is, suggests a gradual change as the local inhabitants adapt to the ways of whatever new culture held sway at a particular period.

At some time during this period of migration and cultural evolution, and certainly before AD 1000, Christian missionaries first arrived in the area, though who they were, when they came or who they met and taught, remains obscure. Some have even suggested that the Christian message came to the area with the Romans themselves in the last days of the occupation, but others look to the near mythical 'Saint Nynia', a Christian bishop from Roman Britain to the south. This St Ninian first established a church at Candida Casa in Whithorn and, according to the Venerable Bede, writing three centuries later, went on to convert the 'southern picts' who probably occupied the territory just north of the Forth. Such a journey, along abandoned Roman roads and across the wall at Camelon, would have brought the missionary and his followers into the Falkirk area around AD 400. Might they have chosen the gentle little hill just fifty yards or so in front of the wall, facing across the valley towards his chosen mission field, to site a little shrine or church? Or did those early inhabitants have to wait for the great mission of St Columba, which radiated from Iona towards the end of the sixth century, for their first introduction to the Gospel message which would have such a profound influence on future generations? Oral tradition certainly supports this view, for the foundation of the church at Falkirk has for many centuries been associated with an early seventh- or eighth-century Celtic missionary called Mo-Aidan or Modan, probably the most famous of several who bear the name. This man, who is said to have 'tamed external senses of sight and hearing that he never experienced the irregular motions of sin', worked in Argyll for a time and may then have served as Abbot of an early foundation at Dryburgh in the Borders. Eventually, or so the legends have it, he came north again and founded a church at Falkirk on the site where the Parish Church has stood ever since.

Whatever the origin of the Church it was its arrival which gave rise to the name by which the town and district has been known ever since. But, like the early history of the settlement itself, the evolution of the name during the confused Dark Age centuries remains a matter for heated debate. From what one scholar called this 'linguistic borderland' came Celtic influences – both the old Welsh or Cymric and the Irish Gaelic – to be overtaken eventually by the middle English of the Anglians. As with so many aspects of the history of this period we must rely on much later written sources. The first reference to the place we know as Falkirk comes in a famous account by one Symeon of Durham written around 1120 but describing events which took place in 1080, not long after the Norman conquest of England:

> In which year the same King William sent his son Robert to Scotland against Malcolm in the autumn. But having turned back when he reached Egglesbreth, he founded New Castle on the river Tyne.

The name 'Egglesbreth' reappears in several later sources following more or less the same form. The 'eggles' part obviously means church and is associated elsewhere in Scotland with early Christian foundations, where it is quite often linked with a personal name giving 'the church of so and so'. In its Latin form of 'eccles' one can think of examples like Ecclesmachan, the church of St Machan. One source does link two 'Welsh' priests or monks with the early church at Falkirk, a Devyyd and, more interestingly, a Brychan, who appeared to have been a martyr for the Christian faith. Though the source is somewhat questionable it does fit with a derivation in which the 'breth' part may then have started life in a form like 'brych' giving us 'eccles brych' – the church of Brych. If this is the case then the church foundation would predate the Columban mission and be placed earlier than the seventh century. Which takes us back again to St Ninian and his followers. What is certain is that when the Gaelic of the Scots from Argyll gradually replaced the earlier Celtic form, Egglesbreth became, not the church of Brych, but Eggles Bhrec, the broken or speckled church, or Varia Capella as the later Latin manuscripts have it. By turn the Gaelic gave way to the language of the Angles so that by the twelfth century the church, and of course the settlement nearby, are described as Faukirk or Fawkirk – the speckled or spotted church. One thirteenth-century document talking about an earlier period says: 'at length we arrived at Faukirke, which had a nearby cemetery about which we inquired, and were then invited into the chapel of the sacred house of Mary Magdalene.'

Later still, the map of the area draw up by the cartographer Timothy Pont in the late sixteenth century and published in Amsterdam in 1654 describes the town as 'Fakirk'. The final touch in the evolution of the name is amusing, particularly to those 'bairns' who still describe their town as 'Fa'kirk'. Sometime in the fifteenth century some pedantic scribe, thinking no doubt that the Scots ba' really meant ball and wa' meant wall, decided to turn 'Fakirk' into Falkirk, and thus it has remained.

The evolution of the name then does suggest an early foundation for the church and, other later evidence talks about the 'ablands' or abbot's lands of Falkirk, a term commonly associated with the early Celtic church. Certainly much earlier than the 'foundation stone' inside the vestibule of the Parish Church which proclaims: 'Fundatum Malcolmo III Rege Scotia AM 1057'. The stone was discovered in 1810 during

7. A section of the Blaeu map of Stirlingshire published in Amsterdam in 1654. It was based on Timothy Pont's survey completed in the 1590s.

the rebuilding of the church and was thought by some to mark the replacement of an early church with a new establishment. Most people now agree that the stone, with its arabic numerals is a forgery, and the finger of suspicion points at the minister of the parish in the early 1800s, Dr James Wilson, who urgently needed such evidence for a lawsuit, and found it in this amazing chance discovery!

8. The so-called Foundation Stone from the Old Parish Church in Falkirk which most believe is a nineteenth-century forgery

In its earliest form the church was probably some kind of monastic settlement with a few missionary monks and an abbot ministering to a small group of people already settled in and around the area of the church. As this form of loose church organisation gradually gave way to the parochial system in the eleventh and twelfth centuries, Falkirk found itself the centre of a vast parish which stretched all the way from Cumbernauld in the west to the Avon in the east including the later medieval parish of Muiravonside. To the south it reached the boundary of the parish of Slamannan, and to the north the river Carron. By the twelfth century it is recorded as part of the Deanery of Linlithgow within the Bishopric of St Andrews. The distinguished historian of Falkirk Church, Lewis Lawson, confirms Falkirk's relative status at that early period:

The Deanery of Linlithgow had thirty-five churches, the most richly endowed of which were St Cuthbert's, Edinburgh, cessed at 160 merks, Falkirk cessed at 120 merks and Linlithgow, cessed at 110 merks. The average yield from all thirty five churches was 41 merks so that the importance of Falkirk is evident.

But this apparent prosperity, probably the result of the sheer size of the parish as much as on its acknowledged fertility, was not enjoyed in the local area for long, for it was soon being expended on the establishment and maintenance of the Abbey of the Augustian Canons of Holyrood, in Edinburgh. The year 1166 confirmed the gift made by the Bishop of St Andrews:

> Richard, by the grace of God lowly minister of the church of St Andrew to the church of Holyrood and the canons serving God there the church of Eiglesbrec which is called Varia Capella and the whole land which we or any of our ancestors had there with all the pertinents of the said church and lands.

And all this for the annual payment of 'unam petram cerae', a stone of wax! Thereafter the spiritual needs of local settlement as well as of the scattered souls of the parish fell to these regular priests who enjoyed great popularity with the kings and nobility of Scotland and whose eighteen houses included Scone, Inchcolm, Cambuskenneth, Inchmahome, and Jedburgh as well as St Andrews and Holyrood itself. What benefit their skills as farmers and builders brought to Falkirk is unknown – they probably followed the usual practice of the time by placing a poorly paid vicar with limited education in charge of the parish with the obvious detrimental effects this must have had on what religious life there was among the people. It probably remained like this for four hundred years though scarcely a word has come down to us to illuminate the daily lives of the people as they worked and worshipped, lived and died through war and peace, famine, plague and plenty. We can be sure though, that the church, however it was managed, remained at the heart of the settlement which was, by the time of the great

wars of independence, firmly established and now quite defi-
nitely called by its English name, Faukirk.

The same darkness which shrouds the early history of Falkirk's
church also obscures the origin of the district's second centre of
power and influence. Less than a mile to the east stands Callendar House, a huge mansion enclosing behind an imposing
Victorian façade, the remains of many centuries, including an
early fortified tower house dating from 1400 or thereabouts. But
the origins of Callendar go back far beyond this period, and once
again, it is the early charters and place-name evidence which
provide the best, perhaps the only, reliable information.

Several sources in the eleventh century, including an account
of William the Conqueror's progress north in 1072, refer to an
area called 'Calateria' identified as the huge tract of land
between the Rivers Avon and Carron, and including of course,
the Falkirk district. We may safely discount a link with the
'Calathros' or 'Calitros' mentioned in accounts of tribal battles
of the seventh and eighth centuries, but it is a reasonable
supposition that before AD 1000, and probably much earlier,
a clearly defined area of vast size in this part of central Scotland
emerged, bearing a name recognisable as a version of Callendar. One particularly attractive account found in a French
romance of the late twelfth century tells of lady who has a
bower in the 'woods of Calitar' where she reposes on a couch
covered by a counterpane of a chequered pattern! Maybe
woven from a bale of the celebrated Falkirk tartan?

From the twelfth century on, versions of the name appear
regularly in royal charters and judgments, which usually link
the lands of Callendar with a ruling family enjoying considerable power and wealth. Even at a time when much low-lying
land was impassable and thousands of acres lay as unusable
marsh, moss and scrub, the lands of Callendar included rich
woodlands and pasturage, fertile plains, river fishings and
saltpans. Confirmation of the power and status of these over-
lords of Callendar comes with the use of the title 'thane' which
appears to have been introduced to Scotland from the south
around the eleventh century – Callendar was one of only two
areas in Scotland south of the Forth to carry such a distinction.

9. An impression of the 'Thanes's hall' (*Drawing by John Reid*)

In 1990 an archaeological dig by Falkirk Museum staff in the area to the east of Callendar House – on the site of the former teacher-training college – uncovered the foundations of a large wooden building which has been radio-carbon dated to the ninth century. Dubbed the 'thane's hall' it was around 80 feet long by 25 wide, its size and construction in keeping with the kind of fortification likely to have been required in the turbulent and disordered society which characterised the emerging Scottish nation at that particular period. Interestingly enough the eminence on which the building once stood has been known for many centuries as 'Palace Hill'.

During the reign of King David I, between 1124 and 1153 the first personal name appears – one Dufoter de Calateria as witness to a charter – and during the same reign we have the first mention of a thane, Duncan by name. During the following sixty years, several others are described as thanes – in 1190 we have 'Malcomo, Theino de Calentar' and in 1226 one 'P . . .' [probably Patrick], Thane of Callendar', witnessed a Lennox charter. The Lennox connection is an interesting one – as well as the extensive lands between Avon and Carron, the thanes of Callendar also held territory in Kilsyth which was within the lands of the powerful Earls of Lennox. This, coupled with the Callendar Christian names – Malcolm, Duncan and Patrick, all familiar royal Lennox names – has led that sharp-eyed observer, John Reid, to suggest that the earliest ruling family of which we have any knowledge may well have been a branch of the Scottish royal family itself.

The last individual described as a thane was another Malcolm who in 1234 gifted lands to the Knights Templar. In the same year, however, it was his lands that were being gifted elsewhere, presumably without his wholehearted support! King Alexander II, conscious perhaps of the growing power of his nobility, or anxious to secure for himself the patronage which huge land holdings would bring, brought the thanage of Callendar to an end. Malcolm was 'bought out' by the crown and received back only a proportion of what his family had once held. The charters covering this change in status make it quite clear who the major beneficiaries of the new arrangements would be:

> Alexander by the grace of God, king of Scots to all men of his whole land, churchmen and laymen, greetings. Let men know, now and to come, that we have given in feu to the canons of the holy cross of Edinburgh for ever all our land in Kalentyr, that we had in hand on the day when we assigned Malcolm, late thane of Kalentyr, forty librates of land.

Thus the same Canons who already owned the small church lands of the 'terrae de Faukirk' in the town itself, and who were entitled to the church revenues from the huge parochial territory, were now also the possessors of the rich lands of what became the 'abbot's carse', later Abbots Kerse. The remainder of the original territory, still large and valuable, remained a considerable inheritance for thane Malcolm's successors as Knights of Callendar.

Among them we know of one 'Alwin de Kalentyr' in 1252, a 'Sir John de Calentir' around 1296 and later another 'Alwyn,' and finally 'Patrick' in the early fourteenth century. They were clearly men of substance playing a significant part in the power play of the emerging Scottish nation in the oasis of relative peace and prosperity which preceded the disastrous wars of independence at the end of the thirteenth century. By then their land holding seems to have been further diminished with the emergence of the Stirling family, who found themselves in possession of a large tract of land north of Falkirk later known as West Kerse and held by them and their successors – Monteath, Hope and Dundas – for over six hundred years. The map shows the probable division of land around the end of the thirteenth century, with Kerse lying east of Falkirk and including a substantial stretch of the Forth, the 'drylands' of Polmont and the summer hill country of the Redding muir. The Stirlings' lands of West Kerse were smaller but included most of Bainsford, including Abbotshaugh and Mungall, along with lands on the south side of the Falkirk–Grangemouth road including Westfield and the area known today as the Bog Road.

10. The land divisions in Falkirk area around AD 1300 showing territory held by Callendar, Abbotskerse and West Kerse. (*Drawing by John Reid*)

The rest was Callendar land with the exception of Dalderse which remained something of an independent enclave within West Kerse.

When the crisis in Scotland heightened towards the end of the thirteenth century the then leading member of the Callendar family, Sir John, and his son, were members of the nobility who signed the infamous Ragman Roll swearing allegiance to King Edward I. It was the prelude to one of the most significant periods in the history of Scotland when William Wallace emerged to challenge English supremacy and once again the Falkirk district was to play a significant part in what was to follow.

CHAPTER 3

Wallace and the Battle of Falkirk, 1298

In July 1298 William Wallace's inspirational campaign to defend Scotland from English domination effectively ended in disaster near the town of Falkirk. We do not know why he chose to face the might of the English army in this particular part of Scotland, though there is some evidence to suggest that he was familiar with the area from an early age. Indeed, if we are to believe the legends, then the great man found his vocation as a freedom fighter in the old chapel not far from the present Hills of Dunipace while still a young man. His uncle, who was the priest there, is said to have taught him to recite the latin verse *Dico tibi verum, libertas optima rerum; nunquam servili sub nexu vivito, fili* which roughly translates as 'I tell you truly, freedom is best of all things. Never live in slavery, my son'. Years later he repaid this debt by storming Airth Castle to rescue the priest from the hands of the English garrison. That was in the spring of the 1298, a few months before he faced the huge army of Edward I who came north bent on vengeance for the humiliating defeat at the hands of the Scots at Stirling Bridge the previous September.

For Edward the campaign began badly. There was a severe shortage of provisions and serious disagreement in the ranks between the English and Welsh contingents. At Linlithgow the night before the battle, the king, sleeping in his armour in the open, had his ribs broken by his own horse but rose to lead his army forward on hearing that the Scots were near Falkirk. Tradition says that Wallace and his senior commanders standing on the high ground now called Wallacestone watched the huge English army as it advanced slowly from the east. Later that same day the English held the same spot and, since it was the Feast of St Mary Magdalene, 22 July, the Bishop of Durham celebrated mass before the advance to Falkirk was resumed.

It is difficult to assess the size of the two armies which came face to face on that afternoon. The English chroniclers like Pierre de Langtoft and especially Walter of Guisborough, using so-called eye-witness accounts, make astonishing claims for the number of combatants on both sides. Langtoft begins his account by claiming that 'the people of Scotland, each with a spear in fist are come to Falkirk in the morning'. Ridiculous figures like 300,000 are not unusual in these accounts but modern scholarship is much more conservative with the most recent estimate by military historian Pete Armstrong suggesting that the total number on both sides combined was more like 25,000. We know that Edward had with him 111 noble families with all their retinues of foot and horse, and that along with men on the royal payroll this gave him a combined strength of around 16,000, including 7,000 spearmen, 5,500 longbowmen, mainly Welshmen, 500 crossbowmen and over 2,000 mounted knights. According to Armstrong they faced a much smaller number of Scots, perhaps 10,000 to 12,000, almost all spearmen supported by a few hundred horse. Despite this 'down-sizing' the battle remains one of the biggest fought on British soil, but where the clash of arms took place remains something of a mystery. Over the years antiquaries and local historians using the few clues available have championed this or that corner of the Falkirk district, but no agreement has emerged despite hours of entertaining debate. Tradition, for what it is worth, places the centre of the battle in the area of the present Victoria Park in the Grahamston area, just north of the town centre. Graham's Muir was said by many to be named after Sir John de Graeme, a local nobleman who fought and died with Wallace that day, but the earliest record of such a place-name is no further back than the eighteenth century. Nonetheless our Victorian ancestors were quite convinced and many of the new streets bear names like Wallace and Campfield. Few people accept this view these days and argue instead for one of several possible sites to the east of the town which better fit the limited information left to us by the observers on both sides who were present. We know, for example, that the Scots were probably drawn up on rising ground, with the town of Falkirk, behind them; the English advancing from the east were separated from the enemy by a water course or an area of marshy ground. Current favourite is the area lying between the village of Redding and the Falkirk suburb of Hallglen with the Scots placed with their backs to the wood of Callendar and the English approaching towards the marshy confluence of the Westquarter and Glen Burns. Another popular contender is the Beancross area which places the Scots on the slope of Mumrills close to the site of the old Roman fort. Below them, again separated by the Westquarter Burn, were the English army advancing towards what is now the Grandsable Cemetery.

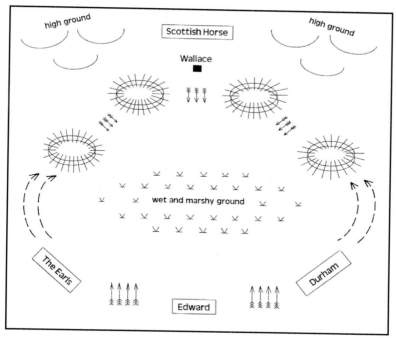

11. The relative positions of the Scottish and English armies at the Battle of Falkirk on 22 July 1298

Unless someone discovers a huge cache of bones of thirteenth-century date then the arguments will continue despite the threatened intervention of that prince of publicity seekers, Uri Geller!

However we do know a good deal about the conduct of the engagement itself which was to prove such a disaster for Wallace and the Scottish cause. The English knights formed three or four columns led by the king himself in the centre, the warlike Bishop of Durham, Anthony de Beck, on the right and the Earls of Lincoln, Norfolk and Hereford on the left. Separated from them by the stream or marshy ground, were the Scots, drawn up into four great schiltroms – massive defensive circles or 'phalanx rings' as they are sometimes called – bristling with ten-foot spears, for all the world like giant porcupines. There may also have been roped stakes of wood stretched in front as an added defence though this is by no means certain. Behind the infantry on the high ground were the mounted nobility, though there were precious few of them with Wallace and even fewer when they were needed most at the height of the bloody battle.

The English attacked repeatedly, using mounted knights skirting round the edge of the marshy ground in an attempt to weaken the schiltroms, but the Scots held. However, the Scottish horse and the archers standing between the schiltroms were badly mauled by the knights in the first attacks and played little part thereafter. At this critical stage Edward called up his archers, whose longbows would later win the honours at Poitiers and Crécy, but who were now put to the battle test for the first time. They rained their arrows down on the helpless Scots and when Wallace looked to his horsemen to scatter them he found that the nobles were no longer there, driven from the field in the first exchanges or perhaps departed of their own accord when the tide turned against them. Whatever, the Scots were doomed. One of the English chroniclers said that they 'fell like blossoms in an orchard when the fruit ripens'. Great swathes were cut in the rings as wave after wave of arrows pierced the defence. And now the knights could do their worst on the open and dispirited Scottish ranks. The rout followed quickly and Wallace with many of his gallant men fled north towards the Carron and relative safety. Many hundreds, perhaps thousands, did not escape and they lie buried today in the common pits near the field of battle as was the custom. But the great and powerful among the Scottish fallen were carried to the kirkyard of Falkirk for burial, and there they remain, their graves marked by fine memorials. Sir John de Graeme, Wallace's right-hand according to contemporary accounts, was, says the inscription on his tomb, 'ane of the chiefs wha rescewet Scotland thris'. Above him they laid a carved effigy of a knight in armour which, having suffered badly from centuries of exposure to Scottish weather, was covered three times by stones set a few inches above each other. Blind Harry tells us that Wallace carried Graeme to his grave with the words:

> My dearest brother that I ever had.
> My only friend, when I was hard bestead;
> My hope, my health, O man of honour great,
> My faithful aid, and strength in every strait.
> Thy matchless wisdom cannot here be told;
> Thy noble manhood, truth, and courage bold;
> Wisely thou knew'st to rule and to govern;
> Yea, virtue was thy chief and great concern.
> A bounteous hand, a heart as true as steel,
> A steady mind, most courteous and genteel.
> When I this kingdom did at first rescue,
> Great honour then, I'm sure to thee was due.
> Wherefore I vow to the great God, and swear,
> Thy death shall be to South'ron bought full dear.
> Martyr thou art for Scotland's right this day,
> Which I'll avenge with all the might I may.

It was scenes like this that made Harry's story such a potent force in shaping Scottish national feeling in the centuries following its first publication at the end of the fifteenth century, and it continues to inspire today. However we can be fairly sure that at the time Wallace was said to be in the graveyard he was already a long way away from Falkirk seeking the safety of the

Torwood where there are many Wallace connections including a celebrated oak tree which was only lost in the eighteenth century and from which radical Scots delighted in fashioning precious objects like the snuffbox sent to George Washington by the Earl of Buchan.

The grave of Graeme was further enhanced by a splendid wrought iron enclosure erected by Victorian admirers in 1860 on which a replica of Sir John's sword was placed nine years later. Less grand is the flat stone which is said to mark the grave of Sir John Stewart of Bonkhill, brother of the High Steward of Scotland, whose gallant men of Bute fell to a man in a vain attempt to save their chief in those first chaotic moments of the battle. The granite Celtic cross now standing in front of the church near the High Street – the Bute Memorial – was another late salute, this time from the Marquis of Bute in 1877. In

12. The elaborate tomb of Sir John de Graeme and the plain grave slab of Sir John Stewart in the graveyard of the old Parish Church

recent years many people from the Isle of Bute have come to Falkirk to honour the men of their area who fought and died on that day and now they have raised a stone in Rothesay which tells the same heroic story.

Though it is difficult to be sure how many fought or fell at Falkirk on that Magdalene's day, we do have the names of many leading men who were captured and later exchanged for prisoners held by the enemy. Among these was Sir John, Knight of Callendar, held by the Scots and freed in exchange for one Reginald le Cheyne, held by the English. Although Sir John and his family continued to support the English crown during the final Scottish triumph at Bannockburn in 1314, they somehow managed to retain their hold on the lands in Falkirk area. However, the period of stability which had followed that famous victory did not survive for long after the death of the Bruce in 1329. In a renewed dispute over the rightful succession, a Bailiol challenger took up arms once again supported by the English and by a section of the Scottish nobility including, predictably enough, the Callendars. The defeat of King David II at Neville's Cross and his imprisonment at Durham no doubt brought brief advantage to the then incumbent Patrick de Calentyre but vengeance soon followed the King's release and restoration. In 1346 all the lands of Patrick were forfeit and given instead to one William Livingston, whose loyalty had brought him to the same English prison as the king. The Livingstons were a family holding lands in West Lothian, but now they moved to the centre of the Scottish stage. In a time of rapidly changing fortunes, William's principal concern was to secure the new possessions for his family, and he did so by the traditional method. Marriage to Christiane de Calentyre, daughter of the deposed Patrick, went a long way to protect the claim of their descendants against whatever the unpredictable winds of political change might bring in the future. Thus arrived a dynasty that would dominate local affairs for four centuries, and ensure that the people of Falkirk would continue to be involved in all the great affairs of the nation.

CHAPTER 4

The Livingstons of Callendar

In the years that followed their arrival in the Falkirk district the Livingstons grew in power and influence. Sir William's son John fell fighting alongside King Robert III at Homildon Hill in 1402 and when King James I was murdered in 1436 it was Sir Alexander Livingston, the next Knight of Callendar who spirited away the six-year-old James II and later became the King's Guardian, Justiciary of Scotland and effective Regent during the King's minority. But power in those turbulent times depended ultimately on an individual noble's willingness to take up arms against others who challenged their position and, on more than one occasion, Sir Alexander and his Falkirk vassals burned and demolished the strongholds of their enemies. He even had the audacity to besiege his erstwhile ally Crichton in the castle of Edinburgh, the very place where the two had brutally murdered a Douglas rival following the notorious 'black dinner' of 1439. But such actions provoke equally ferocious reactions and the Knight of Callendar was often forced to defend his lands and castle from vengeful and ambitious rivals. About 1444 we hear of a young Douglas nobleman attacking Livingston lands in Falkirk and destroying the castle of Callendar, followed by a predictably powerful reply from Sir Alexander and his allies. And, underlining the rapid ebb and flow of fortune, we find just a few years later, both Alexander and his son confined in the Castle of Dumbarton as the king's enemies. His second son, also Alexander, was executed along with another Livingston kinsman, yet within months he was not only free but once again enjoying a position of power at the same king's right hand. Confused and confusing times indeed!

But these were the conditions which a succession of child monarchs brought to Scotland during the next century and a half, and there was always a Livingston close to the centre of affairs, most often playing a full part in the intrigue and double-dealing which marked this particular page of Scotland's story.

Sir Alexander's son, Sir James, was also the King's Guardian and became the Great Chamberlain or Master of the Royal Household. He was rewarded with a Lordship of Parliament by the King and the title first Lord Livingston of Callendar. After James II's death in 1460 he remained as 'magnus camerarius' during the minority of the new king and served as ambassador to the English court. In his later years he was once again involved in intrigue to secure greater control over the young James III and for a period the family's influence at court declined, though they continued to enjoy complete power in the Barony of Callender which was confirmed in 1458.

The original thane's house was probably replaced in the early fifteenth century by a strongly fortified tower house, elements of which remain within the western end of the present Callendar House. The church at Falkirk was completely rebuilt in the 1450s and included a south aisle to house the dead of the new Livingston dynasty, an important step in the growth of their power and status. About this time one brother 'Henricus de Levingstoun' is recorded as Knight Commander of the Order of St John of Jerusalem in Scotland and Preceptor of Torphichen. The order acquired some rights in the south aisle of the church which was converted into a chapel for their order dedicated to St John as well as the last resting place of the feudal lords of Callendar.

The new church building followed the traditional Catholic west–east alignment with a second aisle to the north dedicated to St Michael the Archangel. The western nave, eastern chancel and the two aisles were joined together by a great square tower with 'lofty arches' housing the altar. This square tower survived the rebuilding of 1811 and remains as the vestibule of the present building, though the arches lie buried behind the brick and plaster of a new age. At the crossing point of the church above the altar was a great stone roof boss bearing

13. The pre-Reformation church of Falkirk and the roof boss showing the Livingston coat of arms from around 1450

the arms of Livingston of Callendar, and this has survived and can be seen in the west corridor of the present church. So too have the effigies of two of the feudal lords and their ladies, but they are so badly weathered as to make identification difficult though early scholars thought one pair might represent the king's guardian Sir Alexander or his son.

It was with another Alexander, the fifth Lord that the Livingstons returned to the centre of the political stage, for he was close to King James V and accompanied him to France in 1537 to celebrate his brief marriage to the Princess Magdalene. When the king died

14. The Livingston effigies from the old Parish Church – probably those of Lord William Livingston and his wife from around 1590

in 1542, a broken man whose armies had been roundly defeated by the English at Solway Moss, the care of his infant daughter, Mary, then a few days old, was entrusted to eight nobles, one of whom was Sir Alexander Livingston. It was the beginning of a close personal relationship between the ill-fated Queen and the Livingston family which did not end until her death on the scaffold of Fotheringay Castle forty-five years later.

King Henry VIII of England, like his predecessors, feared the constant threat from his northern neighbour and hoped now to win the Scottish crown for his infant son Edward by arranging a marriage with the Queen of Scots. The Earl of Arran, acting as Regent of Scotland, favoured such an arrangement but a powerful group led by the Earl of Moray and Cardinal Beaton and including Lord Alexander Livingston were bitterly opposed. On 4 September 1543 at Callendar House the parties were reconciled and joined in a rejection of Henry's proposal. From then on Livingston along with Lord Erskine was entrusted with the care of the young queen lest she fall into the hands of the enemy. Thus the Privy Council Register of 5 June 1546 records: 'the Lordis Erskine and Levingstown Lordis chosin to be of Secret Counsel, . . . of the keeping of our Soverane Ladis persoun'.

Henry was far from happy with the outcome and his armies invaded Scotland seeking revenge for the insult given. At Pinkie on 10 September 1547 hundreds of Scots fell in battle, among them Lord Livingston's son and heir John, Master of Livingston, who had led a party of vassals from Falkirk in his father's name. The threat to the queen was increased and in August 1548 she sailed to France to begin a twelve-year period away from her homeland.

As companions Mary had with her four daughters of noble families – Mary Fleming, Mary Seton, Mary Beaton and Mary Livingston of Callendar. These four Maries were about the same age as the queen and were to remain with her for much of her troubled life. The ballad writers, never over-concerned with accuracy, have served the Livingston memory badly for only Seton and Beaton made it into the famous song. Who the Mary Carmichael or the Mary Hamilton of the song's title were, no one is certain. Lord Alexander accompanied his daughter and the young queen to France and died there some five years later. His part in this most famous story is comemorated by a badly worn grave slab from the old Livingston aisle which bears an incomplete inscription which seems to confirm his role as the protector of the young queen in France. The slab also bears the Livingston coat of arms along with the device of his wife, Lady Agnes Douglas. On his death the title Lord of Callendar passed to his son Lord William Livingston who remained in Scotland and was to play a significant part in bringing Mary Queen of Scots back to her Kingdom in 1561.

It was during the Queen's sojourn in France that the stirring events of the Reformation transformed the religious and political face of Scotland, though Falkirk seems to have escaped the attention of the more extreme among the reformers. Indeed it appears that the last Catholic vicar, a man named Hogge, demitted office quietly and his congregation, if he still had one, adopted the new theology without fuss. The new Lord of Callendar was an enthusiastic supporter of the change, but his new-found Protestantism did not diminish one whit his devotion to the young Catholic queen. Indeed he was one of a group of nobles who journeyed to France in 1560 to invite Mary to return to Scotland, which she did the following August.

There followed the best known and most often recounted period in the life of the queen – seven tumultuous years in which she married twice, gave birth to a son and heir, suffered imprisonment, braved defeat on the battlefield and fled to what was to be a long English exile ended only by her execution in 1587. Throughout this period the Livingstons of Callendar were among her closest personal friends and allies. Lord William's wife Agnes was the queen's cousin and sister of Mary Fleming, one of the four Maries, and from the queen's arrival in Scotland in 1561 it was clear that Callendar House would be a regular port of call. In 1565 she was present at the magnificently celebrated marriage of Mary Livingston to John, son of Lord Robert Sempill and, from her the couple were gifted Crown lands, including Auchtermuchty and the island of Little Cumbrae, a wedding dress for the bride and a number of other presents including 'ane bed of scarlet velvot bordered with broderie of blak velvot'. John Knox, ever ready to damn those close to the queen, wrote in his 'History' that 'It was weill knawin that schame haistit mariage betwix John Semphill, callit the Danser, and Marie Levingstoune, surnameit the Lustie'. Not for the first time the evidence does not support this particular charge.

A few months after the Livingston wedding, on 1 July 1565, the queen was in Callendar House for the baptism of one of Lord Livingston's children which followed the Protestant form which Mary found abhorrent. Nonetheless she stayed to hear the sermon preached, we are told, by Knox himself, because, as she told her host, she wished 'to show him (Lord William) that favour that she had not done to any other before'. She remained in Falkirk for several days on this occasion though already her enemies, incensed by her engagement to Henry, Lord Darnley, were on the roads seeking to waylay her and her noble supporters. Three weeks later she married Darnley and began the downward acceleration of her fortunes which ended with her exile.

On the 9 March 1566 Livingston was one of the Lords in attendance on the queen at Holyrood House when her Italian secretary and confidant David Riccio was brutally murdered by associates of Darnley; indeed there is some suggestion that his own life was threatened and with Huntly, Bothwell, Fleming and others he was forced to flee from the palace to a place of refuge. Three months later, as the queen prepared to give birth to the future James VI in Edinburgh Castle, Mary Livingston helped her draw up a list of her possessions which has survived in *Les Inventaires de la Royne Descosse*. It includes numerous references to the Livingston family with details of gifts to the dowager Lady Livingston and her two daughters Mary and Magdalen, who was herself one of the queen's maids of honour after her sister's marriage, and who is always referred to, in the French of the period, as 'Livingston la jeusne' – the younger. On the occasion already mentioned Magdelen was to have received: 'Une aultre montre garny de dourze rubiz et deux grandes saffiz avec une perle pandant au bout'. When the same lady married Arthur Erskine of Blackgrange, himself a favourite royal equerry, she was presented with, among other things, 'Une vasquine de toille d'or cramosysye brodee d'une petitte frange d'or'.

During the month of January 1567, Mary stayed three separate nights at Callendar House – the 13th when passing from Stirling to Edinburgh with her infant son, the 24th when en route to visit the smallpox-ridden Darnley in Glasgow, and the 27th when both she and her husband rested for a night during their return journey to Edinburgh. Two weeks later Darnley was murdered in the Kirk o' Field and James Hepburn, Earl of Bothwell, thought by many to have organised the crime, began to play a major part in the queen's final six months of power. On 24 April he carried her off to Dunbar Castle and she agreed to marry him. On 15 May at four in the morning in Holyrood, the marriage was celebrated following Protestant forms and Lord Livingston was one of only eight noblemen present. The Lords, who opposed both the marriage and the queen, took up arms and at Carberry Hill they defeated her adherents. Mary we are told was hurried on foot through the streets of Edinburgh in her nightgown, supported by her faithful companions Mary Livingston and Mary Seton. She was sent to Loch Leven Castle.

On 29 June in Dumbarton, Lord Livingston and other loyal nobles denounced the queen's imprisonment and called on all loyal people to rise up in her cause. Support was slight and the queen was forced to abdicate the throne in favour of her infant son. The Earl of Moray became Regent and on 10 September he met a deputation of Mary's adherents, including Lord Livingston, to discuss her release. Again they were unsuccessful in their appeals and she remained confined until her escape in May the following year. Livingston, supported by men from Falkirk, fought beside her at Langside and he was with her as she left the country for exile in England. Lady Livingston joined them shortly afterwards.

Of course the Callendar House known to Mary Queen of Scots and witness to many of these great events was quite different from the building we know today. But behind the

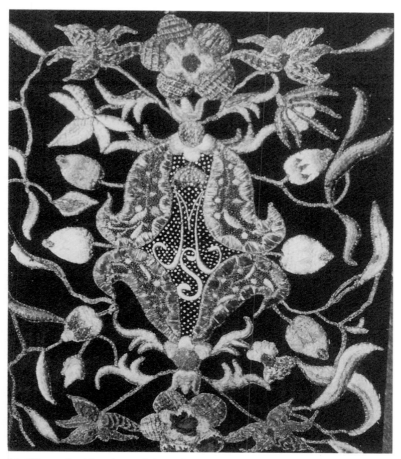

15. The embroidered panel from Callendar House with the monogram MS

Victorian façade at the west end lies the plain oblong 'castle' not much bigger that the square tower with which the house originally began life. For many years from the mid-Victorian era, the apartments said to have been used by Mary were devoted to displays of paintings and engravings depicting her life and times, but these were disposed of by auction in 1961. One fascinating item among the collection was a beautiful example of embroidery with the monogram 'M S' in the centre. It has recently been dated to the mid-sixteenth century and the style and workmanship suggest that it may be from the hand of one of the Maries or even the Queen herself – she was certainly known to be a very accomplished needlewoman and did make gifts of her work to her favourites. Whatever the truth, it remains as a tangible reminder of the link between the House and its most famous visitor.

The devotion of the Livingstons did not end with the departure of the queen to confinement in a succession of English castles and great houses. Both Lord William and his wife spent much of the next twenty years either by her side or on missions, both official and secret, aimed at securing her release and return to power. In 1569 an English agent visiting Tutbury Castle reported that the 'greatest personadge in house abowte hir is the Lord of Levenston and the lady his wife, which is a fayre gentilwoman; and it was told me both Protestants'. Around 1572, while her husband was in France on business for the queen, Lady Livingston returned to Falkirk where she was allowed to use her home on condition that it should not be available as a refuge for 'rebels or declared traitors'. Despite this undertaking the secret work continued and the Lady soon found herself confined in Dalkeith Castle where we are told that 'although things were so evident that she could not deny them, she would confess nothing except by tears and silence'.

The struggle for power in Scotland continued throughout the queen's long imprisonment, centred as ever on the possession of the young monarch. Successive regents faced constant challenges from other powerful rivals as well as from the supporters of the queen. And it was such rivalry that almost brought Falkirk yet another battle to add to the long list of engagements fought in and around this particular stretch of central Scotland.

In 1578 the king, aged twelve, was in Stirling Castle under the control of the regent, James Douglas, Earl of Morton. The so called Marian Lords, especially Atholl and Argyll supported as ever by the Livingston loyalists from Falkirk marched with an army of close on four thousand men towards the town bearing a blue 'sarsnet', that is, silk, banner showing the young king looking through a barred window with the words 'Liberty I crave and cannot have it' and, more menacingly, 'Either you shall have it or we will die for it'. The army, forever after known to their enemies as the 'faction of the Falkirk', came face to face with Morton advancing from Stirling to meet them with a force of equal strength and determination. Another bloody clash seemed inevitable. Archbishop Spotiswoode of Glasgow was an eyewitness:

> When they were on the point of engaging, the men handling their arms, and the chiefs riding from post to post conveying their orders, a trumpet sounded; and, when its echo had died away, there was a pause of a moment, then at another flourish of bugles, Sir Robert Bowes, the English ambassador, rode up attended by his suite, and stationed himself between the hostile ranks. He rode from chief to chief, entreating them to forbear from fighting; and at length, by proposing honourable terms, he succeeded in persuading them to agree to a truce.

But before the treaty was concluded a personal challenge was made, and accepted:

> A cavalier, of the name of Tait, a follower of the Laird of Cessford, who was at Falkirk in arms against Morton, cased in complete steel, rode out between the lines, bearing his glove on the point of his lance, and having thrown it before the enemies ranks, challenged any one of them to break a lance for his mistress. The pledge was lifted by a soldier of the name of Johnston, who was an attendant on the master of Glamis, and the challenge accepted. A place was immediately marked out for the combat; it was a little level plain on the banks of the Carron, on both sides of which river the horsemen stood spectators. It was about sunset on a calm autumn evening, 1578, when the combatants entered the lists; they sat on horseback, and remained at opposite extremitie of the course, till the signal was given, when they couched their spears, and rode at full gallop against each other. At the first shock, Tait was transfixed by his antagonist's lance; his hands lost hold of his arms and his bridle; he drooped his head, tumbled from his saddle, and died.

While these great national events were engaging the energies of
the Lords of Callander and their families, what was happening
to the village or town of Falkirk itself? Only part of the present
town centre – roughly north, and due east of the church, was
within the lands of Abbot's Kerse – the remainder to the south,
including the present High Street, was Callendar territory. The
parish church was of course the common link between these two
centres of power and it seems likely that the early village grew
up, around and away from the church along two roads – one
along modern Manor Street and Kerse Lane, down Ladysmill
towards the lands of Kerse and the other leading to the 'castle'
of Callendar possibly following Manor Street, Silver Row and
East Bridge Street and across the East Burn to Callendar. By
the mid-fifteenth century when the church was rebuilt the small
population, perhaps three or four hundred, probably lived in
an assortment of stone and wooden buildings in closes and
wynds off these narrow thoroughfares. By 1500 some of the land
in the area immediately north-west of the church in modern
Newmarket Street, as well as the land at the east end of the
'Kingis Streite' was being feued by both Holyrood and Callendar. The beginning of the expansion of the town might be
dated from then, for some reports in the early 1800s talk of old
stone buildings on the High Street bearing the date 1513. In
addition, certain old legal titles to buildings on the south side of
the High Street suggest that they were built on feus from the
'hospital at Torphichen' which possessed glebe lands connected
with the south aisle of the church at that period.

Fifty years later the Reformation brought the former church
lands into the hands of a lay commendator who had the right to
draw revenues formerly destined for the canons of Holyrood.
Attempts to take advantage of this reorganisation led to tension
between these new masters and the Callendar faction in the
divided town, and as early as 1566 followers of the two clashed
and blood was spilled. There followed an injunction from the
Privy Council against such behaviour, to be read at the mercat
crosses in Stirling and Falkirk. This is the earliest record of such
a cross in Falkirk which at that time did not enjoy the status
signified by a mercat cross, nor the power to arrange markets,

control trade, license merchants and manufacturers and levy charges which flowed from it. It may be that the commendator had decided to transfer some of the rights of the Barony of Kerse to the town as a way of increasing revenue and that this met with resistance from the jealous Callendar men. In the 1580s control of Kerse passed to a new commendator, Sir John Bellenden, Laird of Broughton, near Edinburgh, and for a period from 1587 onwards the town was officially part of the Barony of Broughton! In the same year there is a record of men trading in Falkirk though the nature and extent of this is unknown.

It is about this period that the five town gates or 'ports' were built. Their location is not certain though it seems likely that one stood on the present High Street near the Lint Riggs; another, Westquarter Port, at the entry to the modern Howgate Centre, one in Kirk Wynd near the Bank Street opening, and the fourth on the Cow Wynd. The last one, the East Port, probably stood near the point where Silver Row met the High Street. Although no trace of these now remains, and no archaeological dig has pinpointed their position, one or two of them survived long enough to have been seen and described by antiquaries in the early 1800s:

> The ports were built in 1585; they were arched gateways of stone, battlemented at top, with arrow or hagbut loopholes in the side walls. It is not long since the East Port was taken down, and one time-blackened arch is still remaining opposite 'the Lodging Yard'. The date, 1585, is discernable on a stone which was taken from the West Port when it was demolished, thirty or forty years ago. This port long hung over the street in a half ruined state, and there was a circular, sloping vizzying hole, through which the armed porter might reconnoitre those who demanded entrance.

Formidable as they sound, there is no evidence that these gates formed part of a full-walled defensive system – indeed later information suggests a series of low stone walls joining buildings or the back ends of properties together as a territorial marker and defence against wandering sheep rather than invading enemies.

By the end of the sixteenth century, Livingston family support for the Stuarts brought the seventh Lord of Callendar, Alexander, to prominence as part of the king's party. Even before he succeeded his father he was a close confidant of the royal favourite Esme Stuart, Duke of Lennox, and acted as a trusted messenger between the two when the Catholic Duke was exiled at the behest of the Scottish parliament. On one occasion in the 1580s he marched with a troop of men from Falkirk and captured the town and castle of Stirling from the king's enemies, and in 1600 he was said by some to have been on hand with his men to help rescue King James during the notorious Gowrie conspiracy. A few years earlier, the young Princess Elizabeth, who in later life would marry Frederick, the Elector Palatine, and in due course give rise to the Hanovarian succession to the British throne, was given into the care of the Livingstons and spent much of her early years at Callendar House. The Scottish churchmen were outraged at this for Lady Livingston was 'an obstinat an profest Papist', but the King had his way. A second royal princess, Margaret, who died in infancy, was also placed with Lord Alexander in confirmation of King James's determination to resist such pressure.

Two very important rewards flowed from this service and the years of loyal support which preceded it. The financially pressed king could not afford to pay the bill for the education and care of his daughters and so offered payment in kind. At the end of 1600 Lord Alexander was created first Earl of Linlithgow, and earlier in the same year the king raised Falkirk, or at least the Callendar part of it, to the status of a free burgh of barony

> granting to its inhabitants power of buying or selling and of creating burgesses, of having a market cross and holding weekly markets on Thursdays and two fair days a year on 29 June and 26 October; with power to the said Alexander to approve guards of the said fairs and market days and with the power of choosing bailies and of building a court

house . . . and moreover he erects the whole into a free regality with the power to hold justice courts.

. . . and all of this in return for 'one pair of gilt spurs to be rendered at the castle of Callendar every year at Whitsunday'. It is in many ways the birth certificate of the burgh of Falkirk: while it did not at that stage apply to the whole town, it laid the basis for all the developments which followed. Any conflict between the baronies which might have arisen was avoided because by 1600 moves to unite the two were well under way. The marriage in 1587 between the then Baron Broughton and Margaret Livingston, sister of Sir Alexander, produced a son, Sir James Bellenden who, in 1606 conveyed the lands of Kerse including his part of Falkirk, to his uncle Sir Alexander Livingston. For the first time since the thirteenth century, the whole of the town lay under one jurisdiction.

CHAPTER 5

Kirk Session and Baron Court

It was in the early years of the seventeenth century, during
Alexander Livingston's time that the first surviving account of
life in the town was begun – the kirk session records of Falkirk
Parish Church, which detail the regular meetings of the minister and elders from 1617 onwards. These carefully maintained
and preserved records provide an invaluable insight into the
day-to-day life of the community, albeit filtered through the
eyes of the stern elders as they dealt with countless 'scandalous
persones for their reformatione'. Elsewhere in the district
similar accounts were being maintained in communities with
ancient histories like Airth, Bothkennar and Kinneil, as well as
Denny and the united parishes of Larbert and Dunipace
created in the early years of the Reformation. Some of these
records will be used later when we look at the stories of these
places, but here we are concerned in the main with the huge
parish of Falkirk which at the time included Polmont, Slamannan and Muiravonside. Much has been written elsewhere
about the kirk session, this uniquely Scottish institution with
its seemingly insatiable appetite for the gossip and general tittle
tattle which formed a substantial part of the agenda for their
fortnightly meetings in hundreds of parishes throughout the
land. Falkirk was certainly no different from all the others
and in charity we should say that the motivation of many,
perhaps the majority was a genuine belief that by calling
sinners to an honest repentance they were doing them the best
possible service. They were certainly following the guidance
given them by the founding fathers who had decreed that a
Kirk Session

stands in reproving and correcting of those faults which the civil sword doth either neglect, either may not punish – drunkenness, excess, be it in apparel or be it in eating and drinking, fornication, oppression of the poor by exactions, deceiving of them in buying and selling by wrong mete or measure, wanton words, or licentious living.

Thus the elders of Falkirk had plenty of scope to search and pry and they used it to the maximum. The swearers and fornicators, drinkers and idlers, the sabbath breakers and disturbers of the peace found themselves regularly summonsed to 'compear' before the Session to answer for their particular brand of scandal. Most came when called, and subjected themselves to interrogation and remonstrance as well as the usual public repentance, normally 'three several sabbaths' at the pillar or stool of repentance plus a public dressing-down from the minister during the service.

Desecrating the Sabbath by doing anything at all except praying brought many an early Falkirk 'bairn' to the notice of the elders. In an agricultural area where nature was no respecter of the laws of church or state, many people worked as the need arose and it comes as no great surprise to find 'stacking of corne', 'shearin', 'picking pease', 'carting divots', 'driving cattle' and 'yoking a pleuch' among the regular charges. Many other Sunday diversions also attracted the attention of the all-seeing session and those who were found 'meeting and talking in the street after publick worship' or 'drinking wi' Hielandmen' or 'fighting in the open fields' or even 'idly gazing from windows', could expect little mercy! Pity the poor soul who was called up to answer the claim that he had been seen 'walking fast on the Sabbath', presumably guilty by implication, in that if you walk fast you are obviously on your way to do something, and that, whatever it might be, was not allowed on Sunday.

Excessive drinking was an early besetting sin of Falkirk people and one which lasted well into modern times. The Kirk's vain attempts to stamp it out, and to eliminate the 'horrid swearing' which usually went with it, are confirmed by regular entries in the records of this early period. Even the church officer was not exempt – indeed he seems to have been allowed to break almost every ordinance in the book before he was finally removed from office –a rare flash of charity in such unforgiving times:

> 16th June 1625
> The Session having taken into consideration the prophane and wicked life of John Dun, occasionit by his druckinnes and evile dispossitioun, and notwithstanding of monie grose and oppin faultis qlk hes bein comittit be him in tyme past to the hie offence of God and evile exampill to uyris . . . of his leudness, filthie druckinnes and wicked lyfe . . . and shameles behaviour under cloude of nicht.

Then there were those who fought in church over a seat, women who nagged their husbands, pipers and fiddlers who played at weddings and christenings against the orders of the session, and even those rash enough to slander their 'betters' like the Falkirk tailor in 1624 who was ordered 'for his misbehaviour and unbreading speiches to Dame Margaret Crawford, Lady Dorrator, to go doune on his kneis and ask hir forgiveness publicklie in the kirk'.

Another musician who fell foul of the Session from time to time was the town drummer, George Brocklay, a cooper whose task was to call the people together for a special announcement at the mercat cross or to lead criminals through the town before their banishment 'furth the paroch of Falkirk'. George was called up before the session accused of 'drinking and tonkering ye drum at unseasonable hours on ye sabbath morne'.

Most often the church punished wrong-doers in its own way but occasionally the civil authorities were called in where some form of corporal punishment was thought appropriate. This usually took the form of a threat rather than an actual sentence, though we may be sure that the drunken cooper was called on many a time to signal the public whipping and eviction of undesirables:

28th May 1635

Nicolas Anderson enacted herself to undergo banishment, and never to be seen in this boundis againe, otherwise to be scourget through the toune of Falkirk or drowned as salbe thoucht most convenient.

Convenient to the session or baillies and not poor Nicolas presumably!

But reform of the Scottish church gave Falkirk people much more than a new range of sanctions on their behaviour. The early years of the seventeenth century saw the beginnings, albeit haltingly at first, of a system of basic schooling and of poor relief. Knox and his colleagues had called for a school in every parish, charged with the task of equipping the 'priesthood of all believers' to read the scripture that would speak directly to them. As a side benefit improved education would assist the development of the community's trade and manufactures.

In 1594 Thomas Ambrose, the first Falkirk 'dominie' of whom we have any information, was deposed for unacceptable behaviour, probably immorality, but soon after he was restored after special pleading from the parishioners. Early in the new century, there is mention of one James Johnstoun, a 'reader' whose 'lyff hes bein good and without scandal' but was not properly qualified to teach. Under pressure from the local presbytery the Falkirk minister 'promises to use diligence to get ane qualified master iff they will find him sufficient maintenance. The brethren thinks it meit that the Erle of Linlithgow, the patrone, be requested that he would give his assistance for the furtherance of so good a work as to have ane shcool their for instructioun and educasun of youth'.

By 1632, this seems to have been achieved because the master, John Dishingtoun, who was also session clerk and precentor of the psalms, was earning £40 Scots. Thereafter the school appears to have become an established part of parochial activity, though where the children met and what they studied beyond reading is not known. In 1644 the session underlined their determination to extend the provision: ' All the children with the town who had past sex years of age should be put to the common schole kept for the present be Mr James Levingstoun and if there wer any whose parents wer not able to pay for them, in that case he should teach them gratis.'

Despite the best efforts of the elders there is evidence that others were offering education for fees and that such adventure or dame schools were drawing children away from the parochial school. In 1656 for example, the session banned women from 'keeping any school', but later, relented so far as to allow a woman to teach sewing and weaving to girls but on no account 'the reiding'. Later still one Grizel Kincaid was forbidden to 'meddle with the teaching of male children'. John Forest, James Nicol, William Drummond and Patrick Renny followed one another as parochial teachers apparently using a succession of unsatisfactory rented houses and constantly fighting to secure the legal salary for the job. It was a situation that would continue almost unchanged for the next two centuries.

The relief of poverty had always been a church responsibility which the kirk sessions of the new reformed church determined to continue and develop. Regular collection and distribution of funds to relieve the hardship of the deserving poor became a regular feature of Scottish church life, with those on the approved parish list being paid a small amount each month. Vagabonds from other areas were denied any support and even begging was licensed, and limited to official parochial beggars!

But in common with kirk sessions in every part of Scotland, the majority of the Falkirk elders' time was taken up with up identifying and punishing what the early fathers called, with commendable bluntness 'fornication'. Later on, the clerks would search for softer expressions like 'uncleanness' or even 'social impurity', but the meaning was the same, and any young Falkirk couple making the mistake of holding hands, might find themselves on the long list of offenders grilled by the elders at every meeting. Three Sundays of public humiliation usually followed, but if adultery, a much more heinous crime, was involved, then a more severe punishment was meted out. The earliest record of such a case in Falkirk occurred on 7 January, 1619 when the couple involved were ordered to pay a fine of five pounds and, 'stand at the kirk dore, bare futtit and bair legit for several Sabathis, from the first bell to the last, and thereafter to pass to the stool of repentence in sec claithis everie day of the said sex Sabathis in tyme of sermone.'

With services lasting three hours in a dark and damp kirk with no heating and a bare earthen floor, such punishment in a Scottish winter must have been almost impossible to bear, yet the evidence suggests that, for the most part, the people accepted the iron rule and were prepared for almost any punishment rather than lose the 'sealing ordinances' of baptism and communion for themselves or their children. Indeed there are even incidents where enthusiasm for the service was itself a cause for disapproval, as when one man was accused of 'misbehaviour and trublance of the Kirk upone Pasche Day, by lowping in at the windo after the dores were clossit and the sermoun began'. The elders accepted his claim that 'it was for the earnest he had to heir the Word preachit and to communicat of the Sacrament'. Such communion services were held only once or twice each year and they were very big affairs, drawing hundreds of visitors to the town from other parishes over a period of three or four days before the 'occasion' itself. The people's determination not to miss out on the big day is confirmed by one of the earliest visitors to the area in 1643. Gilbert Blakhal, described interestingly enough as 'priest of the Scots mission in France, in the low countries and in Scotland', arrived in Bo'ness late at night:

> I went to sie my horse suppe and then called for my bedde, as if I had been wearyed, and paying myn hostesse at night was mounted upone my hors by the brack of day, and passing by the Falkirk, a place where Walas resorted oft, I did see the country people whigging their meres to be tymously at the kirk, as if they had been running for a pryse. They passed me, bidding me spurre my hors to communicat with them, to whom I gave no answer, but did ride softly to the end of the Torrewoode when I did find an ailehouse all alone.

If Gilbert was in Scotland to assess the prospects for a revival of Catholic fortunes he picked a bad time, for by then the country was embroiled in a dispute which would take the church even further from the old style of liturgy and church government. Once again the Livingstons of Callendar were in the thick of the argument.

When Charles I succeeded his father to the united thrones of Scotland and England in 1625 it was clear from the outset that his personal adherence to episcopalian forms would eventually lead him into conflict with his presbyterian countrymen north of the border. In the event more than a decade passed before the affair reached a crisis when an attempt by Charles to force the Scots into submission provoked armed resistance in the so-called Bishop's Wars. For the first time in almost three centuries a Livingston took up arms against a Stewart King. This was James, Lord Almond, who in 1633 had purchased the lands of Callendar from his elder brother Alexander, the eighth Lord

16. James Livingston of Almond, first Earl of Callendar

Livingston. A staunch presbyterian and a very experienced soldier, he signed the National Covenant in 1638, promising to defend the liberty of the Scottish church against the king's encroachments. But like his great contemporary, Montrose, he was both covenanter and royalist, and for a decade he would agonise over every decision which threatened to place the two on opposite sides. In 1640 he joined Montrose and several other nobles in the Cumbernauld Bond, a secret agreement to defend both king and covenant against what they saw as the evil intent of Argyll and the Scottish church party. Despite this he accepted, albeit reluctantly, the post of second-in-command to General Alexander Leslie in the powerful Scottish army which marched into England later the same year. In the face of such resistance the king soon gave way and a peace agreement followed. In the aftermath the king rewarded the leaders of the Scots – Argyll, Leslie and Almond, who was created first Earl of Callendar. In the same year, 1641, he was offered the post of Treasurer to the King, but the Scottish estates, aware now of the Cumbernauld Bond, refused to sanction the appointment.

Despite this easing of the situation the king's determination to have the Scots submit to his religious view kept the new earl on the side of the kirk, and when the civil war in England broke out in 1643 James Livingston was once again among the commanders of the Scots army against the king. The Falkirk session had made its position clear when the new Solemn League and Covenant was signed in the church with great care taken to ensure that all took part:

October 31st, 1643
It is ordained that on Sunday when the Covenant shall be subscribed, the persons following shall attend the several parts if the kirk, viz: To attend the north isle, Wastquarter and Patrick Grindlay; to attend the wast end of the kirk, John Monteath and John Wyse; to attend the east end, Walter Scott and Patrick Guidlat; to attend the wast loft, Alexander Watt and Hew Hall; to attend the east loft, Robert Burn and Patrick Guidlat.

Thus blessed by the local fathers and brethren, James and his
Falkirk vassals marched off once again to war, fighting on the
side of the parliament against the king at Marston Moor and at
Carlisle. When Charles surrendered to the Scots, Callendar was
one of the leaders who spent long hours with the king, trying to
persuade him to relax his religious demands and reconcile
himself with his natural supporters in Scotland. Though unsuccessful in this, Callendar's natural attachment to the royal
cause seems to have led to a personal understanding with the
king, for in 1646 the town of Falkirk was once again elevated in
status. The baronies of Kerse and Callendar were united into a
single free regality with Falkirk as its head burgh. New powers
were conferred on James in relation to the control of trade and
manufacture and the administration of justice within the town,
and for the first time it was in a position to match in prestige
and power, the rival royal burghs of Linlithgow and Stirling.

Within twelve months the earl, disturbed by the way in
which the victorious parliamentarians were acting in both
religious and political affairs, led his battle weary men from
Falkirk to war for the last time in a desperate attempt to save
the king. This great 'engagement', as it was called, was frowned
upon by the Scottish Kirk, including the elders of Falkirk, and
the earl and his men were later condemned by the kirk session
which wished no truck with episcopal Stewart kings. In the
event it was a disaster as Cromwell's new model army swept the
Scots aside with ease. Near Preston in August 1648 the Scots
were crushed and Callendar with his Falkirk cavalry broke out
from the closing circle of the enemy and eventually escaped to
the north and home to the hostile arms of the kirk. James
Livingston himself made his way in disguise to London and
escaped to Holland where he joined the party surrounding the
exiled Prince Charles.

Over the next few years the session dealt with seventy-five
Falkirk soldiers along with officers like 'Sir Alexander Levingstoune, ane leavetennant-colonal to ane regiment of hors' and,
'Sir William Callander of Dorrator, captain-leavetennant to
ane hors troup'. All declared themselves 'sorriful and willing to
obey ye kirk'.

Throughout these stormy events and beyond through the century, the people of the town carried on with their everyday business seemingly undisturbed by the power struggles waged in their name far from home. It is a period rich in source material, for apart from the sessional records, we also have the detailed reports of the Court Book of Callendar from 1638 to 1715, in which the bailies of Falkirk dispense justice in the name of 'ane nobill and potent Lord James Lord Levingstowne of Almont and Callender'. It is an amazing document full of fascinating details which illuminate the lives of the ordinary working people of the district. Here are the indwellers of the town, the 'portioners, feweris and tennentis' along with the tradesmen – 'smithes', and 'wrights', 'fleschors', 'websters' and 'baxteris', 'maltmen', 'cordiners' and 'tailyers' and, of course, the powerful 'mairtchands' –settling disputes, pursuing claims and receiving judgments on matters of slight or great importance by turns. But this was no mighty lord laying down the law to cringing vassals, but bailies who are themselves portioners and merchants, farmers and maltmen resolving disputes among their peers so that a well-regulated trading environment is available for all –or at least all those who bore the official seal of approval:

4th December 1638
Item . . . that na induellar within the said toune of Falkirk use any traffique or mak any mairthandice within the said burgh thairof except onlie those quha is admittit burgesss of the said burgh and hes ressavit from his lordschip burgess tyckettis and quhasoevar doethe in the contrair heirof to pey X li

There many examples of the Court trying to protect community assets:

7th January 1642
The quhilk day it is statute and ordanit That the haill scheipe be put furthe of the towne of Falkirk befoir any peis be sawne under the paine of 40ss and that na bairnes cum within the

said peis in tyme of hervest . . . and that fowles be keipit in
housss fra the first of mairtche untill the first of June.

And there are judgments on the ownership of a horse – or a
house, on money borrowed and not repaid, on goods ordered
but not supplied and cloth supplied but not paid for. Most often
the punishments are financial penalties, in part to right the
wrong but in part no doubt to swell the coffers of 'ane potent
and nobil lord'.

When the people stepped out of line to resolve their differ-
ences in a more direct way, the Court was always ready to make
them pay for the pleasure:

> 5th Appryle 1639
> And anent the complaint gevine in befoir the said bailzies be
> Hendrie Hall in Falkirk againis Patrick Muirhead maltman
> thair ffor casting of ane glasful of beir upone the said Hendrie
> his face . . . unlawit in V lib.

and, if a glass was not to hand, more unusual weapons were
sometimes available:

> 8th February 1639
> And anent the complaint gevine be the said Johne Gairdner
> againis the said Alexander Levingstoune for stryking of him
> wt ane stalfe or golfeclub and blooding of him yrwt upone the
> face to the effusioune of his bloode on the 2 day of february
> instant wt the burgh of Falkirk.

Where the local golfers hit a ball with the club, rather than
their opponents, has not yet been discovered, though a couple
of entries in the kirk session records suggest that the first Falkirk
links were at the 'Cleddens'. No doubt the public executions,
which were also held there from time to time, provided some
diversion for those golfers waiting for the players ahead to clear
the next green.

The picture that emerges from the crowded pages of the
Court Book is of a busy, even a bustling, small town which had

obviously made rapid strides in the relatively short period of its legitimate burghhood. It was considerably larger, with a population of around 1,500 souls living and working in a much more complex network of streets, not very different from the town centre today. A charter of 1645 mentions 'reparations and extensions about to be made in the town of Falkirk', and certainly a good deal of building work was undertaken from then on despite the unsettled times. The High Street was by then established as the principal thoroughfare, with what may have been the former main street becoming, as a consequence, the 'Back Raw', now Manor Street. That part of the High Street immediately to the west of the present steeple became the town market-place where the jail or tolbooth stood, along with the symbol of burghal status, the mercat cross and the official weighing machine or tron. Many street names familiar today, Fleshmarket Close, Wooer (Weaver) Street and Baxter's (Baker's) Wynd, recall the trades of the old burgh, while Lint Riggs, Bean Row and the Cow Wynd of course, remind us that the new prosperity, such as it was, derived in the main from agriculture and would continue to do so for a century and a half. A number of new buildings were erected during this period; the Earl of Callendar himself had a new town house built just off the Kirk Wynd near its junction with the Back Raw and a new Tolbooth with a steeple was built in 1697 to replace the earlier one. The Lairds of Bantaskine, Westquarter and Rashiehill built substantial lodgings on the High Street and visitors to the town at the end of the century talk about a number of new stone lands or tenements under construction in the same area.

In this growing trading community the quality and quantity of what was brought forward for sale was a matter of constant concern to the bailies, and the pages of the Barony Court Book contain many enactments on bread, ale, meat and meal and even shoes. Agents were deputed to visit the market and search out the 'blawne mutton and collapit flesche', or ensure that white bread was sold at 'ane unce for ane penny' and no more. We might these days envy Alexander Watt and John Warden of the Cow Wynd who were appointed as the official 'testeris of aill', duty bound to visit all the suppliers in Falkirk and ensure that their product was worth the fixed price of one shilling and eightpence! And tasters of the unofficial variety found themseles on the wrong end of the law. Witness the sad tale of John Gow and William Baillie who were collecting several hogsheads of claret from Falkirk's official port on the Carron at Abbotshaugh. Having 'ane inclination to taste the berrie they did break up ane of the hogsheids and did drink themselves drunk therewth' –according to the charge they managed to get through three gallons – and were fined thirty pounds Scots for their efforts.

Hard drinking was a common complaint among the fleshers, of whom there were an astonishing number in Falkirk at the time. A great deal of mutton and beef must have been available for sale and this must throw doubt on the commonly held view that lowland Scots people existed on oatmeal and precious little else at this particular period. The fleshers were a constant source of concern for both Baron Court and Kirk Session. Sometimes it was their language which annoyed the elders:

> November 1668
> It was represented to the Session of the horrible and un-christian-like life of the fleshers in this town lived in profaining the Lord's name by cursing and swearing. Therfor the Session has appointed John Moir to wait upon the fleshmercat on Munday, James Sword upon Tuesday, John Mack upon Wednesday and Thomas Burn on Thursday, to remark the banners and swearers and to report.

One has visions of these devout agents listening in at the door of the market and cringing at every expletive from the unruly butchers, but continuing with their sacred duty nonetheless. More often it was the Court which had to deal with the countless assaults involving the fleshers, whose disdain for authority was typified by one John Stirling who was fined twenty pounds for saying that 'he caired not ane fart for any baillie in Falkirk'.

But the authorities' efforts to maintain a safe and peaceful community went far beyond controlling the behaviour of the inhabitants of the burgh. External threats like the plague which visited the Falkirk area in late 1644 produced a swift response from both the civil and religious powers. In December of that year we find the Earl of Callendar writing to his Falkirk baillie urging immediate action to close up houses and guard others and to ensure that those confined are supplied with 'meill and coales'. Since contaminated clothing had to be destroyed, the earl ordered his men to 'try what course cloath can be gottin in Falkirk at 2s or half a croune ane ell, and buy it, and cause all the taylzeours fall a making of four tailed coats and breiches.' Both presbytery and session deemed the arrival of the pestilence a divine punishment and special days of prayer and fasting were ordered. But more practical decisions were also taken, which satisfied both spiritual and earthly requirements –'Banquittas, brydellies and nicht wakes were not decent when God is offendit with the land.' Later it was decreed that no shearers would be allowed in the town without an official pass. The plague stayed for fully two years in the town and there were many victims who were not permitted a burial in the kirkyard for fear that the pestilence would survive and return when lairs were opened. Instead they were carried outside the town to the common land and buried together in what were thereafter known as the Pest Graves. A stout stone wall was built round the spot on Graham's Muir to prevent cattle from eating the grass, but a more en-lightened generation removed all traces the following century. The site lies at the junction of George Street and Russel Street on the north-east corner and few of the inhabitants of the area are aware of its existence – perhaps it is just as well.

James Livingston's exile in Holland did not last long. Soon after the execution of Charles I in 1649, his young son agreed, on Livingston's advice, to accept the conditions offered by the Scots, and become what they had always wanted – a 'cove-nanted King'. The earl thought this new arrangement would restore him to favour, especially as the formidable army of Cromwell was on its way north to punish the Scots for their renewed support of the Stewarts. But he was wrong. The unlawful 'engagement' was still roundly condemned and the forfeiture of his house and lands was confirmed by the parliament. He was classified a 'malignant' and ordered out of Scotland. Three months later the Scottish army was shattered at Dunbar but only after a long argument and with severe reservations did the Estates finally agreed to allow the earl to return and assist the country in her hour of great need.

Personal rivalry coupled with his previous record of vacillation prevented him from playing a leading role in the Scottish army and he was unable to return to Callendar House because the exclusion remained against him. He was therefore spared the immediate vengeance of Cromwell and his hardened parliamentary army which came face to face with the new king and his followers near Linlithgow in the early summer of 1651. Advancing to meet them there, Cromwell's troops drew close to the Callendar castle of his old enemy James Livingston. What happened next is uncertain. One account suggests that Cromwell asked for, and was given, a solemn undertaking that the defenders of the castle would refrain from firing on the English troops as they passed by. In return the building and its occupants would be left alone. As soon as Cromwell's troops came within range, the Livingston guns opened up and the roundheads responded by turning back to punish the perfidious Scots. Other versions of the story have Cromwell and his men marching straight to Falkirk to begin the siege without pause for negotiation. Whatever the truth we do know that a detachment under General George Monck, Coldstream Guards, then known as Monck's Regiment – subjected the house or 'castle' to a considerable bombardment and its defences were blasted down by the superior firepower of the enemy. The castle was, of course, still the plain fortified building of Mary Stuart's time but it probably had crenellations and gunloops as well as a moat, drawbridge and curtain barbican wall some distance in front of the building itself. Despite this it proved no match for Monck's determined veterans, among whom was one Cornet Bayne whose letter dated 19 July 1651 reports on the attack:

> From the camp near Kallender House we advanced again to Fawkirk near to Torwood. We have been here four nights.

Upon Tuesday last about sunset after we had made a breach upon Kallendar House even in the face of the enemy we stormed it and lost a captain of foot, our gunner Robert Hargreave of your troop and 2 or 3 private soldiers. More were slain in the storm. We slew the enemy about 50 persons, and such as had quarter given them were most of them wounded. Little was taken from the house except horses and cattle of the country people.

One account suggests that James Livingston may have watched the destruction of his home from the entrenchments of the Scottish army but there was to be no swift revenge for him. The main armies did not clash and the Scots withdrew to the Torwood and formed a defensive line above the Carron crossing at Larbert.

In the immediate aftermath of the defeat, the town and even the church were subjected to the privations inflicted when a large and unfriendly army are in residence. Some accounts suggest that horses were stabled in the kirkyard and that soldiers slept in the nave of the church itself – the area of the town adjacent to the glebe of the church, which is still known as the 'garrison' may well date from this period. Cattle and sheep went to feed the hungry troopers and many months after the departure of Cromwell's men, locals were still asking for help from the church to offset their losses. For a period the government's Commander in Scotland, General Monck, made his headquarters at Callendar House and he may have began the repairs and restoration of the building which had been so damaged in the encounter.

The final defeat of Charles II by Cromwell at Worcester in September 1651 did not help James Livingston in his quest to regain his estates. For the next five years he moved about the country, sometimes living in 'his house in Pinkie', for several months confined in Burntisland and Edinburgh Castles for suspected contact with royalists and in Aberdeen on secret business which may have involved the loyalist forces in the Highlands. He spent seven months in London in 1655 in an attempt to petition Cromwell directly to lift the sequestration on his Falkirk estates. In the end he was successful and early the following year, at the age of sixty, he was at last restored to the house and lands of Callendar after an exile of nearly eight years. Throughout this period he seems to have retained the loyalty of his Falkirk followers and, according to the Court Book, the Falkirk bailies continued to exercise baronial power in his name. He found the house and estates in very poor condition and his financial affairs in disarray – according to the trustees who had held the estates, the Callendar income per annum was £1,554 and the debts £24,317. He began the process of restoration of both house and lands and spent much of the rest of his life in this task, though he did sit in the Parliament from time to time. He was one of only fourteen noblemen who carried the coffin of the great Montrose to his place of honour in St Giles in May 1661.

One of his first acts in Falkirk was to establish a small refuge or 'hospital' for the aged which stood to the west of Lint Riggs, and tradition has also linked his name with the building of the Cross Well in the market-place near the Tolbooth. As a reward for their loyalty, or so the story goes, the old earl arranged for a line of water pipes made of hollow tree trunks jointed by lead, to be laid from his policies to the south of the town, to the High Street. There a large and handsome well-head of dressed stone was constructed, bearing the Livingston coat of arms, and on one memorable day the earl arrived to hand over his gift to the people. One Victorian antiquarian with an eye for the romantic moment and a style to match, takes up the story:

> He caused his feuars to range themselves at the cross and after thanking them for the gallantry with which they had fought beside him, and reminding them of the many fields through which their fathers had followed his . . . having filled a bicker from the pure well stream which was poured from the mouth of a sculptured lion, the grey haired baron stood up in his stirrups and drank off a quaich 'To the wives and Bairns o' Fakirk giving them the well and all its fountains in present, forever'.

. . . and presumably their nickname as well, for 'Bairns' the inhabitants of the town certainly are, and have been for well over two centuries. Alas for the romantic, the accepted date for the opening of the well is 1681, several years after the death of James, and the arms on the well-head are those of his nephew Alexander who succeeded him around 1674. If we are kind we might say that the events described took place when the water arrived and before the well-head was completed. It was demolished in the early nineteenth century and replaced by the familiar roundal of ashlar which bears the date 1817. After an absence of 12 years 'for repairs' it is now back in place, a tangible link to one of the most exciting periods in the town's history.

Throughout the century when episcopalian and presbyterian held sway by turns, the changing fortunes appear to have provoked only limited defiance in the town of Falkirk itself. While clergy of the wrong persuasion were elsewhere forced from their charges, successive ministers of the parish survived, although the tendency of the masters and ministers to support episcopacy, and the preference of the people for a presbyterian settlement, must have created some real tension. In the early years of the century, for example, the minister Adam Bellenden, brother of the commendator Sir Lewis, was a

17. The original Cross Well from 1681 with its 1817 replacement

staunch presbyterian whose opposition to the continued existence of bishops in the Scottish church brought a brief suspension and a stern warning as to his future conduct. In keeping with the times he went on to experience a conversion, before becoming first Bishop of Dunblane and then of Aberdeen. And in 1638, around the time of the signing of the National Covenant, a woman called Margaret Clelland was up before the Falkirk session accused of 'casting stones at the Bishope of Galloway'! Later, in 1649, after Cromwell's triumph, several people in Falkirk protested at the performance of their minister Mr Edward Wright, whose episcopalian leanings were well known. A two-year suspension was the result, but Mr Wright returned to serve until 1663, after the Restoration of the monarchy. Maybe these relatively mild protests did not turn to violent opposition because the people feared retribution, but possibly the real impact of change on liturgy and church management at the local level was more limited than the stormy national disputes would suggest. Either way, most of the great movements seemed to impinge on Falkirk people only when the call to arms came once more or when soldiers of another power arrived to take over the town.

James Livingston's adventurous life came to a peaceful end around 1674 when he was about 75 years old. Although he left no legitimate heir he did not die childless for we have a record of one son, Sir Alexander Livingston of Dalderse and a daughter, Lady Helenora Livingston of Bantaskin, who were born over half a century before. But the new master of Callendar was his nephew Alexander, the second son of the Earl of Linlithgow, a passionate supporter of the protesting covenanters. The restoration of Charles II had brought a steady return to the episcopal policies which had led to his father's deposition and many Scottish presbyterians took to the open fields to worship in the way they preferred. Presbytery records suggest that such conventicles were taking place within Falkirk parish with the open support of Lord Alexander. Government troops seized Callendar House in 1675 and again three years later when, according to one historian, 'the Falkirk mob rose in great fury and put the intruders to flight'. The following year Alexander's half brother, the 3rd Earl of Linlithgow, who was, by contrast a strong royalist and episcopalian, marched through Falkirk with the celebrated Graham of Claverhouse, the 'Bonnie Dundee' of legend, on the way to the bloody slaughter of the covenanters at Bothwell Bridge.

The government introduced new tests to ascertain the beliefs of people in positions of power and authority and when Alexander declined he was 'put to the horn' in July 1683, denounced at the mercat cross as a rebel and stripped of his baronial power. Two years later he died and was succeeded by Linlithgow's second son, also Alexander. He was, as one might expect, a staunch episcopalian – once again the pendulum had moved, this time back to where it had been for most of the century.

Despite the sustained opposition of their latest Lord, the people of Falkirk parish seemed to have welcomed the final settlement which followed the deposing of the Catholic King, James VII and his replacement by William of Orange in 1688. This, of course, meant trouble ahead and it was not long before the patron and the local kirk were at daggers drawn over who should fill the Falkirk pulpit. The Revd Andrew Slirrie, the choice of Lord Livingston, was rejected by the people and he was deposed by the General Assembly, but the battle continued with the keys of the kirk, and other property like lavers, basins and mortcloths being withheld. Once again a detachment of troopers under Sir Thomas Livingston were sent to the town in case of any disorder, but fortunately harsh words and legal threats were the weapons of choice. This wrangle went on until 1693 before a suitable presbyterian-minded candidate, the Revd William Crichton, was called to Falkirk. He was a long-standing fighter against bishops in the kirk and one of a celebrated group who had defiantly established a presbytery in Bo'ness in the difficult days of the 1680s.

By the end of the century the whole episcopal system was effectively dead in Scotland and from then on the ministers in the Falkirk pulpit were confirmed presbyterians. A period of peace and quiet was what the growing burgh and its war-weary population badly needed, but when the new century dawned it was very much the mixture as before.

CHAPTER 6

Cattle Trysts and Highland Armies

In 1695 the two earldoms of Callendar and Linlithgow were combined once again, in the person of yet another James Livingston, whom fate had decreed would be the fourth and last Earl of Callendar. His early years were marked by periods of crop failure and severe hardship throughout Scotland, and the Falkirk area was no exception. The kirk session reported that 'the number of poor within the parish does dayly abound', and schemes to relieve growing poverty occupied much of their time. No class in the district was exempt from the impact and the elders found it difficult to raise money among the leading men of the parish or even call in the loans made over the years to various lairds and merchants. 'King William's years' as these lean times came to be known, brought Falkirk's steady growth to an end for a time, and prospects as the new century opened were decidedly grim. As a Burgh of Barony, Falkirk was required to pay £10 per annum tax to the Royal Burgh of Stirling but because of 'great scarcity and continual quartering of soldiers on the people' the inhabitants were 'incapable of paying as much as half of what was formerly demanded of them'. The Privy Council reduced the amount due to under £2.

The triumph of presbyterianism brought new severity to the daily life of the people, already oppressed by the vagaries of nature. Puritanism returned with a vengeance and the Sabbath desecraters, fiddlers, dancers and fornicators found themselves pursued with renewed vigour. Public repentance multiplied and the numbers banished from the parish increased. The earliest act of the new minister in 1694, William Burnett, had been to complain about the pillar being too 'great a distance from the pulpit and so darkly situat'. Out it came into the open and business boomed! The old Kirk was in a poor state of repair and efforts by the session to have the leading land-owners, and the new earl, do something about it came to nothing. By 1710 things were so severe that the session ordered 'John Jervay, wright in Falkirk' to prop up one of the walls, and once again appealed for help to rescue the 'ruinous fabrick' of the church. Although he eventually agreed to this, James Livingston's thoughts were elsewhere.

Like most of his ancestors he was a Stewart loyalist and cherished hopes of a return to the throne for the exiled family of King James. He was involved at an early stage in the intrigue of the Earl of Mar to raise a Jacobite army and when the Stewart standard was raised in 1715 he was appointed a brigadier in command of a regiment of horse. He fought in the indecisive battle at Sherrifmuir with Falkirk men by his side, but the lack of a clear-cut victory brought the Jacobite challenge to a swift end. Tradition has it that James returned to his house after the battle, but that a detachment of government troopers arrived in Falkirk soon after to seek him out. Once again the loyal 'bairns' came to his rescue by delaying the soldiers at the mercat cross, with sticks and stones, thus allowing Earl James to escape to exile. With him went the Livingston dynasty, for soon after he was attainted, his lands were forfeited and the earldoms of Linlithgow and Call-endar were extinguished. He died in France in 1725 and the York Buildings Company of London became the proprietors of his ancient house and land at a cost of just £18,751.

In 1723 Alexander Johnstone of Kirkland left a detailed description of the 'village of Falkirk' and the surrounding coun-tryside in the aftermath of the failed rebellion and the hasty departure of the leading landowner. Although his opinion con-firms the general view that 'this place has suffered extremely' he describes the state of the town and its commerce in fullsome terms:

> This village has an excellent weekly market upon Thursday, where there is not only all kinds of vivars to be sold . . . a great abundance of pease and beans . . . with a considerable meal market. There are very good houses here and yeards. I

doubt not but this is as sweet a village considering all things, as is in Scotland.

He remarks particularly on the handsome tollbooth, with beautiful steeple, clock and bell, the well and pond in the centre of the village and the church – 'a very considerable fabrick, finely repaired within, with seats in a regular maner'.

Although the Livingston power was gone, the family remained and still had one last dramatic part to play in the story of Callendar and Falkirk. In 1721 Lady Ann Livingston, daughter of the exiled earl, was allowed by the York Buildings

18. The steeple and tollbooth erected in 1697. It was replaced by the present steeple in 1814. (*Drawing by John Reid*)

Company to rent the house and lands formerly held by her family, on a twenty-nine year lease at £872 per annum. She had earlier married William Boyd, Earl of Kilmarnock, and he now took up residence in Callendar House and more or less assumed the role of first citizen. He was, for example, the Grand Master of the Falkirk Lodge of Free Masons for several years and acted as principal landowner in dealing with the parish church. Though his loyalty seemed to lie initially with the government and ruling Hanoverians, whom he and his family had supported in 1715, his wife was, like her Livingston forebears, a staunch Jacobite, though one anxious to avoid the disastrous consequences visited on her late father. However, when the challenge did come to demonstrate her loyalty she did not fail the test, though, as she had feared, adherence to a lost cause brought her dynasty crashing down in the wake of Prince Charlie's rising in 1745.

Things began well enough. The 'young pretender' passed the night in Callendar House in September of that year on his way to a triumph at Prestonpans and a rapturous reception in Edinburgh. One account says that among the ladies who surrounded the handsome chevalier in his happy days in the capital, Lady Ann was the most dazzling and beautiful. But her participation in the revelry seems unlikely. As Geoff Bailey has shown in his vivid account of these events, *Falkirk or Paradise*, Lady Ann tried to persuade her husband to stay out of the rising for fear that the work she was doing to re-establish episcopalianism in central Scotland would be ruined by association with the venture. But Kilmarnock was swayed by the thought of victory and the restoration of his father-in-law's lands and title and, after waiting for news of the vistory at Prestonpans, wrote to his wife with the news that 'I am in my boots for the Prince'. He joined the other leaders at Holyrood and in late October 1745 left on the fateful journey across the border.

The march south to Derby and the retreat back to Scotland marked the beginning of the end of the Stewart cause. Pursued northwards by a government army the Jacobites passed through Glasgow and on towards Stirling, camping eventually on Plean Muir. From here they began the siege of Stirling Castle which had remained in government hands during the campaign in England. Lord George Murray, second only to the Prince in command of the Jacobites, settled with thousands of Highland clan soldiers in and around Falkirk, arriving on 4 January 1746. There they remained for over a week as the rest of the army besieged Stirling Castle, and all awaited the arrival of reinforcements from the north. Shortage of provisions was an increasing problem and on the 12th Lord George marched overnight with a sizeable force to Linlithgow to seize substantial quantities of food stores and fodder which was meant for the advancing government army now moving east from Edinburgh to relieve Stirling. The stores were removed and carted off as the first red-coated dragoons approached the town and, thus resupplied, the Jacobites returned safely to Falkirk. It had been Lord George's hope that the expected reinforcements would allow him to hold his position in the town but the worrying delays forced a reappraisal and eventual withdrawal towards Stirling on 14 January. The Prince in Bannockburn House was less than pleased by this decision, seeing the move as a further retreat in the face of the enemy. Two days later General Henry Hawley, a veteran of the 1715 rising, arrived in Falkirk in command of nearly nine thousand men making camp on land to the west of Hope Street down towards the present Dollar Park. They too thought they had succeeded in chasing the Highlanders out of the town but Murray had no intention of allowing the redcoats to dictate the course of events. He conceived a daring plan to deliver a counter blow by attacking Hawley's army in their camp, destroying its fighting capabilities and begining a revival in the fortunes of their luckless Prince. On the morning of 17th January, aided by Sir Archibald Primrose of Dunipace – under duress, or so he claimed at his subsequent trial – the Highland armies moved from Plean in a southward circle across the rivers Carron and Bonny to the west of Falkirk. By the time that government scouts realised what was happening the huge force had reached the line of the main road and appeared to be planning a direct march along the road through Camelon to Falkirk. The redcoat dragoons and infantry were hastily assembled in battle order facing west and spread out across the Camelon road beside the present

Dollar Park. However the Jacobites continued to move south, climbing steadily upwards towards the south muir of the town from where, had they not been detected, Lord George planned to launch a dawn attack on the government camp. A mile or so away in Callendar House Lady Ann was entertaining the unsuspecting Hawley, who, on hearing the news, rose from the table – in some disarray, according to one account – found his horse and galloped towards his army to begin a belated response. Now both armies were in motion, aiming to secure the high ground above the town. Over 1,000 dragoons, followed by the struggling infantry, passed through the present Maggie Woods Loan and began the climb in dreadful weather conditions with wind and rain sweeping down the hill into their faces. It was late afternoon in winter and already growing dark as 8,000 men, Highland infantry from all the major clans, supported by cavalry of the Lowland Jacobite gentry reached the top of the rise at the same moment as the first of the dragoons, well ahead of the regiments of foot, appeared in front of them. Chevalier Johnstone was with the Prince and he later recalled the scene as the dragoons of Cobham, Ligonier and Hamilton confronted the right wing of the Jacobite army where the Macdonald clans stood. After receiving a blast of fire from the Highland lines which killed 80 men, the cavalry charged forward:

> The most singular and extraordinary combat immediately followed. The Highlanders, stretched on the ground, thrust their dirks into the bellies of the horses. Some seized the riders by their clothes, dragged them down, and stabbed them with their dirks; several, again, used their pistols, but few of them had sufficient space to handle their swords . . . The resistance of the Highlanders was so incredibly obstinate that the English, after having been for some time engaged pell-mell with them in their ranks were at length repulsed and forced to retire.

It was a ferocious clash, with many of the dragoons riding down their own infantry as they tried to find their positions on the battlefield. On the left wing the Jacobites fared less well as the ravine between them and the oncoming infantry prevented a

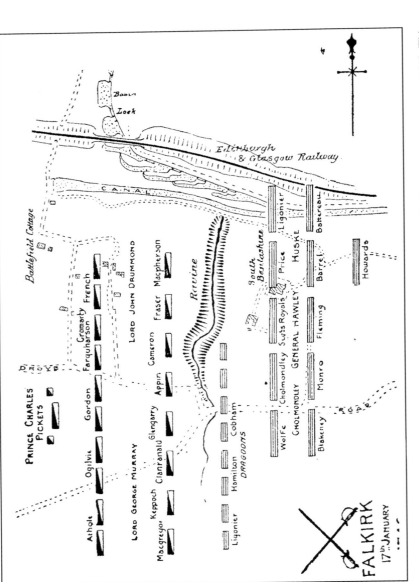

19. The positions of the government and the Jacobite armies at the Battle of Falkirk Muir on 17 January 1746. This particular version of the battle plan was drawn up by a member of the Wilson family of South Bantaskine and shows the battleground set against the layout of the estate in the mid-nineteenth century with roads, railway and Union Canal.

full-blooded charge. While many of the redcoat regiments fled in disarray others like Barrels and Ligoniers stood their ground and then slowly advanced. Now it was the Jacobites' turn to panic and many fled away to the west thinking the day was lost. A few hundred yards away the Highlanders charged hard downhill towards their fleeing enemy and could not be recalled by their commanders who wanted a more controlled advance. But from the confusion which raged for a time it soon became clear that the overall outcome was nearly complete Jacobite victory. Government forces retreated towards Falkirk where they set fire to their tents and abandoned great quantities of equipment. These dramatic events were witnessed by hundreds of people who had arrived in the district drawn by the prospect of a real battle. The people of the town too were keeping an eye on developments from afar as Geoff Bailey tells us:

> Back in the town of Falkirk the people were anxious for news. Some of the burghers and the prominent citizens had taken positions on the battlemented crown of the church's steeple and in the upper floors of the tolbooth steeple in order to gain a better view. From these vantage points they saw the government army enter the misty and storm-covered moor at the top of the hill; then they saw the dull atmosphere thickened by a fast-rolling smoke and heard the pealing sounds of the discharge; immediately they beheld the discomforted troops burst wildly from the cloud . . . and rush, in far-spread disorder over the face of the hill. From the commencement till what they styled 'the break of the battle', they later said was only an interval of about ten minutes.

Within a few hours three columns of Highland soldiers entered through the town ports – Lord George Murray by the Howgate and Roberts Wynd, Lord John Drummond through the Cow Wynd and Cameron of Lochiel by the West Port. A century later the event was commemorated in the beautiful stained-glass windows of South Bantaskine House which stood on the battlefield. Now appropriately enough they grace the Howgate

20. The stained-glass windows from the Howgate shopping centre showing Lord George Murray, Prince Charles Edward Stuart and Lord John Drummond. They were originally made for South Bantaskine House in the 1860s.

shopping centre not far from the point where the Prince's soldiers entered the town and where he spent the night in the 'great lodging', the former home of Livingston of Westquarter. The building at that time was owned by the widow of the surgeon Walter Graham, a strong Jacobite sympathiser, and later housed Watson's shoe-shop. It is now home to Waterstone's book shop.

Casualties were high among the redcoats with between three

and four hundred killed and many more taken prisoner. The Jacobite losses were less, some say as few as forty men. As with the other battle centuries before, great pits were dug the following day and the naked bodies, stripped bare in the night by the country people or victorious clansmen, were laid to rest. A little copse beside Dumyat Drive is thought to mark one of the places where some of the redcoat soldiers were buried and known for many years as 'the English Graves'; another lay close to the present High Station. Several prominent people were buried in the Falkirk churchyard including Colonel Robert Munro and his brother Dr Obsdale Munro, cut down by the Camerons in the rout after brave resistance, and the young officer, William Edmonstone of Cambuswallace.

The Highlanders now settled in the town which they had left just a few days earlier and by all accounts there was little depredation – an old tradition suggests that the Highlanders found the product of the Aitken's ale and porter brewery founded six years before very much to their liking and that they spent much of the next eleven days there! They had, of course, much mopping up to do and for several days redcoat prisoners were brought in from the surrounding country and lodged in the church, the tolbooth or the cellars of Callendar House. Several incidents of note occurred during this period, not least the accidental shooting of Young Glengarry, son of the chief of the Macdonnells, and the execution of the young clansman who was responsible. The Prince returned to Bannockburn House but most of the clan chiefs remained in the Falkirk area and it was in a room in the High Street that they met with Lord George to prepare their memorial to the Prince, explaining why they should resist the temptation of following Hawley's beaten army to Edinburgh. Instead they proposed withdrawing in good order to the Highlands with the promise of a refreshed and reinvigorated army in the spring. The Prince was outraged but recognised where the real power lay and had little choice but to complain and sulk.

The site of the battle on the south muir is today marked by an obelisk unveiled by the Duke of Atholl in 1927. It is a modest memorial of such a great encounter, the last time the famous

21. The Battle of Falkirk monument erected in 1927
(*Photograph by Ronnie Blackadder*)

'Highland Charge' carried the day. A more chilling reminder of the battle can be found in the many eye-witness accounts which survive. Among the most graphic was that of Chevalier Johnstone who was sent with a sergeant and twenty men to guard the captured cannons on the battlefield:

> The sergeant carried a lantern; but the light was soon extinguished, and by that accident we immediately lost our way, and wandered a long time at the foot of the hill, among heaps of dead bodies, which their whiteness rendered visible . . . To add to the disagreeableness of our situation from the horror of the scene, the wind and the rain were full in our faces. I even remarked a trembling and strong agitation in my horse, which constantly shook when it was forced to put its feet on the heaps of dead bodies and to climb over them . . . on my return to Falkirk I felt myself relieved from an oppressive burden: but the horrid spectacle I had witnessed was for a long time, fresh in my mind.

Only once more would British soil witness such carnage and that just three months later on Drumossie Moor at Culloden. On that day Lord Kilmarnock was taken, as the Jacobite cause perished. In August he was beheaded on Towerhill in London and Lady Ann, retreating in abject misery to her husband's family home, lay in a blackened room and, according to one account, 'wept herself blind before dying of grief'.

But the jaunty Highland troops who now left Falkirk had no thoughts of Culloden or defeat but were in high spirits and full of optimism. They were not the first Highlanders to spend time in Falkirk of course, and as the century wore on many more of their fellows would make the town their autumn home as the Falkirk trysts grew in size and importance to become the greatest cattle fairs in Europe. For centuries the cattle of the Highland glens had found a ready market in the Lowlands where arable farming predominated. Increasingly buyers from England too made the long journey north to meet and deal with the Highland drovers whose sturdy 'kyloe' had walked hundreds of miles over grassy drove roads to the great market of

22. William Boyd, Earl of Kilmarnock (reproduced with permission of East Ayrshire Council Arts and Museums)

Crieff. It was probably the continued growth in demand from the south after the union with England in 1707 which prompted landowners in the Falkirk district to organise the first cattle markets which sixty years later would eclipse all others in Scotland.

A large area of common land on Redding muir, acquired by the Dukes of Hamilton from the Bellendens in the aftermath of the Reformation, became the site of the earliest trysts. Unlike the weekly town markets, the annual meetings of buyers and sellers of cattle, sheep and horses had no legal standing. The owners of the land simply advertised the availability of the ground for such meetings and slowly, over many decades, the numbers of livestock on offer increased as news spread by word of mouth. The earliest Falkirk record dates from 1717 and in it the Duke of Hamilton sets tolls for the cattle, horses and sheep arriving for sale at Redding. One account suggests that the profit in the early years did not reach the coffers of the noble proprietor, since it had been 'eaten and drunken by the former factor, baillie and clerk.'

Despite the obvious difficulties encountered by Highlanders during the Jacobite rising the trysts continued to function but a greater threat came with the agricultural reforms which swept the country from the middle of the eighteenth century. Everywhere great areas of common land were being subdivided and brought under cultivation and in 1761 the feuars petitioned the courts to allow the division and allocation of the commonty of Reddingrigmuir and Whitesiderigmuir. Despite an eleven-year fight by the Duke to preserve the trysts, and his income from them, the courts ruled for the feuars and in the early 1770s the great fair had moved to a second location to the south-west of the town at Roughcastle.

But if the enclosure of land forced the move to a new site in Falkirk the same reason lay behind the massive increase in business which appeared at the same period. The great Michaelmas fair held in Crieff each October, where as many as 30,000 head of cattle were offered for sale, began to decline as more of the stances were lost. From then on an October fair developed at Roughcastle along with those held in August and September. This became the pattern for the next century, with the second Tuesday of each month the official sale day.

The great gathering of Gaels in a Lowland town prompted the Highland Society of London to establish a great piping competition at Falkirk tryst in 1781 and it was held there for several years before moving eventually to Edinburgh. But the construction of the Forth and Clyde canal from 1768 onwards caused considerable difficulties for the drovers who had to negotiate yet another obstacle in their journey southwards. By 1785 the Falkirk tryst was once more on the move, this time north of the canal and the river Carron into the parish of Larbert. The site at Stenhousemuir housed the trysts from then on until the last decades of the nineteenth century and are still home to the last remnants of the great gathering, the annual fair and sideshows.

At their height the trysts were a sensational sight, with as many as 150,000 cattle, sheep and horses arriving in great streams from all corners of Scotland and settling in the fields with their drovers, 'great stalwart, hirsute men, shaggy uncultured and wild', perhaps as many as two thousand with ponies and dogs, sleeping in the open or in portable bivouacs. From the borders and from England hundreds of buyers descended on the area, moving among the animals on horseback, sealing a bargain here and spurning an offer there. The bustle and clamour of the market were remarked on by many observers who came to marvel at the scene. One thought it 'a scene to which certainly Great Britain perhaps even the whole world does not afford a parallel'. Supporting the buyers and the sellers was a remarkable tented village of banks, shops and taverns offering all manner of services to the dealers.

> Many kindle fires at the ends of their tents over which cooking is briskly carried on. Broth is made in considerable quantities and meets a ready sale. As most of the purchasers are paid in these tents, they are constantly filled and surrounded with a mixed multitude of cattle dealers, fishers, drovers, auctioneers, pedlars, jugglers, gamblers, itinerant fruit merchants, ballad singers and beggars. What an indescribable clamour prevails in most of these parti-coloured abodes.

Hundreds of thousands of pounds was paid over the counters of these temporary banks during each tryst day and the impact on the local economy must have been very significant. In the 1760s, for example, one dealer arrived in the town from England with a Royal Bank credit note allowing him to spend up to £2,000 – the average price for one cow in that period was less than £2! By the end of the eighteenth century upwards of half a million pounds was changing hands at the three trysts.

And they continued to grow through the first half of the nineteenth century until the arrival of the railways made it possible for dealers to buy off the hill and sellers to transport south on wheels. By then the availability of open ground en route from the hills to Falkirk was decreasing and the fatter, carefully bred and cosseted cattle were less able to take the long walk to market. The tryst did continue but the numbers of livestock steadily declined until by 1900 the great markets were all but dead. One old man living in the town as a boy in the 1890s recalls that even in decline the arrival of the drovers in town was a sight to behold:

> We could hear the bellowing of the cattle and the bleating of the sheep and goats . . . we watched them squeezing their way through the Kirk Wynd which was then as narrow as Roberts Wynd. When we got to Grahams Road there were as far as the eye could see, droves of livestock. We were afraid of the Highland drovers who were wild looking, unkempt crowd of raggimuffins who carried a roll of canvas on their shoulders for their tents, and billy-cans dangling from a piece of string. They were gesturing with their sticks and shouting in Gaelic at their long haired cattle with big long wide horns and wild eyes.

The failed Jacobite rising of 1745 was little more than a memory when the last Livingston house and lands were placed on the open market in 1783. With peaceful times long restored and families no longer subject to the stain of disloyalty, the habit of allowing them to purchase their ancestral lands un-challenged had developed. When the Livingston property was offered in three lots – Callendar, Almond and Carmuirs, it was expected that the same gentleman's agreement would apply. But they did not reckon with the formidable William Forbes. An Aberdeenshire merchant, Forbes had made a fortune in London by providing copper sheathing for the hulls of wooden ships. Now, as was the style, he sought to use his new wealth to buy into landed society. If he was aware of the special arrange-ments he did not allow the thought to divert him from his course. On all three lots he outbid his Livingston rival, the Earl of Errol, offering a total of nearly £90,000. When challenged by the selling agents to establish his *bona fides* as a purchaser he is said to have handed over a £100,000 note from the Bank of England! That will do nicely, Sir, was no doubt the reply and

23. The first William Forbes of Callendar, from the painting by Raeburn
which once hung in the morning room at Callendar House (private collection,
on loan to the Scottish National Portrait Gallery)

soon the Forbes influence was being felt throughout the town
and district. It was the start of almost two centuries of power for
the family, quite different in nature from that of the feudal
Livingston Lords, but just as significant in terms of shaping the
destiny of the town and its people.

The huge land-holding in East Stirlingshire which now fell
under the control of William Forbes was the second-largest in
all of Stirlingshire, consisting of nearly 8,000 acres farmed by
hundreds of individual tenants spread throughout the district
from great stretches of muir in the south to the fertile carselands
along the River Forth. This was the time of agricultural
improvement in Scotland which was rapidly catching up
and overhauling its southern neighbour in its enthusiasm for
reform. Forbes, with his undoubted business acumen, considerable capital and determined, not to say ruthless, character set
about applying the new principles with a vengeance. Although
a comparatively small percentage of his holdings lay on the

fertile carse lands which had been highly productive for generations his powerful influence in the district inspired reform everywhere and a new régime of enclosure, drainage and crop rotation was the order of the day. Above all there were new leases for those tenants prepared to do as instructed and the exit door for the others. Hundreds of workers were shaken from their traditional holdings to uncertain futures in the employ of their erstwhile neighbours or in the growing industrial undertakings which the arrival of the Carron Company and the great Canal, described in the next chapter, had initiated. Forbes enclosed over 7,000 acres of land, creating hedged fields of up to eight acres which were heavily limed and drained, and in the process upset many by his dictatorial and unfeeling methods. One oft-repeated story has William returning to Callendar House from the south in 1797, seeing it apparently on fire and fleeing from what he took to be the revenge of disgruntled former tenants. It turned out to be no more than the fiery glow from the mighty furnaces of Carron Ironworks which had been established some forty years before. John Kay's famous portrait shows 'Copperbottom' – he had brought the nickname from London with him – fleeing in terror!

However there is no doubt that the actions of the new Laird of Callendar brought increased prosperity to the district, though those who suffered might not see it that way. When he died in 1815 William Forbes was one of the wealthiest men in Scotland and the unchallenged master of Falkirk and district. Writing in 1797 the Minister of Falkirk Parish, Dr James Wilson, described the state of agriculture in his entry for the famous *Statistical Account of Scotland*. 'Almost the whole of these estates,' he reported 'is now enclosed and subdivided – the ridges are straightened and the wet parts drained.' According to Wilson's account the population of the town by then was 3,892 including 18 bakers, 22 grocers, 1 physician, 5 surgeons, 2 druggists and 4 clock- and watch-makers! He might well have mentioned the name of James Aitken who had established himself as a lawyer in the town in 1790 and whose former apprentice, James Russel, took over the firm in 1818. As Russel and Aitken from then until now the firm have recorded the rise

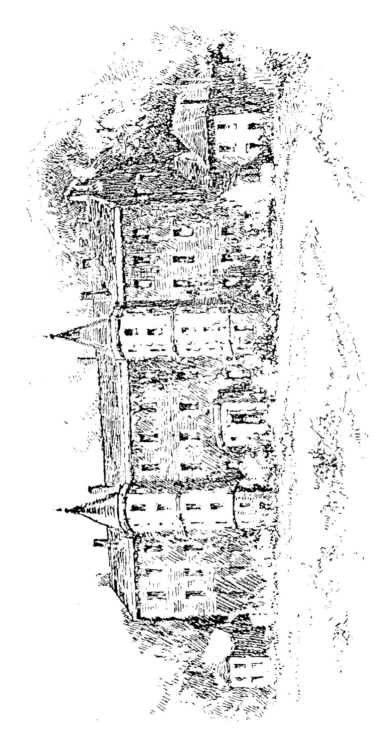

24. Callendar House in 1789, not long after it was purchased by William Forbes

25. *Copperbottom's Retreat* by John Kay, published in 1837. It shows Forbes fleeing from Callendar House thinking his enemies have set it on fire. The flames were actually from the furnaces of Carron ironworks.

and fall of Falkirk's companies and families and their records are a wonderful resource for the student of the past. The Revd Dr Wilson did have a good deal to say about the autumn cattle trysts but reserved his most fulsome praise for two major developments which, taken together, would totally transform the district. The establishment of the ironworks at Carron in 1759 and the cutting of the 'great canal' from Forth to Clyde a decade later, signalled the start of the industrial revolution in Scotland. The birth crucible of the nation in that first Iron Age 1,400 years before was once again the place where the new Scotland was shaped and formed. For fifty years afterwards the town and district remained essentially agricultural but the growing seeds of a new industrial future were already firmly established before the eighteenth century came to an end.

CHAPTER 7

A New Iron Age

On 15 June 1759 Birmingham industrialist Samuel Garbett wrote to his Scottish partner William Cadell in Cockenzie. 'Dr. Roebuck and I,' he said, 'think Carron Water is a situation infinitely preferable to all others.' It is arguably the most important letter written in the history of the Falkirk district, for the direct consequence was the establishment of the iron-founding industry which dominated the lives of the people for well over two hundred years. Britain was at war with France yet again and imports of iron from the Continent were seriously disrupted at a time when demand for munitions was greatly increased. Garbett and his partners believed that the central valley of Scotland offered the perfect location for a new, large-scale works for smelting iron from local ore. Dr John Roebuck, a medical man from Sheffield, was already in partnership with Garbett, making chemicals at Prestonpans, and Cadell was a wealthy merchant with an established timber shipping and exporting business. He wanted to site the new venture near his properties in East Lothian, but the others, especially Roebuck, much preferred land on the north bank of the Carron. There was iron ore available at Bo'ness and limestone supplies not far away in Maddiston and across the river near Dysart and Limekilns. Although timber would have to be brought from the Highlands for conversion to charcoal there was an almost unlimited supply of coal which the far-sighted businessmen knew would, in the form of coke, eventually replace charcoal as the principal fuel for the smelters. Above all there were the two rivers, Carron and Forth providing relatively easy access for raw materials and for the export of finished products and, equally importantly, offering water power to drive the bellows for the blast and the hammers of the forge. A company was formed with 24 £500 shares, 6 each to Garbett and Roebuck and the other 12 held by Roebuck's three brothers and Cadell and his son William who was appointed first manager. Fourteen acres of land were feued from Sir Michael Bruce of Stenhouse, the destroyer of Arthur's O'on, still trying to raise enough money to provide for his large family, and skilled workmen and special equipment were brought to Scotland from England. Construction work began in the autumn of 1759.

There is a tradition fostered by the company over the years that iron was produced on the first day of 1760. We are told that in the presence of many visitors, Dr Roebuck pierced the furnace breast, allowing the stream of molten iron to fill the sand beds spread out beside the furnace. One observer remembered that 'the cheers from the assembled guests were deafening and when they had subsided, Mr. Cadell called for a bumper to the works – "long years of prosperity to Carron and Dr. Roebuck."' The following day the visitors returned to watch the iron converted into bar iron and then forged into nails which were given out as souvenirs to those present. The reality is that it was several months before the works were capable of producing any iron, far less the blast furnace product described in the story; so if this happy event did indeed take place it must have been stage-managed for the entertainment of the visitors. An air furnace was commissioned in March 1760 with the first iron used to produce cannon-balls; the first blast furnace was ready towards the end of the year and tapped on Boxing Day, 26 December. A year later a second furnace was commissioned and along with forges and rolling and boring mills gave the partners all the basic facilities they required to become a major force in the British iron industry.

It had been the demand for ordnance which had inspired the establishment of the works and the partners soon began to produce cannons in a variety of sizes for both the admiralty and the war office. The workers were for the most part brought from England and the works were dubbed 'the English foundry' by the locals who appeared to resent the presence of their southern neighbours. One newspaper reported that more than angry words were exchanged. There was, they said

> a sharp skirmish between some countrymen who were mending the highways and a parcel of the English workmen belonging to the Carron Iron Factory. The origin of the quarrel was some reflections thrown by the workers against Scotland and its inhabitants which the country fellows nobly resented . . . it quickly became a kind of national quarrel and reinforcements continually arriving to both sides.

From the outset the power of the River Carron was crucial. The infamous Stenhouse damhead rebuilt after the stones of Arthur's O'on were swept away, fed water to the Bruce Mill close to new works. It was not powerful enough to work the bellows for the blast or drive the forging hammers, and at an early stage the Furnace lade was constructed which drew water from the river a mile or so away, near Larbert Church, and fed a small reservoir adjacent to the works. Within twenty years this had been augmented by two much larger areas of water to create the familiar 'Carron dams' on which the works was to depend for so long. Giant bellows of wood and leather provided the air for the first two blast furnaces but by 1766, when the next two were commissioned, a water-powered blowing machine devised by the famous engineer, John Smeaton, was installed.

Despite very severe problems in producing ordnance of a standard acceptable to the authorities and frequent financial difficulties, the ironworks grew at a phenomenal rate. By 1762 Roebuck had patented a process which used coked coal as the fuel and the laird of Quarrol, Thomas Dundas, had agreed to sell the company eighty tons of coal each week at 4s. 6d. per ton from his two existing pits, but eventually the company leased these from him and sank a further four of their own. James Bruce, the celebrated Abyssinian explorer, accepted £250 as an annual rent for the coal from his Kinnaird estate, plus 10 per cent of the value of the coal extracted. Later on the Duke of

Hamilton's coal from Brightons and the collieries on former Livingston lands of Callendar and Shieldhill began supplying the works. Coal was carted through Falkirk almost continuously from then on, down the Cow Wynd, which from the late 1700s was known as Coal Heugh Road, along the High Street and then out over the long open road through Grahamston and Bainsford to Carron. So hungry were the furnaces for coal that some reports suggest that each carter on the road could see the back of the one ahead and over his shoulder catch sight of the one coming behind, all day, all week, all year. It was this explosion in demand which brought the greatest change to the people of the wider Falkirk district and the story of the villages, especially in the Braes area to the south, (told in Chapter 15) is dominated by the search for more and more of the black gold which brought prosperity to some and hardship to many.

In 1768 Garbett's son-in-law, Charles Gascoigne, took over

26. Charles Gascoigne

as manager of the works from Cadell and soon he was far more powerful than any of the partners. Having helped oust Roebuck whose side ventures had left him bankrupt, he out-manoeuvred the Cadells and pushed Garbett into a relatively minor role in the Company's affairs. With considerable skill he reorganised Carron's financial structure to ensure that the rapid expansion was adequately funded and in 1773 managed the incorporation of Carron Company under a Royal Charter. For nearly twenty years he dominated the firm and it was in no small measure due to his skill and ruthlessness that Carron survived. It was under his influence, for example, that the Company's most famous product was born in 1778. This naval gun, which was eventually called the Carronade, had a very large calibre in comparison to its other dimensions, and because it was relatively short it could be recharged and fired again much more quickly. Its effect at close quarters was said to be devastating and it soon overcame the reluctance of the Admiralty to trust the unreliable guns from Carron. The Carronade was probably the brainchild of General Robert Melville, but improved and developed by the famous Patrick Miller

27. A naval carronade in action

under Gascoigne's direction. Indeed it was known during development as the Gasconade but by the time it was put on the market its famous name was established. The gun could fire almost four times the weight delivered in one shot by conventional naval guns and it was soon in demand by navies all over Europe. By 1791 they were mounted on 429 British ships and were being exported to Russia, Denmark and Spain. Visitors flocked to the works, which were rapidly gaining the reputation as one of the world's wonders, with the flashing fires of the furnace lighting the sky above for miles around. In 1784 the French Royal Commissioner of Mines, Barthelemy Faujas de St Fond, recorded his amazement at the scene which greeted him in the parts of the works he was allowed to see:

> He conducted us at first to an immense yard – covered with cannons, mortars, bombs, balls – amidst these machines of war, these terrible instruments of death, gigantic cranes, capstans of every kind, levers and assemblages of pulleys. Under the sheds we saw several rows of rampart cannon siege guns and field pieces, destined for Russia.

But more than the products it was the process which impressed him most of all:

> When one observes from some way off – so many sheaves of flame darting to a great height above the high furnace and at the same time hears the noise of the heavy hammers as they strike on resounding anvils, mingled with the sharp whistling of the blast pumps, one doubts whether he is not at the foot of a volcano in eruption.

But the 'terrible instruments of death' were far from the only product cast or hammered out beneath the towering 45-foot furnaces – sugar boilers for the West Indies, stoves of every kind, grates, kitchen ranges, kettles, tea pots, frying pans, spades, hoes, hinges and bolts. This combination of domestic and agricultural tools and equipment, with the guns and mortars for the navies and armies of the world, was a formula

28. The yard at Carron Works in the mid nineteenth century. The bell on the top of the triangle was used to signal the start and end of the working day.

that was to serve Carron well in war and peace for more than two hundred years.

Perhaps the most remarkable aspect of the Carron story in those early decades was its continued growth against a background of financial crises, constant material and power shortages, product failure, labour disputes, complex legal arguments with unhelpful local lairds and bitter personal rivalry among the partners. The sheer scale of the demand for iron products in Britain and beyond, overcame the most serious of impediments and by the end of the century the Company was strong and prosperous. Its influence extended to every aspect of the life of Falkirk district; it became a leading heritor in the parish of Larbert and a powerful voice in the decisions which shaped the economic, social, religious and political future of the area.

But it was the physical impact of such a huge undertaking on the locality which was more immediate. Villages were born, peopled by colliers from Shropshire and masons, wrights and moulders from Derby. Agricultural workers cast adrift by enclosure and improvement on the land were drawn by the magnet of regular employment to labour alongside the skilled men from the south. Ancient mills along the length of the Carron were bought up and, where the miller once ground oats and barley, fresh castings were finished and charcoal dust blackened the ancient stones. Within a year, over six hundred men were employed and a decade later it was said by one visitor to be over eleven hundred. Working and living conditions were deplorable, even by eighteenth-century standards. The Scottish colliers in particular still suffered from their legal status as bonded labour, tied to their pit and employer to be bought or sold like so many wooden props or lengths of waggon rail. The squalor in which they and their families were forced to live so debased and dehumanised them as to provoke all manner of disputes, frequent drunkenness and violence, widespread theft and even full-scale rioting. On several occasions during the early years, troops were called in by the managers to put down the disturbances – the prevailing philosophy of the times regarded concern and compassion as weaknesses likely to provoke idleness and lead the firm to financial ruin. In this the managers regretted the need to depend on the 'undeserving Scots' rather than on the English who were 'sober and commendable and they live in very decent fashion'. All over the district men women and children, some as young as six years of age, found themselves in dank, dark and dangerous places often hundreds of feet below the ground. The plight of the children is particularly shocking and the extent of the inhumanity involved was not fully revealed until 1842 when the remarkable testimonies of the children themselves were reported to the Parliamentary Commissioners. From Redding to Bo'ness, from Bantaskine to Kinnaird came horror stories that shamed all those who perpetrated such abuse. Craig Mair has made a study of the children in the coal mines of Stirlingshire and Clackmannan and he notes that 'In 1769, the Dunmore Colliery near Airth employed 102 people of whom only 28 were male adult hewers, supported by 23 wives, 29 daughters, 17 sons and 5 others.' In Falkirk Rebecca Simpson, aged 11, worked underground along with her sister pulling hutches of coal weighing 7 cwt up a 200-yard slope 14 times a day: 'If it is difficult to draw, brother George [who was 14 years old] helps us up the brae'. Not far away, in Redding Colliery Thomas Walker a 13-year-old coal hewer who had started work aged 10, usually worked a 13 hour shift, beginning at about 2.00 a.m. After cutting the 20-inch seam he was required to 'push four hutchies [each weighing nearly half a ton] to the pit bottom. It requires some strength to do the work.' In the same place a 7-year-old trapper called David Guy sat for hours operating a ventilation door by hand when wagons came through: 'It's no very hard work, but unco lang, and I canna hardly get up the stair-pit when work is done'. One of his fellow workers at Redding, 9-year-old James Watson, found the pit 'gai dark . . . an awfu frightsome place', and one of the inspectors visiting Stoney Rigg colliery met 17-year-old Margaret Hipps and was appalled by what he found: 'She draws a bogie weighing 250 to 350 pounds along a passage 26–28 inches high . . . it is almost incredible to believe that human beings can submit to such employment, crawling on hands and knees, harnessed like horses, and over soft slushy floors more difficult than dragging the same weights through the lowest common sewers . . . the inclination is frequently 1 in 3.' Serious accidents were common, death frequent and concern for the well-being of the workers almost non-existent. As Mary Sneddon from Bo'ness reported: 'Brother Robert was killed on 21st January last: a piece of roof fell on his head and he died instantly. He was brought home, coffined and buried in Bo'ness kirk-yard. No one came to enquire how he was killed; they never do in this place.' Although the coal mines have attracted most attention the iron works could be just as unpleasant and dangerous. The Commissioners criticised Carron Company for the conditions faced by boy moulders, most of whom were illiterate and as young as nine years of age who faced 12-hour shifts at the red-hot furnace mouth with only one 20-minute break. Despite all of this there was no shortage of applicants ready to take both mining and foundry jobs. Wages, though poor, were higher than the going rate for children in agriculture, and as we have seen, work there was in decline as improvement reduced opportunities. When legislation restricting the employment of children followed these reports many of the working men themselves were among the most vociferous opponents, such was their dependence on the labour of their childen to secure a living wage as a family. But there was a new spirit in the air, inspired in part at least by the French Revolution with its message of equality and freedom. Industrial unrest increased throughout the country and especially in the west where in December 1819 the weavers were talking of revolution and organising themselves for a fight. In Falkirk, Miss Helen Heugh, daughter of the family of Gartcows, wrote to her sister who was in Paris with her new husband, George Meek of Campfield, as part of a European tour:

> You may think yourselves fortunate in being away at present for the country seems in a dreadful state . . . things are growing everyday worse . . . there is a great meeting of Radicals to take place at Glasgow tomorrow which is causing great alarm . . . the town and every place around for many miles is filled with Military to be in readiness if any riot should take place and even at this distance there is a troop of cavalry stationed who keep a constant communication with Glasgow and sleep in their clothes that they may be ready at a moment's notice, and all the respectable inhabitants of the place have enrolled themselves as special constables to search for arms and prevent unlawful meetings . . . what will you say when you return if Campfield should be divided amongst a parcel of reformers who won't think of paying any rent?

It wasn't long before the disturbances feared by Miss Heugh reached the Falkirk district. In April 1820 at Bonnymuir near Bonnybridge a battle, perhaps a skirmish would be a better word, took place between a group of those Glasgow weavers supported by local sympathisers, and a troop of the Stirlingshire Yeoman Cavalry and the 10th Hussars. The 'radicals' armed with pikes and muskets were *en route* to Carron Ironworks where they hoped to seize the ordnance with the support of the workers there. Their aim was no less than the overthrow of the government, but they were betrayed and misled, falling into the trap prepared for them. In the immediate aftermath of the rising, forty-one men were taken into custody, of whom over a third came from Camelon and Falkirk. They were nearly all nailers. Twenty-seven were tried for treason at Stirling in August, including eight locals, and all but two of the Camelon men, John McMillan and Andrew Dawson, were found not guilty. These two, with their leaders, John Baird and Andrew Hardie from Glasgow, and eighteen others were sentenced to be hanged, drawn and quartered but in the end only the two leaders were executed and the others transported. It was a severe reaction which quieted the scene for a period and the eventual passage of the great Reform Act in 1832 brought some measure of correction of long-felt injustices.

Among the middle classes like Miss Heugh the fear of political reform was almost as frightening as an armed insurrection. The rise of the chartist movement was one such spectre as the minister of Denny, the Revd John Dempster, reported in 1841:

> Unprincipled newspapers are the chief cause of any discontent that exists. The public morals and peace are at this time both suffering from what is called Chartism. The principles of Chartism, as exhibited here, are infidel and anarchical. Few, happily, countenance them.

Despite the steady advances in representation, the attitude of such persons as the Revd John Dempster meant that appalling working conditions remained and low wages and insecurity inspired repeated strikes and unrest as the century progressed. In 1856, for example, as coal prices fell following the ending of the Crimean War, the coal owners combined to reduce miners' wages from five to four shillings per day and a widespread strike followed. In the Falkirk area the Redding colliers took the lead, arguing that

> The old rate given is scarcely an equivalent for the severity of their labours and for the privations they have frequently to

endure. The work is of such an onerous description that they cannot as a rule work more than four days a week, and that £1, instead of being too great a remuneration, is barely sufficient for their wants.

Marches and demonstrations followed, which for the most part were peaceful though the authorities took no chances, and once again the 90th Highland Borderers and the 7th Dragoons were standing by just in case. Most of the fury was directed at the few colliers who remained at work and on more than one occasion this spilled over into violence. The house of one man in Redding and later another in Easter Shieldhill were attacked with stones and the windows and doors were broken by a huge crowd of strikers. Effigies were burned and for a time there was a danger of the houses themselves being set on fire. Arrests were made in both places by the police and military and the men involved were fined the equivalent of a week's wages: 20 shillings. However the overall impression of the events from the press is of a peaceful, even respectful, though determined protest. Large meetings were held in Falkirk and at Carronshore where the men were even addressed by Colonel Dundas who was said to have been 'conciliatory'. The men in return conducted themselves in 'a remarkably orderly manner'. At national level it was the Falkirk area delegates who urged others to refrain from attacking working miners and to maintain their dignity and solidarity. It did not work. The power of the combined employers supported by the authorities was too great and amid great hardship the strike dragged on for twelve weeks before the defeated colliers returned to work for the lower rate. In Redding one immediate consequence was the formation of the Free Colliers described later in Chapter 15.

But the early problems at Carron Company did not all lie with a discontented workforce. The managers too were frequently at odds and in 1786 Charles Gascoigne left for Russia with many of the firm's designs, a good deal of their special gun metal and many skilled workmen. Unfortunately for Carron he decided to stay there and set up an iron foundry for the Tsarina Catherine the Great for which he was suitably rewarded.

However this loss was overcome by the appointment of Joseph Stainton as manager in Gascoigne's place. He was soon a powerful shareholder and able to promote the interests of other members of his family incuding his nephews Joseph and William Dawson. Between them the Staintons and Dawsons ran Carron for nearly a hundred years and their canny and intelligent, if slightly dubious, management of affairs ensured Carron's continued prosperity despite an increase in competition from other foundries. It is a story very well told by Brian Watters in his 1998 book *Where Iron Runs Like Water* and any reader interested in the inside story of nineteenth century Carron will find it all there.

Carron was, of course, only the beginning of the story of Falkirk's iron revolution. The first new company to be formed in the district after Carron was the Dalderse Foundry Company established by George Sherriff on the north bank of the new canal at Abbotshaugh in 1804. Sherriff had worked at Carron and with Matthew Boulton and James Watt in Birmingham and he judged the markets strong enough to support a second producer in the district. He met with only moderate success and the firm closed its doors just six years later. In the same year a more determined bid to compete with the giant was launched by a group of gentlemen who recruited skilled men from Carron to form the Falkirk Foundry Company, with premises on the Falkirk side of the canal next to the main road. As Falkirk Iron Company in the decades ahead it would spearhead the development of the Falkirk district as the nation's greatest centre for light castings and profoundly influence the lives of every child born in Falkirk for the next hundred years.

CHAPTER 8

The Transport Revolution

The revolution in agriculture and the first stirrings of industry in the mid eighteenth century put an added strain on the nation's appalling transport system. Everywhere existing roads were extremely difficult in good weather and virtually impassable in bad. According to both law and custom they were maintained by the labour of those who lived on the land through which they passed, but it was a duty more often neglected than observed. As is ever the case, economic advantage promoted change and in November 1751 'An act for repairing the Post Road from Edinburgh to Glasgow' was approved by Parliament. This so called 'turnpike road' was promoted by local landowners who raised money from shareholders who stood to gain from the payments charged to the users of the roads at the toll barriers at Linlithgow Bridge, Laurieston and Bonnybridge Toll. It was a beginning, and though progress was slow, further acts did follow involving roads from Falkirk to Stirling. Falkirk had had a post office for over a century by then, since 1689 in fact, but road conditions meant that deliveries from Edinburgh through Falkirk to Glasgow and Stirling were made by men on foot once a week. One of the first benefits of road improvement brought horse and coach posts on a much more regular basis, and though the villages still had to be served by runners from Falkirk there was a real sense of closer connection with the world beyond the district. Coaches carrying passengers and mail became common as the eighteenth century progressed, as the following surviving handbill from the late 1700s illustrates:

Falkirk Stage-Coach to Edinburgh
RALPH POTTS INN-KEEPER
Without the West-Port, Falkirk
Returns his most grateful acknowledgements to his Friends
and the Public in general, for the encouragement he has
hitherto been favoured with at Linlithgow, and earnestly
solicits and hopes for the continuation of their friendship, and
no pains shall be wanting on his part to merit it.
   He now proposes to run his Coach three days a week. To
set out from his house in Falkirk every Monday, Wednesday
and Friday at six oclock in the morning and leave Edinburgh
precisely at four o'clock in the afternoon of the same days.

He goes on to detail the charges – 5 shillings each way – and
the luggage allowance –14 pounds – before promising 'good
entertainment for Company may be depended upon at his
house in Falkirk, and good stabling for horses etc.' A further
sign of the times is the footnote which points out that on the
days when Ralph is not *en route* to Edinburgh he drives his coach
back and forward between Falkirk and Carron.

   However, the most significant transport change involved not
roads but canals, and there is no doubt that it was this initiative
even more than the arrival of the Carron Company that
triggered Falkirk's transformation from an agricultural to an
industrial centre. The spirit of the times which had inspired the
Carron venture gave rise to an explosion of enterprise across
Scotland and led directly to renewed proposals to cut a waterway from the Forth to the Clyde in the 1760s. The short neck of
land between the Irish and North Seas which the Romans had
crossed with their great wall had been identified as early as the
1660s as the ideal place for a canal, but it was not until
economic and social conditions were right a century later that
the work was begun. In 1762 the great engineer, Robert
McKell, surveyed a route on behalf of a group of Glasgow
merchants and shortly afterwards John Smeaton was invited by
the Board of Trustees for the Encouragement of Fisheries,
Manufactures and Improvements in Scotland to produce
an alternative version which was the one finally adopted.

Smeaton's proposal, modified in several ways after it was first produced, envisaged a 35-mile canal over 50 feet wide and 7 feet deep from an eastern terminus where the Carron joined the Forth, to the Clyde near Bowling. A series of locks would carry the barges across the carse immediately north and west of Falkirk, from Middlefield to Bainsford and on through Camelon to Bonnybridge. From there a further four locks would lift the canal up to its highest point at Wyndford Lock near Castlecary over 150 feet above the sea. Thereafter it was stepped down through a further 19 locks across to the Clyde north of Glasgow. A cut from the canal into the city would ensure that the produce of the east coast would have a path to the rapidly expanding commercial heart of the west coast.

In 1767 a public company was formed with 1,500 £100 shares subscribed to by the most powerful and influential figures in the land. There were six dukes and seventeen earls, as well as the Lord Provosts of both Edinburgh and Glasgow, but by far the biggest single shareholder was Sir Lawrence Dundas of West Kerse, with £10,000 worth of stock. The canal

29. The bascule or lifting bridge on the Forth and Clyde Canal at Camelon

would begin its journey on his land and, as a result, he stood to gain in every way from its success. Parliament approved the proposal in 1768 and in the same year the work began. It was a colossal undertaking, the greatest civil engineering project in Scotland since the Roman builders completed the Antonine Wall over the same ground over 1,600 years before. Smeaton was appointed as chief engineer with a salary of £500 and Robert McKell, his assistant, was paid £375. These were princely sums in the mid eighteenth century when one of the thousand men engaged to dig the canal was to be paid less than one shilling per day. McKell certainly earned his pay, for he was in charge of the day-to-day work – searching out and buying timber, stone and clay, engaging skilled masons and bridge-builders as well as scores of untried labourers. These navigators or 'navvies' who by all accounts, fought, drank and dug themselves from Falkirk all the way to the Clyde were not the easiest of workforces and McKell must have envied his Roman predecessors with military discipline available to keep their building squads in line.

One can hardly imagine the impact on a small town of the arrival of these huge armies of workmen, living in temporary accommodation and disrupting the life and disturbing the peace of the inhabitants like the soldiers of previous centuries. Such annoyance no doubt contributed to the hostility shown by locals to the whole project, but the real reason was the threat to the livelihood of the carters of the district represented by the canals. The arrival of Carron ironworks had increased the number of carters in the Falkirk area from four to over a hundred and now the canal looked likely to deprive many them of their new-found prosperity. Canal Company records report regular vandalism, dams and locks destroyed, equipment stolen and workers attacked. Even worse was the breaking down of the top lockgate at Lock 16 in Camelon which released four miles of water between there and Lock 17 at Castlecary. By 1770 over 1,500 men were working and the Canal had covered over 14 miles. By 1775 the canal was completed as far as Stockingfield near Kirkintilloch and there was water in most of the eastern end so that trading along this part could begin.

Financial difficulties delayed the completion of the final stretch until July 1790, when a ceremonial hogshead of Forth water was poured into the Clyde near Bowling. By then developments were already under way with small workshops and warehouses, tile works, timber yards and coal stores established along the length of the canal from the new village of Grangemouth in the east to Camelon and Bonnybridge in the west. More than any other development the cutting of the canal transformed Falkirk from the market town of the carse to a centre of industry with a wide range of new manufacturing activities and a growing population. But it was not always plain sailing. Relations between the partners at Carron iron works and the Canal Company were strained and for some years they were refused permission to make a special cut from the River Carron to the canal at Dalderse. This was eventually completed sometime before 1775 and greatly improved Carron's access to the sea until the course of the river itself was straightened a decade or so later.

More and more vessels which had once used the established port of Bo'ness now landed raw materials and finished goods at Grangemouth, where they were loaded onto barges for the journey west. In the opposite direction came the imported goods of the great Glasgow merchants for onward transmission from the Forth to the rest of Britain and Europe. Initially goods were moved on horsedrawn barges but the inventive genius of the age soon found an outlet in the harnessing of steam power to the task. In 1789 Patrick Miller of Dalswinton, whose involvement with the Carronade has already been noted, brought his 60-foot-paddle boat *The Experiment* to the canal west of Lock 16 where there was a clear four-mile run free of locks. It was fitted with a steam engine designed by William Symington of Wanlockhead and made in Carron. After several unsuccessful attempts, during which Millar began to lose faith in the whole idea of steam navigation, *The Experiment* did finally sail on the canal on 25 December 1789. Miller was absent and he refused to support the venture further.

A decade later the sheer volume of shipping trying to use the completed canal led the Canal Company to think once again

30. William Symington's *Charlotte Dundas*, the world's first practical steam-powered boat

about the possibility of steam tugs. Lord Thomas Dundas, son of Sir Lawrence, was by then the Governor of the Company and early in 1800 he asked Symington, who was once again working at Wanlockhead, to design a new engine. The following year, a wooden-hulled craft, probably designed by Captain John Schank of the Royal Navy and certainly fitted with Symington's steam engine, was built by Alexander Hart of Grangemouth and launched with the name *Charlotte Dundas*. Contemporary reports suggested that the 58-foot by 18-foot boat had successful tests on the canal but the project was expensive and not without serious technical problems. In 1803 a second boat, probably also called *Charlotte Dundas*, was built to a modified design with an improved engine. Early the following year Symington tested the boat along the whole length of the canal and on 28 March, witnessed by a number of important guests, the boat towed two large barges weighting some 130 tons a total a distance of 18½ miles in just over nine hours. It was generally regarded as a satisfactory if not spectacular performance, but the fears of the Company that the boats would damage the banks of the canal persisted, and the project, and Symington, were eventually abandoned. The boat served as a dredger before it finally rotted away at Tophill near Lock 10. Symington himself became the manager of Falkirk's Callendar Colliery for several years and lived in Kinnaird House, Larbert. He died in near poverty in London in 1831 aged just sixty-eight. His work preceded that of Henry Bell and Robert Fulton and he is entitled to be remembered as the father of steam navigation, though it was many years before steam-powered boats sailed on the Great Canal.

In the same year as the Forth and Clyde was completed the scarcity of coal in the capital led the then Edinburgh city fathers to look towards the rich Lanarkshire coalfields for future supplies. The advantages of a waterway linking the city to the west was obvious and several possible routes were surveyed between 1793 and 1797 by distinguished engineers including John Rennie and Robert Whitworth. Involvement in the French wars delayed the project and when planning was resumed in 1813 a further plan by Hugh Baird was commissioned. This envisaged a line linking Edinburgh and Falkirk, where the two canals would join together. Despite many reservations from those who preferred an independent waterway from Edinburgh to Lanarkshire, the plan was eventually accepted. Work began in Edinburgh in March 1818 and continued, following the contours of the land right through to Falkirk, a total distance of 31 miles. Where valleys lay in its path great aqueducts were built such as the twelve mighty arches of the Avon aqueduct over 80 feet above the river and stretching for 900 feet. But the barriers were not always physical. The Forbes family went to extraordinary lengths to ensure that the canal would not be visible from the grounds of Callendar House. The campaign of opposition included producing a print and plan showing the effects of the development which was sent to every member of parliament in Britain. It was successful and engineers were forced to change the route which involved cutting a 690-yard tunnel under Prospect Hill.

31. The mouth of the Union Canal tunnel at Bantaskine
(*Photograph by Ronnie Blackadder*)

It was not the first canal tunnel in Scotland but it was ten times
longer than anything attempted before and was constructed by
digging holes from the hill above and blasting and driving
through solid rock. Even in this high technology world the
'dark tunnel' as it is known remains a marvel, as astonishing in
its day as the Falkirk Wheel is in ours. The squads of navvies
engaged in digging and lining the canal for over 31 miles were
the same hard drinking, hard living gangs of displaced workers
from the Highlands and later from Ireland who had already
made the Great Canal and would one day drive the railways
across the length and breadth of the land. One observer was as
concerned about their behaviour as he was impressed by the
techniques involved. Writing from Falkirk to New York on 20
September 1818 he describes the project:

Their is a Cannal going throu from Falkirk to Edinburgh
and they are cutting a tunal belaw grany from west side of

our moar all the way to the glen burn about half a mill . . .
they sunk pits about 100 yards from each other to the level of
the cannal and then cut east and west till they met below
taking all the stuff up by windlasts . . . a great deal of Irish
men came over and is employed at it and several accident has
happened at it and 2 was killed by the face of the brea faling
down on them . . . few of our countrymen is at it as in general
they cannot stand the work . . . they are mostly irish young
men and a bad set they are.

At the Falkirk end of the canal a flight of eleven locks bridged
the gap to Lock 16 on the Forth and Clyde at Camelon where a
basin was constructed at the junction. The whole expensive
project with its marvelous aqueducts and 62 over-bridges,
linking locks and half-mile tunnel was completed in 1822–23
when the city centres of Glasgow and Edinburgh, and the
estuaries of the two great rivers were joined at last in a waterway system which was almost as important as a symbol of man's
ability to overcome and tame the natural world, as it was an
element in the economic development of the nation.

If the carriage of coal and lime, iron ore and Baltic grain,
tobacco and woollen plaids, earned the shareholders dividends
and fired the industrial revolution, the canals also linked
communities and offered passengers the opportunity of seeing
their country in a way that had not been possible in the past. As
early as 1822 a traveller's guide to the Edinburgh to Glasgow
journey was produced, pointing out the sights to be seen to
north and south of both canals – the forest of masts at the new
port of Grangemouth, the elegant villas and 'gentlemen's seats'
and parklands, new church buildings and the flaming furnaces
of Carron. It explained how passengers would disembark at
Falkirk and walk the few hundred yards down to the basin and
partake of refreshment at the new Union Inn while the barges
passed through the chain of locks and basins ready for embar-
kation and a renewed journey to Bonnybridge and the west.

But the Union Canal, as it came to be known, was never as
successful as the Forth and Clyde which remained the Great
Canal in every way. The coming of the railways in the mid

32. The Union Inn and Lock 16 at Camelon where the two canals joined together

century changed everything, but the Forth and Clyde especially continued as a key route for shipping, goods and passengers, remaining financially sound until the early years of the twentieth century. Ironically in the light of future developments, it was the canals that first brought railway locomotives to the district. In 1840 at the Union Canal terminus at Causewayend a line of coal trucks from Airdrie arrived along the new Slamannan Railway. By all accounts a goodly crowd walked from the town to see the iron horse enter the district for the first time – now the servant of the bargemen but soon to be their master. A year earlier an experiment had been conducted on the section of the Forth and Clyde Canal, west of Lock 16, earlier used by Symington with a small locomotive called the *Victoria* running along a single track pulling barges and passenger boats at respectable speeds. But again the Canal Company feared for the structure of their precious waterway and the experiment met the same fate as those of Symington.

Three years on and the railway age for Falkirk began in earnest. A passenger train carrying 1,000 enthusiasts of the

Glasgow and Edinburgh Railway reached Falkirk High Station, half a mile from the town, after a journey from Glasgow lasting one hour and a quarter: 'The sides of the railway were lined with admiring spectators, the bridge across the line, the station and every height which commanded a view of the train were crowded and young and old rent the air with their cheers.'

The locomotive was fed with 'fresh water and coke', given a second engine and cheered on its way into the mouth of Falkirk's second long tunnel. Shortly thereafter four trains per day left the station to each of the great cities – first-class fares were four shillings and sixpence and third class, just half as much. The public had been admitted at a price to the new tunnel before the service commenced. The rough and ready track, named from its function as the Cow Loan, re-named for the same reason as Coal Heugh Brae, now became in part at least the High Station Road and passengers were collected by horse buses for the bumpy journey to the town centre.

In 1847 the Caledonian Railway Company linked Glasgow to Carlisle adding a branch to Greenhill, near Bonnybridge, the following year. Here it joined the newly laid line to Perth operated by the Scottish Central Railway, and in 1850, with the opening of the Stirlingshire Midland Junction Railway, a branch line through Grahamston linked Polmont to Larbert and the north. The celebrated Skew Bridge at Laurieston was built to carry the line across the Edinburgh Road but the main road north from Falkirk to Carron had only a narrow footbridge for passengers with the horses and their heavy loads redirected round the arc of McFarlane Crescent to rejoin the road fifty yards further on. Unsatisfactory as this was, it was not replaced by a proper stone bridge for another fifty years. The railway era heralded by these developments brought intense rivalry between the two companies which came to dominate the Scottish scene. The North British Railways Company took over the Edinburgh and Glasgow Company in 1865, and with it the Union Canal, while the Caledonian Company acquired the Forth and Clyde Canal just two years later. With the North British taking control of the Grahamston line and the Caledonian running between Glasgow and Larbert, the battle for the lion's share of passenger and freight traffic in central Scotland was joined with a vengeance. This led inevitably to wasteful duplication of facilities, but the scramble to extend rail services brought lines into every corner of the district. Soon new and expanding firms sought out sites near the track and great sidings and marshalling yards were built in the industrial heart of the town and networks across the district linking collieries and iron foundries.

It would be hard to overstate the impact of these developments on the economic and social life of the Falkirk district in the decades after 1750. Local landowners were well rewarded for the necessary land sales and way-leaves; there was high expenditure during the construction phase with many jobs, however transient; and there were many opportunities for providers of local services. Then there were the jobs created by the operation of the new road, waterway or line. Inns and stores, building yards, stations and toll houses appeared at points throughout the Falkirk area, creating new communities and giving new life to old ones. Finally, and perhaps most significantly, the new importance of fast transport of goods and raw materials led to a mushrooming of enterprise in the vicinity of the new networks. By the middle of the nineteenth century the district was ready for industrial take-off and with it came a population explosion which transformed the district from little more than a collection of rural villages into a powerhouse of Scottish industry.

CHAPTER 9

Stentmasters and Feuars

During the second half of the eighteenth century when Carron Company and the Great Canal were reshaping Falkirk's industrial and commercial future, the town's municipal affairs were in the doldrums. The ending of Livingston power after the first Jacobite defeat and the trauma of Prince Charlie's rising in 1745 had left Falkirk in disarray. It seems that the power to appoint bailies was retained by the Earl of Errol who occupied Callendar House until the purchase of the estates by William Forbes. But this was done infrequently and the bailies' powers were extremely limited. Eventually such appointments ceased and the town was left in a pretty parlous state. Eye-witness accounts are few and contradictory – one visitor in 1820, for example, was shocked by what he found:

> The streets are narrow, irregular and dirty. Except the principal one, which is itself no very high proof of the taste of the inhabitants, the rest is not worthy of comparison even with the Cowgate in Edinburgh. It is impossible to conceive a more dull or miserable looking scene. A stranger would suppose it a large prison house, rather than the residence of a commercial people.

And of the 'lower and uneducated classes' he added: 'it would be difficult to name a place of equal population where the disgusting vices of drunkenness and profanity so much abound.' But there were others who thought the old town had a bit more to offer. Just five years after that damning verdict the town was being described as having 'a very good appearance' with well-built houses, an elegant steeple and a new church. The elegant steeple referred to was the crowning glory of the one group of men who did exercise a limited authority within the town. These 'stentmasters', who had emerged some time during the seventeenth century as custodians of the burgh's water supplies, represented the merchants and craftsmen of the town and were elected by their fellows with four merchants and two each of the ten trades – masons, wrights and hammermen, weavers, tailors and shoemakers, brewers, fleshers, bakers and whipmen. In addition from 1788 the four quarters of the town – 'Eastburn Bridge, Westburn Bridge, Vicar's Loan, and the Randy gate' as Kerse Lane was then called, were each allowed one member. The twenty-eight men met from time to time to 'cast the stent', that is, to fix an assessment which they expected the inhabitants of the burgh to pay towards the common services – especially water – provided in the town. There was no real legal authority to back their decisions and only immemorial usage or 'use and wont' provided a justification for their activities. An estimate was made of an individual's ability to pay and a 'stint' of a pound or two set. The officer of the committee tried to collect what he could – his own wages depended on his success – but there was little attempt at enforcement beyond cultivating the notion of municipal pride and shared responsibility. Neither seem to have cut much ice with the canny bairns and the kitty was seldom full. In the 1720s, for example, the kirk session was approached by James Bowie, described as a bailie in Falkirk, and Richard Muirhead, the clerk, who wanted to borrow £20 for two months 'to meet the claim of the plumber for laying the pipes because they were unwilling to be hard upon the residents of the town untill the harvest be over.' The loan was granted.

Very occasionally a special effort was called for, though the result was often the same. In the early 1800s the wooden pipes of the original water supply were in such a poor condition that the stentmasters decided to replace them with cast iron and to build a substantial cistern near the town centre. A piece of the garden ground behind the tenement lands on the south side of the High Street near the market place was obtained and in 1805 a wooden cistern was erected to hold 13,000 gallons of water drawn from the coal workings a mile to the south. After twenty years it was so decayed that the stentmasters were forced to replace it with a more substantial structure of stone and iron which remained in use until 1895 when it was converted into a public convenience. The street in which it stood was known as Cistern Lane until well into this century.

But, as already noted, the most celebrated venture of the stentmasters was the erection of a new town steeple in 1814. Falkirk had, from the late sixteenth century at least, been a town with a tolbooth steeple. The first was replaced in 1697 by a building which adjoined the court and prison close to the present site in the High Street. In 1776 a clock was installed and this is shown in a later woodcut of the building. In 1801 Forbes of Callendar allowed one William Glen to use the cellars of the Steeple and other buildings on condition that he did nothing to disturb the foundations. He did, of course, and soon after, the steeple listed 15 inches eastwards; deemed dangerous, it was

33. The Cross of Falkirk around 1820, from a contemporary engraving

'cast to the ground' and the stentmasters valiantly set about raising the necessary funds to replace it.

After a long legal wrangle with Glen they commissioned the celebrated architect David Hamilton, later the designer of Larbert Church, to produce proposals for a new steeple with clock, bell and prison rooms to house 'strolling vagrants and people who commit petty crimes'. The appeal for funds went to 'landed properties, merchants, farmers' who, it was assumed, would want to 'subscribe liberally to such a laudable and useful undertaking'. The target was nearly £1,500 and predictably, less than a third of this was subscribed. Nonetheless, local builder Henry Taylor undertook the construction work and by June 1814 the 146-foot steeple was completed. The town's self-appointed managers fell further into debt but despite this they celebrated their acquisition with the greatest possible gusto. Their new steeple certainly distinguished the town and was much admired by the many visitors – 190 years later it still is.

In 1829 a group of businessmen in the town combined to form the Falkirk Gas Works Company with the aim of supplying private subscribers in the centre of the town. Nearly £1,700 was required to erect a gas-works at East Bridge Street but it was operational by January the following year. The stentmasters, ever anxious to spend money they did not have, immediately set about trying to raise enough to erect gas lights in the same area. As usual they were only partially successful but nonetheless 56 lamps were eventually provided. Keeping them lit remained a costly business and for most of the summer and on moonlit nights the lamplighter stayed at home. Despite this prudence the debts of the stentmasters continued to grow just at the time when real central power in the town was most needed.

The steady growth of the town's population in the early decades of the nineteenth century, the total lack of central control of industrial development and building and the lack of such basic services as sewerage, adequate water supply or street paving or lighting, placed burdens on the stentmasters which they were incapable of handling. Their influence waned and

34. A view of Falkirk from the south in 1824, showing the new steeple, the new Parish Church and the octagonal Tattie Kirk

the state of the town declined alarmingly. But by the time the stentmasters had launched their appeal for funds to replace the steeple, a powerful new group had emerged in Falkirk to challenge their position as the sole municipal authorities.

In 1807 William Forbes of Callendar, continuing his policy of enclosing grazing land and bringing it under cultivation, turned his attention to the 150 acres of land to the south of the town which had been the common muir of Falkirk since the medieval period. The rights to graze stock, gather 'feal and divot' and quarry stones on this land were originally held by the 15 inhabitants of the burgh who had obtained feus of land on which the old town was built. By a process known as 'sub-infeudation' the 15 had by 1800 multiplied to over 200 and each of these 'feuars' as they came to be known could claim some part of the rights which were once the entitlement of the first fifteen. As Forbes' application to the Court of Session proceeded an offer emerged which formed the basis of the final settlement. He would enclose 120 acres for his own use and 20 for the use of the feuars. The balance of 10 acres would be kept as common land for the feuars' use, much as before. In addition the feuars would have one acre of land in Falkirk town centre where from 1801 the Horsemarket had been held, now Callendar Riggs, as well as the small customs or charges on grain and stock sold at the town markets. According to the legal decreet all of the income generated from land and customs had to be used for the benefit of the town or the feuars, a distinction which would cause many difficulties over the succeeding decades. At first the feuars were content to let the stentmasters collect the rental raised on their land and the customs, but within a few years, possibly fearing for the safety of their assets, they established a small committee to administer their own affairs. It was the start of a long period of strained relations between the two bodies which varied from close co-operation to open hostility and back again and was not resolved for 50 years. We are fortune that John Reid has had access to the surviving records of both the feuars and the stentmasters, and his enthralling accounts of their machinations published in the local history society journal *Calatria* have greatly enhanced our understanding of this period in the town's history.

At first the feuars' committee did little with the small sums raised by the customs and land except making the occasional donation to special causes, including, it must be said, the stentmasters' gas lamps. But the farmers of the carse whose crops were displayed on open tables at the weekly markets in the High Street began to complain about paying charges for no obvious benefit. A proposal to buy and sell outside the regality boundary spurred the feuars to action and in the late 1820s the search for a market site began. As usual there were great arguments and disputes before the small piece of land known as Dr Corbert's garden on the north side of the parish church was offered to the feuars by two of their own number. On this site the 'new market' of Falkirk was erected, consisting at first of 15 'shades' or sheltered areas for grain display and sale, later supplemented by a small granary of brick and wood. The ancient pathway across the glebe of the kirk now formed the south boundary of the new market area – that is the present Newmarket Street. Though this new arrangement proved far from satisfactory it secured the customs income for the feuars for the time being and it certainly seemed to attract new business – in 1807 the duties had been only £22 but by 1851 they were over £100 per annum. By 1847 one observer was clearly impressed by the scale of activity:

> This day's market is the second I have witnessed since it was held in its present place at the back of the Parish Church. I counted sixty-five horses and carts all laden with grain standing in a row along the Glebe dyke, the backs of each cart to the footpath and the horses heads all in a line. They reached from the Minister's barn on to the gate of Aitken's Brewery. I never saw such a sight in Falkirk before.

But by the time the new market was open for regular business in 1830 the municipal arrangements such as they were had been given yet another shake-up. In 1832 the great Reform Bill passed through Parliament and the following year the Scottish measure saw Falkirk, including the villages of Grahamston and Bainsford, erected into a Parliamentary Burgh sharing a Member of Parliament with Lanark, Hamilton, Linlithgow and Airdrie. It was a moment of great rejoicing throughout the land and in Falkirk there was a grand procession of tradesmen with their banners, as one commentator observed:

> The Tanners waved aloft their Bull's Head, and the rich flags of Carron were proudly carried by the iron workers as they joyfully marched along to the end of the Callendar Riggs. They were joined by the men from Camelon, who as beseemed the 'Mariners', carried the model of a ship, which was so tall that it would not pass under the triumphal arches.

In the same year a new municipal constitution came into force which allowed for the election of a provost, three bailies and eight councillors, but gave them only the most limited powers to raise money by assessing the property-holders of the burgh. This amounted to a maximum of three pence in the pound, a trifling sum which could do no more than pay for the expenses of the administration. Even their modest judicial role was diminished the following year by the appointment of a Sheriff Substitute for the Eastern District of Stirlingshire, resident in Falkirk and presiding in a court house in the town. The frustration which was no doubt felt by successive administrations increased as the needs of the town strained the resources of the penniless stentmasters and the canny feuars. Falkirk was in a mess – three sets of managers without money or power and a steadily deteriorating fabric, failing water supply, inadequate lighting, unmade streets and an unhealthy population unable to resist the ravages of cholera which visited the town in the 1830s and 1840s, and other killer illnesses that found a warm welcome in contaminated water supplies and overcrowded, insanitary hovels.

The turning point for the community was the publication in 1845 of Falkirk's first newspaper, the *Herald*, which quickly began to draw attention to the short comings of the town and asked questions of the so-called managers. Who organised the feuars? Was their money being used for the good of the community? Why did other towns adopt special measures to improve their facilities and not Falkirk? Stung by the criticism the feuars embarked on a programme of major improvements between 1851 and 1859. The most significant was the causewaying of the High Street which was laid with granite blocks, and given pavements and a covered drain to carry away surface water. Over £1,000 of the feuars' funds went into this project along with subscriptions from gentlemen in the town, especially those with houses or business premises in the street. The feuars also contributed nearly £300 to assist the stentmasters in maintaining the gas lamps in the burgh, and over £100 to help search out new water supplies. But their biggest expenditure was to come. The continued increase in grain brought to their market led to renewed demands for better facilities. The feuars, conscious of the pressure they were under from their critics on the Council and in the local newspaper, made a bold and expensive move. In 1858 the shades were removed and a substantial new Corn Exchange was built to the design of Alexander Black of Falkirk. The feuars borrowed around

£1,500 to fund the new building in what might be seen as a desperate attempt to convince the people of the district that they had the good of the community at heart.

Pressure was certainly mounting to bring about fundamental change. Between 1848 and 1852 three attempts were made to convince the electors to support the adoption of a General Police Bill which would have given the necessary finance-raising powers but these were rejected. By 1858 a new admin-istration under Provost Thomas Kier was ready to try again, this time with a Bill tailor-made for Falkirk's special circum-stances. It was introduced into Parliament the following year as 'An Act for Improving, Paving, Draining and Lighting the Burgh of Falkirk and for Regulating the Supply of Water within the Burgh and for Providing for the Transference of the Property of the Stentmasters and Feuars of Falkirk to the Magistrates and Council'. On the face of it, the aims seem so obviously desirable that a quick passage of the Bill should have been the outcome. Nothing could have been further from the truth. In 1859 the simmering hostility between feuars and stentmasters erupted into open warfare, and the battle was fought, not in a room in Wilson's Buildings or Rankine's Folly, but in the committee rooms of the Houses of Lords and Commons in London. It was a poor advert for the spirit of co-operation of a Scottish town but a goldmine for the historian of the burgh, for in page after page of charge and counter charge, the leading men of Falkirk described their town, with all its defects and deficiencies, in the minutest detail.

Foremost among the proposers of the Bill were Provost Kier and Robert Henderson, solicitor and clerk to the stentmasters. They described the iniquities of the arrangements with three bodies managing affairs with no real power. But it was the general sanitary condition of the town which gave them great-est concern. Everywhere in the town, on the High Street and in the back closes and wynds, were accumulations of filth, human and animal refuse and mud. Lack of drainage left 'large quantities of stagnant water, green in colour and offensive to the smell' especially in Grahamston and Bainsford but also in many parts of the old town. A water supply of around three gallons per day per person was only a quarter of what was required and it had to be carried from the public wells. It was too hard for washing purposes but could be drunk, though 'sometimes it comes to the town the colour of porter or nearly so and it takes several hours for the mud to subside.' Robert Henderson complained that 'at times the scarcity has been so great that the water of the Union Canal has been used for domestic and culinary purposes. Water is in summer occasionally sold from barrels brought into the town.' With 'vegetable growth' in some of the pipes and 'frogs found in the wells' it was obvious that the health of the people was at considerable risk.

Lighting too was totally inadequate. The 56 gaslamps in Falkirk were less than half of the number required. There were 12 private lamps in the Main Street in Grahamston but none at all in Bainsford which was lit by the constant glare from the flashing blast furnaces of Carron half a mile further north. And these dark and dirty streets were the haunt of 'thieves and vagrants' from Edinburgh and Glasgow, along with 'thimblers and cardplayers' who cheated the Falkirk 'bairns' out of their hard-earned pennies. Another witness was the Procurator Fiscal, John Gair, who claimed that his own office in the High Street had been broken into three times recently and that most houses and business premises were the regular target for burglars. There were by 1857 a superintendent, sergeant and three police constables based in Falkirk but they were responsible for an area much greater than the Parliamentary Burgh and were still answerable to the Commissioners based in Stirling. There was no night watch in the town.

Perhaps the most telling evidence of all came from Mr James Girdwood, a surgeon with a large practice in Grahamston and Falkirk and from the Revd Lewis Hay Irving, minister of Falkirk Free Church and Chairman of the Sanitary Committee of the Parochial Board and one of the town's most influential citizens. Both were enthusiastic in their support for the Bill and scathing in their criticism of the town managers who allowed such deplorable conditions to continue. Mr Girdwood argued that the foul emissions from uncovered and blocked drains were responsible for high mortality in certain particular black spots.

Many houses without any kind of toilet facilities were so filthy that many died of fever, croup and cholera. The Revd Mr Irving also claimed that many of the working people lived in buildings which were not fit for human occupation – he particularly highlighted a drain on the south boundary of the graveyard next to the back walls of High Street houses. Surface water drained through the lairs of the kirkyard into this open sewer which was many feet above the level of the houses. All manner of foul and poisonous substances then found their way to the homes of the people in the very heart of the town. Typhoid fever was often the result. Fifty yards away on the junction of Wooer Street and the Back Row, in one common lodging house it had claimed the lives of 50 people just a few years before. All the witnesses were clear as to the cause of the scandalous condition of their town, and all agreed on the solution. A single group of councillors with power to levy substantial assessments on the property owners of the whole burgh would raise the large sums needed to pave and drain and light the whole Parliamentary Burgh and provide an adequate and dependable supply of good water.

They presented a powerful and persuasive case but did not have it their own way by any manner of means. The opposition was formidable. The feuars mustered many of Falkirk's most influential figures and the picture they painted for the Lords and Members of the Commons was very different. Damning their opponents for gross exaggeration they claimed, quite rightly, that the public of Falkirk, including the vast majority of the few hundred qualified electors, were opposed to the Bill and especially the extra burdens it would place upon them. It was a 'most unnecessary and uncalled for Bill' said lawyer Adam Smith because 'Falkirk is so well governed already'. Auctioneer James Neilson was outspoken in his defence of the feuars' record and of the town whose 'Main Street is the cleanest street I ever saw in my life'. Former Provost, Robert Adam, himself a feuar and one-time supporter of such reforms, was incensed by the attempt to take away the feuars' property and rights and use it for people 'outside the blue line', that is, beyond the old Regality boundary in Grahamston and

Bainsford. From the other side of that line, Bainsford black-smith William Drummond took a different perspective. The people of Bainsford didn't want the stentmasters' debts (or the feuars' for that matter, although he did not say so) – nor did the village need drainage, water supply or causewaying. The shocked advocate for the proposers suggested that Bainsford sounded like 'a garden of Eden', which Drummond did not dispute! As far as lighting was concerned, Carron's flames were a blessing: 'The darker the night, the greater the illumination . . . at all times of dark nights it is illuminated so much so that I believe a Gas burner would be like the Moon when the sun is shining.'

A second medical man, Dr David Hadden, disputed the claims of surgeon Girwood. He too regularly visited throughout the district and found the people to be healthy and the state of the town not injurious to their well-being. Statistics were produced to show that the town's mortality rate a year or so before had been lower than that of Stirling, Airdrie, Lanark and Campsie and well below the overall Scottish figure. All in all it was an uncompromising and determined opposition summed up by Adam Smith: 'I would not,' he said, 'be disposed to entrust such powers to a Municipal body, but with respect to a Community like Falkirk it would be perfect madness.'

Madness or no, it came to pass, for the Bill was approved in August 1859, with the feuars retaining their Corn Exchange and land but losing the power to collect customs. The stent-masters' property, steeple and water pipes and wells, and their debts passed into the hands of 'Commissioners' as the municipal councillors were to be called for a period. Perhaps the obvious sincerity of Dr Girdwood and the Revd Irving had carried the day against a group so obviously out to protect vested interests and prevent a fair sharing of the burdens. A telling remark by Adam Smith underlined the prevailing attitude and perhaps helped to sway any doubters who remained. Asked if he would approve even a three-farthing increase in the rates to improve the High Street, he replied: 'If the town were my own and I wished to give it all the amenities of a private house fitted for a genteel family I would . . . but with reference to the Inhabi-tants, I think the three-farthings is too much.'

The Parliament decided that men like Smith should no longer manage the affairs of the 'inhabitants' and put their trust in those whose aims were more in tune with the times. It would be difficult to exaggerate the importance of the Bill in changing the course of Falkirk's history. If the charter of James VI in 1600 was the birth certificate of the burgh then 1859 was its coming of age. After a long and painful adolescence the new burgh was set fair for a period of unrivalled prosperity.

CHAPTER 10

Church and School in Victorian Falkirk

In the early eighteenth century, at the same time as the Livingston's baronial control was extinguished in the district, the power of the one remaining authority, the Church, was diminished by division and secession. The promise of freedom for sessions and presbyteries which the national settlement of 1688 had offered had been dashed in 1712. The Patronage Act of that year more or less restored the power of landowners to impose ministers of their choice even when sessions and church members disagreed. Several serious disputes arose but the first major challenge came in 1733 when Ebenezer Erskine of Stirling and three other ministers formed an Associate Presbytery independent of the Church of Scotland. Seven elders of Falkirk Parish asked for the supply of a minister and in 1742 they acquired 'all and whole, that big yard lying on the north side of the town near the east', that is, on the high ground between High Street and Manor Street on what was Silver Row. A plain 'meeting house' with accommodation for 950 'sitters' was erected and became the second church of the town. The whole area has been transformed by modern development though the Antonine Hotel stands close to the site of the first Erskine building. Of course the new kirk session claimed all the power of the old, with the rights and duties that went with it. This included of course bringing the Sabbath-breakers and the rest to public repentance, with this time one added serious offence – attending services at the established church. Such a split obviously reduced the absolute authority claimed by the minister and elders of the Parish Church; it was easy now to dismiss a call to 'compear' by claiming adherence to the opposition.

35. The Silver Row building of the original Erskine Church which later housed the Roxy Theatre. The Antonine Hotel and parts of Callendar Square occupy the site today.

The power of the established church in Falkirk, thus diminished was further reduced forty years later by a second secession. This time a small group of ministers led by Thomas Gillespie in Dunfermline, established a new Presbyterian church free from the oppression of state or any other interference. He found support in Falkirk and in 1767 a 'Relief' congregation was established in the town. Thirty years later they had their own permanent place of worship at the west end, later known as the West Church. This building served a variety of Presbyterian groups for two centuries until 1991 when it became the Falkirk home of the People's Church, a lively and growing evangelical congregation. It remains the oldest public building in Falkirk and local historians as well as the people of the town must be delighted to see it continue serving the community in the way its founding fathers had intended.

The departure of still more of its active members dealt the Parish Church another blow at a time when it had difficulties enough to contend with. The old kirk building was wearing badly. Some repair work had been done and a new steeple added in 1735, but it was what it was, a 300-year-old building, cold and dark, damp and cramped, built for a style of worship no longer appropriate and incapable of accommodating the congregation it was meant to serve. A new age demanded new and better facilities. The money to provide improvement was available and it required only a catalyst to spark the session and the reluctant landowners into action. In 1794 a new minister, Dr James Wilson, was called and the difficult task fell to him.

From his arrival in Falkirk until his death 35 years later, he was an energetic and controversial figure provoking hostility and opposition from large numbers of his congregation and affection and regard from as many others. He quickly settled to what seemed to him the principal task facing the parish – the replacement of the old inadequate church which by the 1790s seemed beyond repair. The new minister was quite clear in his own mind that the crumbling edifice had to go and he set about convincing the principal landowners of the parish, whose responsibility it was, of the need for a new church. At first he was reasonably successful and most of these 'heritors' including

Lord Dundas agreed to the proposal. In 1797 he was in confident mood as he wrote the Falkirk entry for the famous *Statistical Account of Scotland*: 'The building is . . . far from being sufficient for the accommodation of those who wish to attend; but it is hoped something will soon be done to provide a remedy for this inconvenience.'

But he had forgotten the formidable William Forbes of Callendar who had other ideas and was, like Wilson himself, not easily diverted from his own particular path. At his insistence surveyors were asked to report on the possibilities of repairing the church, and while they did agree that it could be done they were doubtful if any extension was possible without great additional expense. The debate dragged on and the years passed. Forbes changed his line. He would agree to the rebuilding of the church on a new site selected by him – he offered the

36. The Parish Church built in 1811. The square tower which was retained from the pre-Reformation building shows the gable marks of the old south aisle where the Livingstons were buried.

corner of Hope Street and Newmarket Street where the Sheriff
Court now stands. Wilson and his Session were firm in their
resistance – the ground of the old kirk was hallowed by
centuries of worship and it would not be abandonded lightly.
Eventually the dispute reached the Court of Session and from
the welter of charge and countercharge a compromise solution
emerged far nearer the wish of the minister than that of his
principal parishioner. The tower of the old church would
remain and all the rest would come down. A new building
designed by Gillespie Graham of Edinburgh, of oblong shape
lying east to west abutting the tower on the north side, would be
built to accommodate a congregation of over 800 seated in
semicircular form facing in towards the pulpit in the centre of
the new north wall. In 1810 work commenced and the present
church began to take shape. By the following August it was
ready for occupation and the heritors met to share out the
seating in proportion to the value of their property holding in
the parish. Not surprisingly then that the first seating plan,
which survives, is dominated by Forbes of Callendar and Lord
Dundas who have the use of most of the places for themselves,
their families and the more fortunate of their tenants. The early
estimates had costed the new building at £3,593 2s. 6d. but in
the event over £5,000 was expended before that great day
when we are told that the new kirk was opened 'with due
solemnity upon Sabbath, the eighth day of September, one
thousand eight hundred and eleven years amid a great con-
course of people.' Dr Wilson's drive and determination had
secured the new building but his moderate approach to discipline particularly did not please all his congregation. The grip
of the church on the people was slipping and more and more of
the new industrial workers found themselves with neither
church nor minister near enough or concerned enough to serve
their needs. Those who pined for the tough old days of stern
unbending pastors found their way to the breakaway groups
though once the habit of splintering is established it is difficult
to stop. The original Erskine group divided and divided again
so that by the early years of the nineteenth century there
were congregations in the original Silver Row church, an

'antiburgher' group in the curious little octagonal building in the Cow Wynd known to later generations as the 'Tattie Kirk', and still another in a building in Cistern Lane behind the High Street buildings. All claimed to be the real Church of Scotland, true to the reforming fathers' vision, and all claimed power to assist the poor and maintain discipline. Along with the Relief Church and the Parish Church that gave Falkirk five separate Presbyterian congregations, but for the divided establishment much worse was to come.

The 1830s were a time of growing difficulty for the national church with more and more ministers and lay members joining the chorus of protest over what they saw as the State's interference in spiritual affairs. This dispute once again turned on the vexed question of lay patronage, that is, on who had the right to nominate a new minister for a vacant charge. But there was more to the growing polarisation among fathers and brethren than mere questions of interference and spiritual freedom – it was a struggle for the very soul of the church

37. The Tattie Kirk, an unusual octagonal building which housed the Antiburgher congregation from 1806 until 1879 and still survives as a store

itself with the protest led for the most part by the evangelicals and rejected by more moderate elements. By 1840 it seemed that a breach was inevitable and their new minister, William Begg, warned his Falkirk congregation that many ministers would have to 'give up their livings for conscience sake'. He strongly supported the protest and seemed set to join the objectors when the great Disruption finally came. But the period was a complex one with many different standards of opinion woven and twisted into a tangle which no short summary can unpick. Suffice to say that for some ministers a middle way emerged which meant they could sustain their protest yet remain within the establishment. Begg was one of them, and though his friends were greatly disappointed at his decision, it is a considerable tribute to his personal integrity and standing in the community that he retained their friendship and regard. Indeed, when that great break came at last in May 1843 and thousands of ministers, elders and lay members abandoned their churches to support the new Free Church, relations in Falkirk remained reasonably close, unlike many other areas where acrimonious dispute further scarred an already damaged Presbyterian reputation.

The day before the final Disruption took place, a meeting was held in the Baptist Chapel in Bank Street at which two Falkirk elders, John Burns and Thomas Hardie, took the platform – many people attended and pledged themselves to follow the leadership into the new Free Church. How many did so is uncertain, though we do have recorded a telling remark from one elder who remained within the established church and who told a leading free churchman in the town that 'your numbers are not great but you have the cream of the congregation with you'. This new congregation met first in the church in Cistern Lane moving eventually to Garrison Place and finally to Newmarket Street in 1896 – the present St Andrews Church.

In the same year as this great Disruption shook the church to its very foundations an event took place almost unnoticed which was in its way as revolutionary and far reaching in its effect on the religious life of the district. In May, Father Paul

MacLachlan from Glenlivet officiated at the opening ceremony of the first Roman Catholic Church in the district for nearly three centuries. The Catholic religion had been all but extinguished in the years after the Reformation but the great public works, the roads, canals and railways brought large numbers of immigrant workers from Ireland and the Highlands for whom there was no place of worship or ministering priest. Father MacLachlan, who was responsible for the whole of Stirlingshire, began visiting the town in 1831 and occasionally held services in private houses and public buildings like the Assembly Rooms in the Pleasance or in the Railway Hotel on the High Station Road. By 1840 there were 180 in his congregation which was meeting weekly and the new church in Hope Street dedicated to the missionary St Francis Xavier was the culmination of years of struggle. Designed by the architect William Stirling of Dunblane, it was described as 'an elegant structure in the Saxon style which forms a conspicuous object in the thriving town of Falkirk'. The building, which had seating for 600 and had to serve a huge area of east Stirlingshire, was lost following a fire in 1955 and replaced by the present modern building in 1961.

Many other churches outside the Presbyterian fold were established from time to time. Some flourished briefly, declined and closed down, but others were more persistent and their descendants remained active until well into this century. A host of public buildings were pressed into service to accommodate new congregations – a hall in Swords Wynd off the High Street housed an early Baptist group, there was a synagogue in Burns Court and Congregationalists met in what later became the Bank Street premises of Young's Stores. In the same street the Evangelical Union finally settled in a new building, later St Modan's Church, and now, after a spells as a picture house and a bingo hall it is the lower storey of a night club called 'The Carron Works'.

The Episcopalian tradition which had suffered in the final settlement of the religious question in 1688 had survived in the hearts and homes of some of the gentry, but it was probably the arrival of a large contingent of skilled English workers and their families which led to the revival of services in the area. Certainly there are records of fortnightly meetings in Carron in the 1790s and visits by the Earl of Dunmore's chaplains to Wilson's Buildings and other halls during the following century. In 1863 a fine new church was built in Kerse Lane to the design of the celebrated Edinburgh architect, Sir Robert Rowand Anderson, then at the start of an illustrious career. Financed in large measure by Forbes of Callendar and other leading landowners it remains one of the most beautiful buildings in the whole Falkirk district.

Badly buffeted by winds of division and opposition the Parish Church nonetheless held on and began to grow once more. The rapid increase in population brought repeated demands from the outlying areas of the burgh for a church and minister of their own. It was a remarkably complex legal and financial matter to achieve this laudable aim and most had to wait years and suffer great neglect before their wish was granted. Grahamston, for example, which had experienced a huge growth in population throughout the century, had its first church, the present Grahamston United congregation, in 1875, and a new United Presbyterian church, now St James, was opened in 1898. Bainsford had no established Church of Scotland congregation but the Free Church did open the present Bainsford Parish Church in 1875.

As we have seen, the role of the church in society had changed steadily over the years as fragmentation reduced personal adherence to one particular congregation. Discipline of the kind familiar in earlier years disappeared and cutty stools and pillars faded into memory. A gentler message offered in more pleasant surroundings was the way of the new age, still harsher than our own era perhaps but nonetheless a transformation for all that. Stained-glass windows, delicate architectural details, carved wooden pews, harmoniums and organs, gas mantles and warm welcoming Carron stoves appeared throughout the town as congregations, wealthy from the flourishing iron foundries and fertile lands of the carse, erected handsome new premises.

The plain Relief Kirk at the west end was given a fine new entrance in 1883, the old Tattie Kirk was abandoned in 1879 and a new building (demolished in 1990) built in Graham's

Road. And so it went on – a new Congregational Church in Meeks Road opened in 1893, a handsome Methodist Chapel in James Street in 1892 and a Baptist Church in Orchard Street in 1897. It is plain that the church, taken as a whole, was continuing to play a very significant part in the life of the population despite more than a century of division, but its traditional role in affairs was certainly changing.

By the middle of the century poor relief, once the exclusive province of the kirk sessions had more or less passed into the hands of other agencies and in 1872 parish schools were detached from the control of the church and handed over to new School Boards. But the new bodies still relied heavily on the energy and expertise of ministers of the town churches. Men like Lewis Hay Irving of the Free Church, who has already been encountered in his role as proponent of the Bill to change the deplorable state of the town, William Begg of the Parish Church and James Aitchison of the Erskine, were involved in a wide range of activities, helping to establish schools for poor children, building asylums for the very old and insane and encouraging further beneficial public works. These ministers, along with the powerful and wealthy men on their sessions, remained the leading figures in burgh affairs in an era when the growing division between the haves and have-nots plagued the industrial areas of prosperous Victorian Scotland.

They and their earnest congregations did what they thought best, though it seems pitifully little with hindsight. Each Monday from the first week of November for example, ladies of the Dorcas Society gathered to make clothes for the needy to ease the special problems of winter. In January 1884 for example, they distributed '25 petticoats, 4 shifts, 13 dresses for the women and girls, 5 pairs of boots, 6 shawls and turnovers, 14 boys shirts and 5 semits'. A few years earlier the Falkirk Session had noted that '88 people in the town had each received 3/6d'.

But despite the best intentions of ministers and congregations, despite new church buildings galore and more active communicant members than ever, the Church as a whole was slowly losing the battle. The growing urban population, many living in wretched poverty, were finding their solace in other ways and Falkirk, regardless of its fine new fabric, was increasingly the scene of drunkenness and violence and what a later age would call multiple deprivation.

We have already encountered the parochial schoolmasters of Falkirk in the century after the Reformation struggling to fulfil the lofty vision of the founding fathers against the indifference of the majority of the heritors of the parish. These leading landowners were legally obliged to find a schoolhouse and a master but most often they sought to provide the bare minimum demanded by the law and sometimes even less. In the early eighteenth century we find the school in a slightly better situation. Moving from the Kerse Lane to 'my Lord Callendar's lodging' near the junction of Vicar's Loan and the Back Row. Here in the old town house of the ancient family it remained for fifty years with a succession of masters offering a diet of reading, writing, arithmetic and religious education, with the more able children going on to study Latin and sometimes Greek. Although the term 'Grammar School' of Falkirk appears first in 1712, it was many decades before the two streams – the elementary 'parish school' and the more advanced 'grammar school' were clearly identified. In 1761 the session agreed to rehouse the school in the unused nave of the church to the west of the tower. This was 25 feet long and for the princely sum of £20 the elders refurbished the building and created two classrooms. But with demand for places at the school continuing to grow the heritors were forced just 14 years later to provide a completely new building in the Back Row. It was this school which drew the praise of the Revd James Wilson in his report for the *Statistical Account* in 1797. 'The grammar school of Falkirk,' he said, 'is justly held in great reputation' and, in an aside which would no doubt find an echo in educational circles in every age, he concluded: 'Though populous and flourishing situations like Falkirk yield a decent competence for the support of respectable schoolmasters, yet in few situations are they paid in proportion to their usefulness in society.'

There were already several adventure schools running successfully in the town, and the hostility which the session had once shown had given way to an acceptance that the official schools could not possibly cope with the demand from seven or eight hundred children.

By 1803 the Falkirk School was in a 'ruinous condition' but repairs kept it operating, though overcrowding continued to be a feature for another forty years. An additional building was acquired in the Pleasance with one large room for the teaching of English, but just six years later the master, Thomas Downie, petitioned the heritors, complaining about the size of his room and the inadequacy of the furnishings for the numbers attending – more than 100 pupils in a room 18 feet square! He claimed then that his health was threatened by this situation and it was possibly his early death five years later at the age of just thirty-nine that first prompted the heritors to look once again at the situation.

Certainly the new master, James Burns, was far from happy with his facilities. He pressed the heritors for some action and in response they appointed an investigating committee which soon confirmed the schoolmaster's opinion. They found both the parochial school in the Back Row and the English school in the Pleasance in 'a miserable state – damp, low-roofed, small in size and a very bad situation'. The English room which Downie had found so oppressive, plus another large room close by, now contained over 200 children. In an astonishing account Burns described his day-to-day situation:

> Of these 133 write in the following order: 54 write on tables, 24 write on forms, kneeling on the floor: 45 stand, who have neither tables nor forms, but I endeavour to give them fifteen or twenty minutes by making them change places with some of those sitting at table or lying at forms. I have sufficient forms for 130 only and there are 72 who have no seats.

Despite this damning indictment the heritors continued to resist the demand for a new school though they did ask the magistrates of the burgh to assist them in solving the problem. The outcome was a decision in 1844 to build a new school in the town and after much wrangling a site to the north of the Back Row 'an out of the way, low and unwholesome place' according to one of the objectors, was acquired for the purpose. Two new streets were opened up, linking the school to the rest of the town – Park Street running north from the Back Row and Weir Street running west from Vicars Loan. Despite the refusal of the feuars to contribute to the cost, £1,500 was raised by the heritors and through voluntary donations, and on 18 May 1846 the children marched in a procession from the Pleasance to Park Street where many of the leading men of the town joined them in celebration. The building remained as the Grammar and Parochial School for more than fifty years and later housed the County Mining Institute. Now as the town centre base for the Community Education service it continues to serve the educational needs of the people of the district.

From 1846 the Grammar and Parochial Schools flourished under the guidance of a succession of outstanding masters. By 1860 the list of subjects available included French, German, arithmetic, book-keeping, mathematics, writing, drawing and

38. The Grammar School of Falkirk in Park Street. It is still used for educational purposes.

music as well as English, Greek and Latin. From age six to ten children attended the parish school, with the most able remaining in the Grammar School section. By the 1850s there were nearly 400 pupils in all and a decade later an extension was required to alleviate serious overcrowding. But if the Parish School was the heart of Falkirk's educational system, it was very far from the only provision. As early as 1800 there were fourteen teachers in the parish with small schools in Camelon, Grangemouth, Bonnybridge and Laurieston supported by individuals or groups of business people in each location. Thereafter a number of highly successful and long-lasting institutions emerged to serve the needs of particular groups. The Bainsford Self-Supporting School lasted from 1797 until it was absorbed into the Northern School eighty years later. At its height it offered elementary education to nearly 200 children. Half a mile away in Grahamston a Subscription School was established by the inhabitants in 1810 and it provided both day and evening education to children and to young bank clerks, apprentice merchants and surveyors, or seamen who came to learn the arts of mathematics and navigation. There was a Free Church school in Meeks Road from 1851, a Catholic school in the Back Row from 1853, and a Charity school supported by active church members, offering basic education to around 70 children of poor families. From 1813 onwards it offered Bible studies, reading and writing, and so many people wished to support the work that a new school in Pleasance Square was built in 1851. Six years later another church initiative, this time from the Revd Irving saw the establishment of a Ragged and Industrial School to provide for the orphans, waifs and strays of the district. By 1869 fifty boys were effectively in the custody of the master in the school in the Kerse Lane, where bible study and basic education and useful work was the diet intended to reclaim these least favoured of all the bairns of the industrial burgh. Their building served this century as a model lodging house and was demolished in the summer of 1991 and replaced by flats.

But of all the educational initiatives in Victorian Falkirk the one that most seems to catch the popular sentiment of the age

39. Silver Row, from the Callendar riggs, showing St Francis Catholic School built in 1880 to replace the original which was in Manor Street or the 'Back Row' as it was called then

was the school run in Bryson Street, Bainsford, for over fifty years from 1820 by James Grossart. He was the most celebrated teacher of his day, though he had no formal qualifications. Grossart's school was a mecca for people of all ages seeking instruction in a bewildering variety of subjects. One former pupil remembered Grossart's classroom as a place of wonderment.

Above the entrance door was a music board, which had always some new song or hymn on it, in staff or sol-fa notation. They saw the walls covered by maps, mostly of his own painting. Above the fireplace were illustrations of the principles of mechanics. At the south-west corner, over the slate press, was a working model of a steam-engine in sections, all made by his own hands. The centre ornament of the roof was the mariner's compass, with all the points carefully painted in true position. The remainder of the roof was covered with various constellations of the starry firmament. All of these were at hand for illustration in his teaching, and many others besides. He managed to keep a crowded school going in full swing, from the infants in one corner to the sailors in the other, learning navigation, with no pupil-teachers, only a monitor appointed now and then to call out the names of bad boys, who got their reward at his convenience. Whoever heard Mr Grossart recite 'Mary, the Maid of the Inn', and did not feel every hair standing up and their blood curdling? He seemed to throw his whole soul into it, and photographed the picture on their minds.

Grossart's combination of education for the sheer pleasure of learning with the development of practical skills of real value, seems the very embodiment of the intellectual spirit of the age and many of his pupils went on to play a leading role in the rapid expansion of the town's industry and commerce after the middle of the nineteenth century.

But despite the excellence of such individual efforts the whole picture in the district as well as the country as a whole, was a patchwork of quality and insufficiency, high standards and deplorable inadequacy, depending in large measure on charity or the forced contribution of unwilling landowners. It was ripe for change and in 1873, following the Act of the previous year, most of Falkirk eighteen schools were removed from the control of sessions, private groups or individuals and placed under Parochial Boards elected by the ratepayers of the burgh. Most benefited greatly from the change, though there was great regret that under the particular terms of the Act the Grammar School was reduced to no more than one of many providing elementary education. For several years pupils capable of higher study were forced to travel to the cities, but the Revd James Aitchison, minister of the United Presbyterian (Erskine) Church, campaigned tirelessly for a change of heart. In 1886 he was successful and the old Grammar School was redesignated as a High School and soon over 350 pupils were in attendance. A decade later the old buildings proved inadequate and in 1889 a superb new school was opened in Rennie Street which served as Falkirk High for more than 60 years.

Another new school provided by the Parochial Board was Comely Park, opened in 1879 with over 300 children, most of whom had attended the Charity School in the Pleasance. Known by many as 'Cochrane's Academy' after its first Headmaster, it was soon too small for the number of pupils and required to be extended early in the new century. In 1909 it had a role of over a thousand pupils.

In 1827, in common with many Scottish towns, Falkirk saw the establishment of a Mechanics Institute under the name of the School of Arts. In one of the earliest statements of aims the founders proposed 'the instruction of mechanics and others in Popular Science and the Useful Arts – by means of lectures, apparatus, models and a library'. Meeting first in the versatile Assembly Rooms – rented for £2 15 shillings, 'coal and candles not supplied' – the school soon had over 100 members and well known lecturers were engaged to give talks on various branches of physics, as well as astronomy, anatomy and zoology. By the 1830s it had moved on to the larger Independent Chapel in

40. Comely Park School

Bank Street and the lectures were attracting more than two hundred. Despite this there were always financial difficulties and for a period from 1844 the school ceased to function. When it reopened a few years later the trend away from scientific subjects towards literature, music, philosophy and history became even more marked and the school changed from an educational institution for artisans into a culture club for a more leisured class. By 1862 very large musical evenings were being held in the new Corn Exchange in New Market Street and this continued through to the Town Hall which replaced it around twenty years later. By then there were a number of other organizations, particularly church groups offering 'soirees and conversatziones' with musical interludes as well as talks and lectures on all manner of subjects. In the face of this growing competition the School of Arts ceased to exist after 1891 but by then the town had a substantial building knows as the School of Arts and Sciences opposite the old Grammar School in Park Street. It was opened by Lord Rosebery in 1878 as a response, no doubt, to growing demands in the rapidly expanding iron industry for skilled designers and technically competent workmen. A few years after Park Street Grammar School became the new Falkirk High, the School of Arts and Science building became a department of the school.

With fine new schools for children of all ages as well as for adults, and the legal and financial framework to support the work of the teachers, Falkirk was at last freed from the piecemeal provision of the previous centuries. The reformers' dream of adequate education for every child in the parish, no matter their means, was fulfilled at last. It had taken only three hundred years.

CHAPTER II

Building a New Town

Despite the enormous impact of the ironworks, the canals and railways, the town of Falkirk in the mid-nineteenth century was still primarily a market centre serving the landward area of East Stirlingshire and the villages of the carse. Population growth over the previous fifty years had been steady though not spectacular and was just under 9,000 by 1851. Describing the town around the same period, the Falkirk lawyer James Burns claimed that 'with the exception of leather, no goods are to any extent manufactured in the town'. But he went on to list the works which had grown up on the outskirts of the old burgh, especially along the line of the canal – a sawmill in Bainsford 'wrought by three steam engines' employing fifteen, two pyroligneous acid works in Grahamston making 'iron liquor for the print fields and vinegar', and a distillery at Rosebank. Forty-two men worked in the town's four tanneries and there were of course the collieries, woodyards, cornmills, brick and tile works and James Aitken's ale and porter brewery. One in five of the workforce was already engaged in the iron industry and in the second half of the nineteenth century this increased dramatically as the population almost doubled to over 16,000. More than a dozen new foundries opened their doors as the national and international demand for domestic cast iron multiplied. In 1856 Abbot's Foundry opened on the site of the short-lived Dalderse Iron Works. This was followed by Burnbank in 1860, Cockburns in 1864, Grahamston close by in 1868 and Callendar in 1876. By 1900 these five were employing over 1,000 men, using iron from the Carron blast furnaces to produce an enormous range of goods, from pots and pans to stoves, grates, boilers, pipes and ranges. Outside the town the same thing was happening in Larbert, Denny, Bonny-bridge, Camelon, Laurieston and Bo'ness and there seemed no limit to the markets for their products. Many of the foundry employers built houses for the workforce and men were attracted to the town in large numbers by the prospect of steady employment no matter how punishing or unpleasant. In the face of the challenge, Carron Company, itself enjoying a boom period, decided on a huge programme of reconstruction. Under the leadership of Andrew Gordon and later David Cowan, the works were completely rebuilt in the late 1870s with new blast furnaces, foundries and brickworks and that splendid office block which was the subject of much argument in recent years. The battle to keep it standing while all other vestiges of the great undertaking disappeared, was ultimately in vain. Only the central bay remains but without the rest of the building it has lost the dignity and style it once enjoyed.

At the end of the century four out of ten men in the burgh were employed in the iron industry and east Stirlingshire was firmly established as the nation's principal centre for light castings. It was to remain so for another fifty years and for

41. The 1880 office building of Carron Company

42. The new building of James Aitken's brewery opened in 1900. By then they had been brewing on the same site for well over 150 years.

much of the time the vast fortunes earned by the companies were retained by the families who owned and managed them, and who invested substantial sums in the religious and commercial life of the burgh.

Employment in agriculture and the manufacture of goods associated with the land declined markedly over the same period as the old market town became a thriving new industrial centre. Two firms which prospered from the growing band of thirsty ironworkers were James Aitken the brewers who by the early decades of the nineteenth century were firmly established on the large site on the north side of Newmarket Street, and Robert Barr, whose mineral-water works were located on the other side of the High Street at Burnfoot. Aitken's Ales enjoyed tremendous popularity throughout Britain, and as demand increased towards the end of the century the brewery was completely reconstructed. The magnificent red brick building with its familiar high chimney came to dominate the skyline and the aroma which cloaked the town on brewing days was as much a part of Falkirk as the Steeple bell or the distant fire of the Carron furnaces. Barr's story began in 1830 when the first Robert Barr began a business cutting corks by hand on the site at Burnfoot. Among his customers were several aerated water manufacturers and when, fifty years later, machine-cut corks drove his son out of business, Robert Barr junior switched trades and a legend was born. By the end of the century the company had prospered to the extent that it had branches in Glasgow and Lanarkshire and was soon able to buy out many of its Falkirk competitors.

Although both Aitken's and Barr's were located close to the town centre, it will be clear from the foregoing that the bulk of the rapidly expanding industry was based in the burgh's northern suburbs of Grahamston and Bainsford which lay east and west of the 'great north road' from Falkirk to Carron and beyond. The population of these two 'villages' increased dramatically as the foundries, brickworks and timber yards, and, of course, the railway network which supported them, attracted huge numbers of job seekers from all over the land. The Parliamentary committees in 1859 heard a great deal about Grahamston and Bainsford and not much of it was complimentary: housing was in short supply and many of the problems of overcrowding and insanitary living and working conditions described earlier were the result. But, as ever, it was the incoming workers rather than the successful businessmen who suffered most. At one time, when power and wealth lay in the hands of a small number of landowners, they lived in the landward area and kept town houses within the burgh. The rest, whatever their station, lived together in the crowded streets and wynds. But as the century progressed

43. The celebrated Glasgow Buildings in Williamson Street, demolished in the 1960s

the new men of affairs, the lawyers and bank agents, ironmasters and brewers began to acquire fine new houses outwith the old burgh limits. Old mansion houses like Thornhill, Kersehill, Arnotdale and Gartcows were rebuilt or restored, and many handsome new villas were constructed in Arnothill. Later, in the Meeks Road and Woodlands areas, north and south of the railway line through Grahamston, large numbers of villas and cottages were built for the traders and business people and in 1888 the Town Council erected lodging houses and 'artisans' dwellings' for 200 at a cost of nearly £10,000. One of these blocks in Williamson Street was the famous 'Glasgow Buildings', a well-known spot in Falkirk folklore, which was demolished in the 1960s. This was the first example of municipal housing in the burgh and, commendable though it was, it left vast numbers in miserable conditions. The efforts of architects and masons were for the most part engaged in a quite different activity.

Within the burgh it was new public buildings which began to appear from the mid century on, reflecting commercial success and growing municipal pride and self confidence. The first of these was the new Sheriff Court House on the corner of New Market and Hope Street. For many years from 1834 successive sheriffs dispensed justice in a variety of inadequate public halls like the familiar Assembly Rooms, Wilson's Buildings and the Red Lion Inn in the High Street. In 1852 the Temperance Hotel, the building on the south side of Bank Street which later housed Young's pram store, was purchased and converted into a proper court building and police station. But plans for a more permanent solution incorporating prison cells were already under way – by 1850 the familiar west end site had been acquired from the Falkirk Brewery Company, and despite long years of wrangling between the Town Council and the Stirlingshire Commissioners, the new building was finally ready in 1868. Designed by the Edinburgh architects, Brown and Peddie, in the popular Scots baronial style, it cost nearly £8,000 and served for over 120 years. It closed in 1990 and the business was transferred to the fine new building in Camelon Main Street.

A decade after the new Court House opened for business the

44. The Sheriff Court building opened in 1868 at the west end of the town. The police station on the left was added a few years later. The Gentleman Fountain was removed in 1923.

Town Council, anxious to find a permanent home for its growing band of officials, commissioned local architect William Black to design a building for the corner of Newmarket Street and Glebe Street. The result was the attractive baronial-style building still known to most Falkirk folk as the 'Burgh Buildings' which served as the municipal centre for nearly a century. In 1975 it was scheduled for demolition as part of the redevelopment of the brewery site but a determined campaign led by that doughty fighter James Middlemass eventually succeeded in saving the building. It did more than that – it proved to the people that it was possible to resist the worst excesses of the planners if the will was strong enough. The unnecessary destruction has continued of course, but not with such ease or contempt for the views of the public. The building is now home to the Registrar of Births, Deaths and Marriages, the Town Centre management team and one or two other voluntary agencies.

In 1877 the feuars of Falkirk, bereft of much of their power but still influential in the affairs of the town, decided to replace the Corn Exchange. It was less than twenty years old but the demands placed upon it for public meetings and entertainment

45. The Town Hall in Newmarket Street opened in 1879 and was demolished in 1968

were steadily increasing and the building could not cope. It had been built as a grain market with some use for public purposes – now its replacement would reverse the scheme – a Town Hall for the burgh with some space set aside for the diminishing corn trade. Again the architect was William Black and the Town Hall and the new Masonic Lodge of Falkirk next door were completed in 1879. The feuars expressed the hope that their new hall would 'in generations to come, be looked upon as the home of music in our town and from which would proceed elevating and refining influences in this and the sister arts'. For almost a hundred years it was at the heart of the community, constantly thronged for political meetings and election results, choral and orchestral concerts, displays and demonstrations, school prize givings and church socials. Great public appeals were launched within its walls and many of the most famous performers in the land graced its stage. With the possible exception of the Old Kirk and the Steeple, no building in Falkirk was so prized, but that did not save it from the bulldozers in 1968. With a new, modern building in West Bridge Street, the old hall was surplus to requirements, or so it was said. Down it came, and with it the back wall of the Parish Church! Further building on the site was deemed impossible without more permanent damage and plans to build a church hall were abandoned. The space stands empty today – a constant reminder to those who still recall the Town Hall with affection and regret. But all that was in the future. In 1879 the feuars may have thought that the investment would restore their power, but only eleven years later the Falkirk Corporation Act was passed by Parliament which transferred all their properties to the Town Council. This, of course, included land which has remained in use as public property ever since: the thirty acres on which Lochgreen Hospital and Princes Park were later sited, the Blinkbonny or 'Low' Park and the 'Washing Green' on High Station Road, which later housed the burgh stables and then the electricity power station. In the town centre there was the one acre remembered as the 'market square' in Callendar Riggs and now a multi-storey car park, and of course the grand new Town Hall. All passed out of the hands of the feuars who by 1890 had effectively ceased to exist.

The new Sheriff Court, Burgh Buildings and Town Hall were all inspired by municipal authorities of one kind or another, but the independent commercial interests in the town were equally anxious to take a larger stake in an increasingly prosperous community. Nothing in Victorian Scotland demonstrated confidence and success more than fine, stone buildings in classical or baronial style and many were built in Falkirk. Thankfully, a goodly number have survived, like David MacGibbon's magnificent baronial building at the junction of Vicar Street and Newmarket Street completed in 1863 for the National Bank, and a similar design at the west end of the town by Peddie and Kinear in 1879. Both are now solicitors' offices. Elsewhere there was the Post Office building in Vicar Street, completed in 1893, the nearby red sandstone office of the British Linen Bank from

46. Silver Row in the early years of the twentieth century. This section nearest the High Street was demolished as being unfit for human habitation soon after.

1899 and the earliest of all, the Commercial Bank building on the High Street opposite the Cow Wynd, opened in 1831. But as these monuments to prosperity multiplied their magnificence must have been in stark contrast to the prevailing squalor of the Back Row, the Howgate, Silver Row and dozens of other dingy closes and courts. There, a rapidly expanding population lived and worked at all manner of dirty and dangerous occupations with little concern for health and public safety and precious little sympathy or support from those who prospered from their labours. The power of the trade unions was increasing and Falkirk was often a battleground between determined iron-workers and the powerful masters who banded together to lock-out the workers and force wage reductions when profits were threatened. Strikes were frequent and when the men thought their national union was failing them they formed the Central Ironmoulders' Association in 1889 which thereafter led the fight for better conditions and security of employment. A year later they helped form a Trades Council in the town which played a significant part at national level in creating the Scottish Trades Union Congress with the aim of bringing unions together rather than 'battling against each other'. Although the STUC, which still represents the interests of Scottish workers, did not meet officially until 1897 it was born in Falkirk a year earlier at a conference called by the Trades Council and addressed by William Strang of the Central Ironmoulders' Association who warned that 'The masters could now dictate to the workmen whether they should work at all, and where they should work, and all this tended to show that the workmen must federate to keep pace with the employers' and to get 'a more equitable share of the fruits of toil and better opportunities in the race of life.' In the decades that followed there were many opportunities to test this new resolve for the iron foundries which earned fortunes for the masters still offered unremitting, back-breaking labour in the foulest of conditions and the coal mines and brick works were often even worse. Only a genuine pride in the quality of the workmanship compensated those thousands of men whose life expectancy was cut short by their labours, and that was far from enough. As far as housing was

concerned the passing of the 1859 Improvement Act did strength-
en the hands of those who demanded change and a great deal was
done in the decades which followed to tackle some of the most
pressing problems, but another sixty years and a World War
would pass before the worst of the slums were removed.

In the meantime the people had to survive as best they
could and, sadly, many found relief from their labours at the
bottom of a whisky glass in any one of dozens of Falkirk pubs
which stood along the length of the High Street and from
Newmarket Street to Bainsford Bridge. There was the Swan
and the Cat, the Pie Office, the Red Lion and the Black Bull,
the King's Arms and the Crosskeys, whose most famous
resident, the poet Robert Burns, visited the town in 1787.
And that was only on the main street! Hidden away up wynds
and closes were the King's Head, the Steeple Bar, the Guild-
ford Arms and, of course, the Wheatsheaf in Baxter's Wynd,
the only one still operating and the watering hole of choice for
all self-respecting local historians. Many of these hostelries did
survive well into the modern era until the departure of the
working population from the town centre to the outskirts
brought about their gradual decline. At one time in the late
nineteenth century, Falkirk was said to be second only to
Airdrie as the most drunken town in Scotland and certainly
the Sheriff Court reports in the *Falkirk Herald* testify to the
truth of this particular claim to notoriety. But there were other
diversions. Sports of various kinds attracted a considerable
following and if curling tended to be a major interest of the
well-to-do then bowling had a more universal appeal, and
quoiting, pronounced 'kiting', absorbed whatever surplus energy the miners and moulders had left after their day's graft.
This was no namby-pamby pastime like the genteel game
played on the deck of a luxury liner! The great iron rings with
built-in handles were hard enough to lift, far less to throw, but
throw them they did at iron pins set in clay beds on special
'kiting greens'. Miners from Plean tackled moulders from
Carron in formal league matches before large crowds of
spectators at the Boyd Street green, while look-outs watched
for the 'Polis' lest the illegal side-bets were confiscated and the

culprits marched off to the jail at the top of Hope Street. Cricket was a surprisingly popular team game with the earliest recorded match at the Pikes in 1836, but it was not until near the end of the century that golf began to tighten its grip on the local community. The first course, the Tryst in Larbert, opened in 1885, followed by Glenbervie and Falkirk Golf Club after the First World War.

But in the end it was the spectator sport of football which won the hearts of most of the Falkirk faithful, though their East Stirlingshire rivals in Grahamston and the 'Warriors' in Stenhousemuir generated an amazing loyalty quite unrelated to their performances on the field. The 'Bairns' were established in 1876, the 'Shire' five years later, and while both began their existence in other parts of the town it is Brockville and Firs Park with which they will always be identified. These teams have specialised in breaking the hearts of their supporters for well over a century but like prodigal sons we forgive them again and again! The story of their survival against the odds in the twentieth century is told later in this book.

For those who disliked sporting activities nineteenth-century Falkirk offered the occasional dramatic presentation in places like the Assembly Rooms, Burns Court Hall or Wilson's Buildings. Often these took the form of colourful 'tableaux' saluting heroes like Nelson or General Gordon and glorifying the British Empire in words and song. As we have already seen, the new Corn Exchange and Town Hall took over many of these activities from the mid century on, and great affairs like the annual Volunteers' Ball danced on 'a linen carpet' purchased from Wylie and Lockhead's in Glasgow, were the social highlights of the gentry's year.

The work of improving the town's environment continued to preoccupy the Town Council in the last quarter of the century. In the 1870s a new cemetery in Camelon more or less ended burials within the town, and the opening of a new slaughter house in Kerse Lane in 1873 stopped the foul business of butchers killing animals in premises all over the burgh. But the provision of an adequate supply of fresh water was their single most important undertaking, though it was also the most costly and contentious.

Valiant attempts were made up to the early 1880s to extend and develop the supply of mine water from the traditional sources south of the town, but with a much greater population now demanding up to ten gallons a day per head a new solution was required. Proposals were made and rejected, the ratepayers were consulted, the Provost and many councillors resigned, new proposals emerged and were rejected and old ones were unearthed, dusted down and offered once again. One account talks of a meeting held in the Town Hall to examine the proposals yet again in 1885 at which buckets of water from Summerford, Bells Meadow, Earls Burn and Faughlin were passed round and councillors and ratepayers tasted the product for the sake of comparison. Later it was whispered that all had been filled in the horse trough outside the Hall but it mattered little. The decision – no decision!

The whole water saga was a classic example of the way in which local politicians went about their business during the period. Nothing was ever as simple as it looked and if it was it would not remain so for long. Eventually in 1888 the Falkirk and Larbert Water Trust emerged, charged with solving the problem and the same year settled on a small reservoir on the Faughlin burn near Carronside which would trap the water of the Denny Hills. From there the new supply would be piped via larger reservoirs and filter plants to the town. Agreement was reached and the work went ahead amid great enthusiasm. The scheme was officially opened in 1891 by the Duchess of Montrose and newspaper reports talk of great celebrations, triumphal arches and processions and small boys catching the water in their caps at the town wells and offering it to the adults in the vicinity. By the end of the century consumption had increased to over 40 gallons per head per day with many houses having their own piped supplies. But it would be well into the new century before the bulk of the population would be freed from dependence on town wells, though at least now the quality and quantity matched the demand.

For centuries the burgh was marked out to east and west by open burns. The West Burn running from Gartcows to the foot of Cockburn Street, where it was known as Jenny Mair's, then

east to Burnfoot Lane where it turned north to serve the
tanneries in West Bridge Street or Tanners' Brae before continuing on towards the Carron. The East Burn arose to the
south of the town in the lake at Callendar Park, crossed the
parkland to the south of the House under the main road at East
Bridge Street, flowing north through the meadows to Lady's
Mill, where it had once powered one of the corn mills of the
early barony. When Callendar Road was constructed in 1829,
replacing East Bridge Street as the main entry into the town
from the east, the burn was piped under the new road. A third,
known as the Adam's Gote or Goat Burn ran past the Poorhouse, along Hodge Street to join the West Burn near the
present Erskine Church. It once marked the southern boundary
of the burgh and it was the discharge of sewage from the
Poorhouse into the Gote which prompted a few gentlemen
to gather subscriptions which eventually saw it and the West
Burn piped underground in December 1870.

Another constant source of concern was the narrowness of
most of the main streets of the burgh and from the mid-1850s
through to the outbreak of the Great War in 1914 strenuous
efforts were made by individuals as well as by the authorities, to
rectify the situation. The Cow Wynd was for centuries the
principal road southwards from the town and successive generations condemned its inadequacy. At its junction with the
High Street the Wynd was just 13 feet wide and one observer
recalled that its surface was 'the dread of all who had to
conduct vehicular traffic through it . . . there is a tradition
that more than once Carron coal carters threw down their
whips, declining to guide their horses through its miry way'.
Little or nothing was done until the local newspapers turned
their attention to the problem in the 1860s, with the result that
over a thousand tons of slag were rolled into the surface and
covered by half as much again of whinstone. By then one of the
dilapidated buildings at the High Street end had been removed
and replaced by a new block, at the same time increasing the
width to twenty feet.

Bad as the Cow Wynd had been it could not compare with the
Back Row for human squalor and misery. At its junction with

Kirk Wynd and for thirty yards eastwards it was only ten feet wide and was the first street to be tackled by the Town Council in its improvement campaign. Common lodging houses, rickety old buildings, some dating from the 1600s, housed an assortment of immigrant labourers, street entertainers, second-hand dealers and public scavengers. So bad was the reputation of the Back Row that the Free Church sent a missionary to work among the people, but he soon gave up the task and set off for Bainsford where he enjoyed greater success. Eventually the Town Council bought up properties on both sides of the street and after demolition a new building line was fixed. As the street slowly improved its ancient name was cast aside and Manor Street adopted in 1898. A rose by any other name indeed!

The first decade of the new century saw the same policy applied to the Kirk Wynd and Lint Riggs, which was scarcely wide enough to allow a cart to pass through from the High Street to Newmarket Street. The Burgh Surveyor of the period, David Ronald, recalled his involvement in all these schemes in his memoirs. The state of some of the properties in the Lint Riggs made a particular impression on him: 'The rag store had an abundant colony of rats and on a wet day after a dry spell we used to look across from the Burgh Building to the store and count the number of rats drinking water in the rhone. Thirty was not an unusual number – we used to keep a record.'

Again properties were bought, demolished and the street widened to its present condition, but it was becoming an expensive and time-consuming activity with all manner of legal impediments to be overcome. A great deal remained to be done when war broke out in 1914 and plans were shelved for the time being.

The legacy of years of neglect which had inspired the proposers of the Act in 1859 had left Falkirk an easy prey to the ever-present fevers which were the scourge of industrial Scotland from the mid century on. As early as 1847 an outbreak of fever amongst the workers on the Midland Junction Railway had prompted the town and its new Inspector of the Poor, John Beeby, to open a small 'temporary' fever hospital on the south muir of the town. This was the original of what would become the 'Burgh' or 'High' hospital which treated scarlet fevers, diptheria and tuberculosis until well into the following century.

It began as a simple structure of wood and brick with just two wards, and despite the ravages of cholera nothing was done until 1881 when the hospital was rebuilt in a larger and more satisfactory form, though even then there was a ferocious row among the ratepayers about the need for the expenditure

The newly rebuilt hospital was, of course, owned and operated by the Town Council and people in the landward area controlled by Stirling County Council were treated there at a price paid for by the county authorities. In the 1890s they decided to open their own place in Camelon to cover the eastern district of Stirlingshire. Designed by Falkirk's leading architect William Black, who must have been the busiest man in the district, the new fever hospital was officially opened in December 1896 by George Ure, the ironmaster from Bonnybridge. It served the community for many years until its closure in 1958. It is now a day centre for adults with learning difficulties, run by Falkirk Council Social Work Department.

Back in late Victorian Falkirk, infant mortality remained high and life expectancy at birth low, although improved water supplies and a start to slum clearance began to bring about some improvement. But there were still occasional threats from the deadly smallpox disease as the *Falkirk Mail* of March 1888 testified: 'the public vaccinator Dr Peake will make a house to house visitation in the rural villages for the purpose of making enquiries as to parties requiring vaccination or re-vaccination and will perform such gratuitously.' At the same time they noted that the Sanitary Inspector would set out to find those who failed to manage their 'piggaries, dungsteads and privies' in a proper fashion.

But sickness arising from non-infectious disease or as a result of the frequent accidents in foundry and mine attracted no such municipal action. For the victims there was little help available beyond the support of a close community of fellow workers assisted by the occasional generous doctor, prepared to offer free medicine and treatment to the poorest and most defenceless. As the nineteenth century wore on Victorian 'gentlemen and ladies' began to acknowledge that their great wealth brought with it a duty to help ameliorate the condition of the poorest in society, and by the 1880s their efforts turned most often to the plight of the sick-poor. Foremost among them was Mrs Harriet Gibson, wife of the owner of Salton Ironworks, who was herself a regular visitor to the homes of the sick in the town. In 1884 she appealed for help in the *Falkirk Herald*:

> Let us hope that another year will not pass without our making an effort to have some place, though it were only one room with a few beds, where accidents could be attended to without causing the poor sufferer the added pain incurred by a journey from Edinburgh to Glasgow.

Although several years did pass before the proposal was taken up in earnest, she persisted and eventually won the support of many of her powerful and influential friends. An appeal was launched in October 1887, and soon over £1,300 had been collected or pledged. The following year William Black was asked to design a new hospital with twelve beds around an existing cottage on a

47. The first Matron, Miss Joss, and her staff at the new Cottage Hospital in 1895

site in Thornhill Road. There was a furious response from local property owners who took the strongest possible exception to a hospital for the poor in their neighbourhood. A petition demanding a new site was circulated, and a vitriolic campaign, supported by Mr Fred Johnston, proprietor and publisher of the *Falkirk Herald* got under way with an editorial blasting those 'secretive men' who, behind closed doors, had developed a scheme to site the hospital 'a respectable distance from Arnothill': 'The hospital has started very inauspiciously in having the opposition of the entire district in which it is to be placed and the adverse feeling of a large section of the general public who will be looked to for its future support.'

But the project went ahead and by the summer the hospital was ready. On Saturday, 27 July 1889, before a 'large and brilliant gathering' watched by 'a curious crowd of spectators attracted by the long string of carriages', Mr Thomas Dawson Brodie of Carron Company declared the new Falkirk Cottage Hospital open. Much of the rancour which had accompanied the planning disappeared in the wave of enthusiasm with which the gentry of Falkirk greeted their new acquisition. Outside, as the last of the carriages departed, those less fortunate responded

48. Falkirk Infirmary in Thornhill Road before the First World War

in like manner. 'In the evening,' declared one observer, 'a very large number of the working classes inspected the building.' Twenty-four patients were treated in that first year and, as support from doctors and the public increased, the numbers seeking admission multiplied so rapidly that within a few years an extension was required. In 1900 and again in 1906 successful appeals to the public allowed new buildings and more and more beds to be provided, so that almost 1,000 'indoor and out-patients' were treated each year and over 600 operations performed in the splendid new operating room.

When Parochial Boards accepted responsibility in 1845 for the operation of a poor relief system, the Falkirk Board calculated that it would need to raise £1,400 each year to assist the poorest in the town. Four years later the figure was almost three times higher and in desperation the Board resolved to build a Poorhouse which would reduce expensive outdoor relief as it was called, to manageable proportions. Land was obtained in Cow Wynd where the new Comely Park School now stands. The building was opened in January 1850 and soon after a section for 'lunatic paupers' was added. 'The Poorhouse' served for over fifty years until the opening of a modern version, later Blinkbonny Home, in 1905 in the Gartcows area. Both buildings served the people of the town in various guises until their demolition – the Comely Park site became 'Woodside Home', a working men's hostel and eventually the County Trades School. It was demolished in the 1980s. Blinkbonny was an old folk's home between the wars and more recently Windsor Hospital. It was demolished in 1991.

Of course the ranks of the regular poor were quite often increased by the vagaries of trade or even the severity of the weather, and in the dreadful winter of 1894 the country lay in the grip of freezing conditions for more than four months. In Falkirk the foundries were closed and the men laid off. Public works ground to a halt and the municipal authorities were forced to extreme measures to support the workers and their families. In December David Ronald, then working for the Burgh Engineer, was ordered to establish a soup kitchen in the Burgh Stables across the road from the Poorhouse. Two large boilers, formerly used for boiling food for the horses, were employed, and Ronald went out round the butchers and grocers of Falkirk collecting donations of meat, bones and cereals for the pot.

Tickets were issued by the ministers of the town and two women were employed to make the soup. Soon over 100 people each day were queuing in High Station Road, and as time passed it became more and more difficult to gather the necessary ingredients. David Ronald takes up the story:

> One day I was at the Slaughter house on some business and happened to mention my difficulty to the Superintendent. It was just a casual talk to start with, then he said 'Why should you not use the good part of the carcasses which have been condemned for tuberculosis?' The condemned carcasses at that time were buried behind the Slaughter House. I consulted the Medical Officer, Dr Griffiths, about the proposal, and he said that so long as the flesh was subjected to boiling-point temperature for about an hour, it would be all right, but that it would be better to say nothing about it, and so the meat problem was solved. We still got a small quantity of meat from the butchers, but the bulk of it came from the Slaughter house.

So popular was this concoction that the numbers doubled and at the end of the day two old men came across with a pail and carried the leftover soup to the Poorhouse. No study has yet been done on the incidence of tuberculosis in the years which followed, but it might make interesting reading.

No doubt during the great freeze-up the inhabitants were grateful for the rapid growth in the town's supply of gas. As noted earlier in the account of the stentmasters' travails, the first Falkirk gas company opened for business in 1829 with its works in East Bridge Street supplying mainly street lighting in the town centre. Less than twenty years later it had a competitor in the shape of the Falkirk Joint Stock Gas Company operating out of premises near the canal on Grahams Road. Competition forced down prices and after thirty years of expansion the original company was taken over in 1878. But there was a growing sense that energy supply was such a crucial community asset that it should not remain in private hands. In 1894, the Town Council successfully promoted the Falkirk Corporation Gas Act which saw all the assets of the gas company purchased for £77,000 to be run thereafter by the town authorities. Emboldened by this success the councillors turned their attention to the new marvel of the age – electricity.

No development symbolised the close of the old Victorian era and the beginning of a bright, new age than the first electric generation in the town. In the 1890s several enterprising businessmen had installed electric generators to light their premises and supply a few customers in and around the centre of the High Street. At the great Free Church bazaar in 1896 in aid of funds for the Newmarket Street church building, the Town Hall, the Masonic Lodge and the Church were lit for three days by electricity as a novelty, and thousands of people came to see and wonder at the power of the new age. In 1901 the Town Council decided that Falkirk should have its own 'electric light' generating station and, despite contrary advice from their officials, opted for a building on land adjacent to the Burgh Stables in High Station Road which they owned already of course. The great coal-fired boilers and the generating dynamos were installed with a chimney over 120-feet high dominating the south of the town. Many technical difficulties had to be over-come and more than £25,000 was spent before the first Falkirk electricity flowed to the shops, business premises and the occa-sional house in the town. Inevitably demand expanded rapidly and the capacity of the plant was continually increased to provide both light, heat and power throughout the burgh. By 1912 there were 467 customers with electric lighting and 63 with heat and power as well. In addition there were 74 street lights. But despite this growth, gas continued to dominate for many years to come. For example, in that same year gas was supplied to 4,519 customers and there were 946 gas lights in the streets.

Ironically the most celebrated new consumer of electricity did not use the new town generating station. When the electric trams first began their thirty-year run through the streets it was

Bonnybridge Power Station, then owned by the Tramway Company, which was the monopoly supplier. Before 1898 horsedrawn brakes and buses holding up to 36 passengers linked the town with the surrounding villages, but in the spring of that year a local businessman formed the Falkirk and District Motor Car Company Ltd with three eight-seater Daimler cars running from Falkirk to Stenhousemuir at half-hourly intervals. In June of the same year they were following the familiar circular route from Falkirk through Grahamston, Bainsford, Carron, Stenhousemuir, Larbert and Camelon back to Falkirk. The Company was wound up two years later after a legal wrangle, but by then proposals to cover the same route using electric trams were being prepared for Parliament's approval.

The major problem for the proposers was the need to replace the old wooden bascule bridges over the Forth and Clyde canal at Bainsford and Camelon and the stone bridge over the Carron close to the ironworks. Planning difficulties delayed the project and in 1904 the original proposers were replaced by a new company owned by Bruce Peebles, owners of the Scottish

49. One of the first trams passing the Burgh buildings in 1906

Central Electric Power Company which had been formed to provide power for the County of Stirling. They owned the new Bonnybridge station. Construction work began in January 1905 from Larbert Cross with rails laid to a unique four-foot gauge with 21 double-track loops to allow passing. The erection of the overhead power supply began in May the same year and progress was very rapid. The new Carron bridge cost nearly £4,000 which the Town Council funded, assisted by Carron and the Tramway Company; it was ready in September 1905. The Motherwell Bridge Company supplied the new turntable bridges for the canal crossings designed to open in under one minute to allow boats to pass through. Fifteen French-built double-decker tramcars were in Falkirk by the autumn and on Sunday, 21 October, members of the Town Council made the first circular journey through streets thronged by hundreds of enthusiastic Falkirk bairns. In September 1909 the powers that be were once again celebrating – this time the departure of the first tram from Falkirk to Laurieston – a service which lasted until 1924. The major engineering work here had been the lowering of the road to allow the cars to pass beneath the Skew Bridge, though some widening in Falkirk High Street had also been necessary.

It was the beginning of a love affair for Falkirk people, for seldom has an institution provoked such retrospective affection and sincere regret at its untimely demise in 1936. But that was a long time in the future. In the first year of operation over 3.5 million passengers were carried, and though the numbers did reduce from this very high figure the trams were firmly established as the major mode of transport within the Falkirk area. The cheap and swift service now available to the people in the villages brought them in droves to the shopping centre of Falkirk, which rapidly resumed its traditional role as the market centre of east Stirlingshire.

That first decade of the twentieth century offers local historians and other lovers of the district a rich feast of images not available in such quantity or quality before. The advent of the illustrated postcard sent for a halfpenny and delivered several times a day produced hundreds of photographs of the old town

50. Newmarket Street around 1900, looking east, showing the Town Hall and
Free Church on the right-hand side

and the surrounding villages which help to bridge the years in a
way that the written word cannot. Here are moustached men in
bowler hats outside long-demolished buildings, horses, carts
and traps, elegant women in Edwardian finery and children in
school smocks or Eton collars. And trams! The photographers

51. The west end of Falkirk around 1910

High Street, Falkirk, Looking East.

52. Falkirk High Street, looking east, around 1910

could not resist the sight of the electric wonders of the new
century rattling through the streets carrying the visitors from
far and near to sample the delights awaiting them in town.
A glance through the trade directories for the period reveals
the wealth of choice awaiting them; lovers of 'my Lady
Nicotine' were invited to visit the High Street premises of
James Clarkson, while the musicians could find 'everything
from a pipe organ to a penny whistle' at Sowdan and Forgan's
shop in Vicar Street. Health enthusiasts might try Thomas
Lyon's 'crebanus borax and eucalyptus soap', visit Alexander
McDonald the 'tonsorial artist' where the 'hair brushing is
done by machinery' or even pass an hour or two at the new
Waverley Public Wash-house and Baths in the Howgate,
described as 'a much desiderated convenience, and a marvel
of moderation in respect of tariff'. But when it came to serving
the inner man Falkirk really came into its own. There was Mrs
Tod's shop in the High Street where the 'smoked hams have a
reputation all of their own and are sliced for the purchaser with
a skill that provokes admiration' and not far away 'the denizens
of the deep' were laid out for inspection on the spacious slabs

53. Brodie's butcher's shop at the bottom of the steeple just before the First World War

of Sutherland's fishmonger's shop. Under the steeple stood Brodie's popular butcher's shop and patrons were reminded that it was Mr Brodie himself who had helped introduce a painless cattle-killer to the Falkirk slaughter-house 'a fact which speaks volumes for his humane disposition'! Those with a few pounds to spend and an eye for high technology might purchase a bicycle called the 'Brockville', manufactured by Malley's, or even a collapsible one-man turkish bath from Miller's of Vicar Street.

Most of the shops have long since ceased to trade in the town but there were some like Zuill and Stewart, Dillon's, Anderson's and Alexander's Stores operating until comparatively recently and quite a few which still serve the people of the town nearly a century later. Johnston's butchers, Inglis' printers, and Malley's and G.W. Smith's bicycles are still going strong, along with 'Mr R. Mathieson's bakery and tearooms' which around 1900 were 'the happy hunting ground of weary commercials and hungry farmers, and, in the summer months of whildom batchelor or grass widower, when sea-side attractions take mothers and wives away'. But all too soon it was not the wives and mothers, but the sons, fathers and brothers who were away, this time far from the sands of Ayr or Portobello, but among the mud and rain of Flanders fields. The optimism with which Falkirk had entered the new century perished along with much else there, and those fortunate enough to return safely found a different town and a much changed world waiting for them.

CHAPTER 12

Falkirk at War

The outbreak of war with Germany in August 1914 brought the fever of public works in the burgh to an abrupt halt. In common with the population in villages and towns throughout the land, the people of the Falkirk district devoted themselves to the business of supporting the war effort by whatever means was most appropriate to their particular talents and situation. The rush to the colours among young men was as marked in the district as anywhere else and the *Falkirk Herald* reported amazing scenes just days after war was declared:

> The Patriotic Spirit has spread like wildfire and the rush of intending recruits has been so great that at times it has been impossible to cope fully with it. To facilitate the work an office has been procured in West Bridge Street where the men desirous of serving King and Country may have themselves enrolled as defenders of the Empire. The scenes witnessed at the West Bridge Street Office have been nothing short of remarkable; for hours at a stretch the eager volunteers for service forming lengthy queues in front of the premises.

Reservists reported to their barracks and hundreds of territorials were called up and trains from Grahamston and Larbert Stations carried them off amid scenes of great patriotic fervour to an uncertain future, though the popular slogan 'home for Christmas' deceived few who understood the nature of modern warfare. The press urged the men of the district to come forward in even greater numbers and berated Larbert and Stenhousemuir for only enlisting 601 by November. Men in certain key occupations like mining were encouraged to stay put, but this didn't stop many from joining the queues at West Bridge Street and elsewhere. In his excellent account of the Falkirk area at war *Heroes Departed* (1994), John Dickson says that:

> As many as one in four of the younger miners in the district, and perhaps one in seven of the total, enlisted in the first months of the war. This probably says as much about conditions in the mines as about patriotism, but it relieved the unemployment situation and meant that for the rest of the war the mines were working full time.

Other workers were less fortunate. The port towns faced immediate disruption with the docks at Grangemouth and Bo'ness placed under military control, and many men were laid off. Both imports and exports were disrupted and things deteriorated in November when all non-military shipping on the Forth above Queensferry was banned and for the next four years vital raw materials and finished products crossed the country by rail to and from ports further east. The district soon filled up with military personnel and Falkirk became, as it had been often in the past, a garrison town. Church halls and other public buildings including schools were requisitioned and the normal life of the community gave way to a frenzy of war preparation and support.

Church groups threw themselves into fund-raising, gathering parcels full of comforts for the troops and knitting socks and scarves galore for the men at the front. Children too were encouraged to share in the effort and in early 1915 there was an exhibition in Grange Public School in Grangemouth showing just what 'comforts' the pupils had prepared for 'the men who are undergoing hardships in the defence of the Empire'. As well as the predictable sleeping socks, mittens, gloves and mufflers each parcel contained 'some useful article such as soap, cigarettes, boot laces, pencils, pens, writing paper, blackening, toffee. The whole was inscribed with the name and address of the giver and the parcels are to be made up into two lots, one for "Tommy" and the other for "Jack" and will be distributed to both the army and navy.'

Occasionally the children added little messages and one nine-year old patriot caught the prevailing mood in verse:

> A wee Scotch lassie sends you these,
> I knitted them for you.
> And if you meet the Kaiser,
> Just cut him into two.

Falkirk infirmary in Thornhill Road was designated as an auxiliary hospital attached to Stobhill in Glasgow, and by November had added two wooden huts as temporary wards, each holding twenty beds. Three wounded Belgian soldiers were the first war casualties to be treated but the nurses and doctors found the bulk of their time given to the needs of territorial men recruited in the district who were not immediately fit for active service. In the first six months for example, over 180 men were in-patients, suffering from anaemia, sciatica, rheumatism, haemorrhoids, varicose veins, flat feet, hammer toes, scabies and eczema, and the surgeon conducted '62 operations on soldiers to fit them for active service and 50 to enable men to enlist'. But soon the men with gunshot and shrapnel wounds began to arrive and the impact of the real war began to sink in. Up to February 1915 there were 33 overseas soldiers treated for fractures and bullet wounds as well as bronchitis, rheumatism, frost-bite and ague. In that year over 500 military patients were treated, almost half the total number passing through the infirmary. Several big houses, including Wallside in Camelon, Hillside in Arnothill and Carriden House were designated auxiliary military hospitals and for two years convalescing soldiers were sent to Inverleny House in Callandar which was for a time an official annexe of Falkirk Infirmary. At the end of 1916 an urgent request from the Red Cross for more beds for soldiers meant the conversion of the existing recreation hall into a new ward and, as a replacement, the managers purchased the East Stirlingshire Cricket Club pavilion for £150 and installed it in Thornhill Road.

As well as the knitting and gathering of parcels the people of the district threw themselves into the business of fund-raising. This was something that Scottish towns were particularly good at, and Falkirk was among the very best. Few new churches in the preceding decades could have survived without the obligatory three-day bazaar when tens of thousands of pounds were raised for each particular good cause. Now with a war to be won these energies were harnessed by the Red Cross and others. John Dickson recalls that: 'Hardly a week passed without a flag day, whist drive, jumble sale, bazaar or concert somewhere in the area. When new equipment like X-ray vans or ambulance trains was delivered it went on tour and the public was charged admission to inspect it.'

In the final years of conflict the tank became a symbol of the new warfare and a great wooden model mounted on a fire-engine chassis rolled round the district collecting money for new tanks. The 'Bairn' as it was called travelled under the slogan 'Better meddle wi' the Deil than THE BAIRN o' Falkirk', and it was a huge attraction which helped raise thousands of pounds in 1918. But long before then the true nature of the war being waged in the mud of Flanders was all too evident to the people of the district.

Every week the *Herald* carried a 'For King and Country' column with pictures of the latest local casualties, and as the numbers mounted the enthusiasm for enlistment declined, and by 1916 men between the ages of 18 and 41 were being conscripted. There were exemptions of course, including rail and mine workers, but the impact of huge loss of manpower caused serious problems for employers, especially in the foundries where, as in previous wars, business was booming. Shells, mortars and grenades by the millions were expended in the campaign in France and the Falkirk foundries worked round the clock to satisfy the demand. Despite the opposition of the Trade Unions to what they saw as 'dilution', women and semi-skilled men were drafted in to replace those who had gone to the colours. In 1919 Falkirk Iron Company published a remarkable series of photographs showing young women working in Castle Laurie Foundry making all kinds of bombs and shells,

54. Women at work making munitions for Falkirk Iron Company (*By courtesy of John Walker*)

and these remain as a chilling reminder of the foundation of much of Falkirk's prosperity. And prosperity for some was certainly one of the side-effects of the war. No doubt the ironmasters, mine owners and others supplying the military accumulated small fortunes, but there was also a steady rise in wages which outstripped the increase in living costs. For the first time young women found themselves in possession of both money to spend and a measure of independence and this was to have a profound effect on the society which emerged when the war was over.

Over 1,100 men from Falkirk burgh were lost as the mindless carnage on the Western Front dragged on and on. Every town and village in the district paid a similar price, from eight lost in Blackness in the east, to a staggering 87 in little Longcroft in the west. In all, over 3,000 men died. And who knows how many thousands more fell beneath the iron rain of shells made by the decent, honest working-men and women of Falkirk? It was the nature of the age, and those who worked here as well as those who fought overseas believed in what they did with little reservation. When it was all over at last they mourned their losses, honoured the survivors and celebrated their contribution to the victory. But by then many of them understood.

In 1919 returning soldiers were honoured by the Town Council for their service while congregations and town officials laid plans for permanent memorials to the fallen. In April 1923, for example, a packed congregation in the Parish Church witnessed the dedication of a memorial stone canopy with

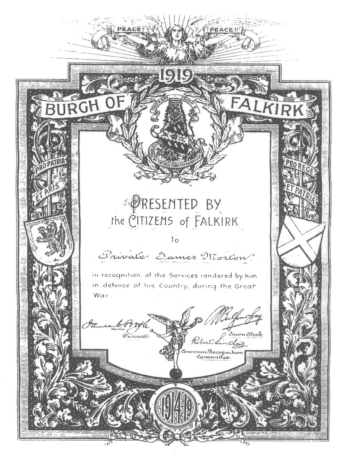

55. The First World War Certificate of Honour presented to Private James Morton by the Burgh of Falkirk in 1919 (*By courtesy of Robert McLaughlin*)

56. The Dollar Park War Memorial, first dedicated in 1926 (*Photograph by Geoff Bailey*)

the names of 97 members of the congregation who perished. Each name was solemnly read aloud by the minister – the husbands, sons and fathers of the congregation. Even after eighty years the description of that service never fails to move and chill in equal measure. And it was a scene repeated in every village and town as the people tried to come to terms with their loss. Between 1920 and 1924, seventeen memorials were raised by public subscription – crosses, obelisks and plain blocks of stone, each one a reminder to the community of its sacrifice. Falkirk Town Council chose a plain cenotaph situated on the Camelon Road in Dollar Park, designed by local architect Leonard Blakey. It was unveiled on 13 June 1926 by the Duke of Montrose and cost £1,100, ironically just a pound for each life lost. Every year since that day the men of Falkirk have been remembered – 'Over Eleven Hundred Bairns died for their King and Country and in the Cause of Freedom, 1914–1919. They died that we might live'. It was the war to end war, or so they thought at the time.

With the ending of munitions contracts the foundries struggled to restore their order books and short-time working and layoffs were the inevitable result. The women who had turned their hands to moulding in the emergency found themselves back in the ill-paid drudgery of pre-war years and shortages of basic foodstuffs made life extremely difficult. But things slowly improved and by the 1920s industry was once again strong and prospects brighter. But the picture in the wider area was more patchy. In 1921 the *Scotsman* reported that work in the Falkirk area was plentiful but that things were much bleaker in Bo'ness where 'the long queue of unemployed at the office of the Ministry of Labour afforded striking proof of the large amount of unemployment, chiefly among the labouring classes in the district.' In the same year there was a major strike in the local coal mines, with over 5,000 men idle though high coal stocks allowed the foundries to stay open. By 1925 one trade union official claimed that the light castings industry was in a most prosperous condition, better than for 25 years. There was not an unemployed iron-worker in the district, or so he said. This was due in no small measure to Government action in 1919 following a Royal Commission report on the state of housing in Scotland, reinforced by the Housing Act of 1925 which funded municipal authorities to clear slums and build new houses. Over 500 were built in the Burgh up to 1927 and

57. The moulding shop at Carron Works in the early years of the century

since over three-quarters of the output of the Falkirk foundries went into producing ranges, baths, water pipes and grates, the housing boom meant security for Falkirk's workforce as well as substantial new houses for themselves and their families. Even the General Strike of 1926, when the local coal mines were closed for many months, did not seriously disrupt the output. Although 8,000 people gathered in Victoria Park to hear the famous miners' leader, A.J. Cook, speak on the strike, the Falkirk moulders remained at work. New gas-fired plant and imported coal sustained the foundries and the crisis passed. But within a few years, with a new Conservative Government reducing the housing subsidies, demand again began to fall and 1927 brought short-time working and wage reductions. The following years saw serious industrial unrest including a major strike involving 2,000 men. Businessmen in the area were alarmed and together launched the Falkirk, Grangemouth and East Stirlingshire Development Association with the express aim of attracting new industry to the area by stressing the availability of land, skilled labour and good communications. In 1922 Cockburn's Gowanbank Foundry had formed a grouping with several English iron-works and now, with the industry under pressure, the group expanded to twenty-three and became Allied Ironfounders. Seven of the firms were in the Falkirk area including the giant Falkirk Iron Company with over 1,000 workers, Cockburn's, Callendar Abbots, Forth and Clyde, Sunnyside and Dobbie Forbes. The object of the merger was to allow specialisms to develop and reduce wasteful competition, and in this it was successful, for most of the Falkirk components survived and prospered until the middle of the century. The 1930s brought further increases in unemployment and with 5,000 on the dole a special initiative by the great and the good tried to encourage workers to help themselves through what they called the 'Falkirk Mutual Service Club' based around Parkhouse Foundry. A number of small workshops were opened offering baking, firewood, hair-dressing and shoe repairs in a kind of barter system. By the end of 1932 over 100 workers were involved and an allotment scheme was added to the list of activities. The scheme continued through the 1930s and attracted a great deal of interest from outside the town, with delegates from different parts of Scotland coming to see what had been achieved. However, it was probably more of a morale boost for the promoters than a real attempt to address the deep-seated problems in the local economy. Against this background it was somewhat surprising that the local water authorities unveiled their ambitious plan to solve the district's water supply problem once and for all. The Carron Valley scheme, costing £250,000, which was launched in 1934 involved the construction of a dam across the river and the creation of a huge reservoir. The work was completed in1939 just before the outbreak of war.

The second Labour Government of 1929 had produced yet another Housing Act and once again the Falkirk Council pressed on with slum clearance and new building, and although the foundries were again the beneficiaries, difficulties remained throughout the 1930s. A new town began to take shape as the worst of the town centre slums were emptied and pulled down and new housing schemes rose up on the fringes of the old burgh boundaries. Merchiston Avenue, the Millflats and Thornhill areas, and further away at Carmuirs in Camelon were gradually covered by new buildings and by the mid-1930s a plan for a further 800 houses was approved. The Bog Road scheme was the last to start before war once again slowed down material supplies and reduced the progress to a snail's pace. By then the High Street had been widened by the demolition of the East End including part of the Silver Row. The Callendar Riggs had been totally transformed and a new street bearing the name was cut through the hill. Millions of tons of sand and earth were removed in the process and modern shops were erected along its length with a bus depot owned by the rapidly expanding Walter Alexander company behind them. Next to this, according to one observer, 'is in course of erection a palatial terpsichorean hall by Mr John Doak, the well known Falkirk dancing expert'– in terms of significance for the future well-being of the town and its people, this new arrival was surely as important as any new steeple, bank or store.

Elsewhere two new streets were formed. In 1933 Newmarket

Street was joined to Park Street and the east of the town by Prince's Street opened by the Prince of Wales, the future King Edward VIII. The previous year the High Street at the West End had been opened up to allow a new road to the south to be created which joined Cockburn Street near the bottom of the Howgate. New streets meant new buildings in the style of the period and Falkirk has several fine examples of art deco from the 1930s – the great ocean-liner shape of the Grand Theatre in Prince's Street, later the Regal Cinema; the bow-ended shops and flats known as Kidd's Buildings at the top of Cockburn Street and the restored Co-operative Super Store in Kirk Wynd, now the Clydesdale Bank – a rich harvest indeed from that last great period of design before the wheels came off in the fifties and sixties. There was a new school too, the 'educational palace' of the Technical School, later Graeme High, opened in 1932 and at long, long last, new public baths replacing that good and faithful servant, the Assembly Rooms in the Pleasance. These new baths were themselves demolished in 1989.

However the new building which provoked the greatest interest was the Infirmary at Gartcows opened by Prince George in January 1932 in front of thousands of celebrating bairns. Behind its plain and practical façade lay one of the most remarkable stories in the whole history of the Falkirk district. The old Thornhill Infirmary had been extended several times and still could not cope with the demands for its services. By 1922 nearly 1,000 patients had been treated with twice as many outpatients and 900 operations. The experts advised a new hospital on a new site and so began an incredible decade of fund-raising involving people of every rank in the community. The present site was purchased for around £6,000 and on 27 April 1925 over a thousand people crammed the Town Hall for the official launch of the Great Appeal.

It was the prelude to an astonishing five-year spell in which every conceivable method of fund-raising was employed, and hardly an organisation or individual failed to participate whether wittingly or not. If they attended a play or pantomime, part of the receipts went to the fund. The same applied to football matches and dances, school concerts and bus trips,

58. Three of the art deco buildings from from the 1930s: Kidd's Buildings in Cockburn Street, the former Co-op Superstore in Kirk Wynd and the old picture house in Princes Street (*Photographs by Michael Middleton and Ronnie Blackadder*)

picnics and whist drives. There were collecting boxes everywhere – outside hospital wards, in public buildings, in private
houses, in shops and business premises. The overwhelming
impression which comes through from newspaper articles
and official reports, concert programmes and souvenirs is of
a great and happy collaboration of all the people of the district
in securing 'their' Infirmary. Every square yard of the site,
every brick of the buildings, every stick of furniture and
equipment and every penny of wages and salaries would be
provided by the people. 'Touch ane, Touch a' proclaimed the
Infirmary motto, and the response was the most eloquent proof
of the truth of its message.

A glance through the local newspaper for 1926 and 1927
reveals a frenzy of fund-raising activity. One might, for example, enjoy 'The Merchant of Venice' at the Dobbie Hall,
'Floradora' in the Grand Theatre, or 'She Stoops to Conquer'
in the Town Hall. There was a 'Fancy Fair' and 'six penny
bazaar' in the YMCA hut, 'Mr Martin's Orchestra Dance' in
the Gymnasium, Camelon, 'Music in the Garden' at Arnothill,
a 'Vocal Recital' in the Masonic Temple and a 'Palais de
Danse' in the Temperance Café. For sporting types there were
football, cricket and tennis competitions as well as the chance to
see a 'Great Boxing Gala in Jim Paterson's new and commodious Pavilion' to see 'a four round contest between Spowart's
midgets' along with Falkirk's own 'Fatty Wells, Young Connell
and Butcher Anderson'. There were road races, grand penny
trails, watch-winding competitions, Highland gatherings, popular lectures, community singing, open days at mansion houses,
jumble sales and silver-paper collections. There were official
'Infirmary Weeks' with great carnivals of students in fancy
dress and decorated floats parading through the streets of the
town. The list was endless. A small book was produced entitled
'Seventy Three Ways in Which You Can Help Your Infirmary'
and it included as number 32: 'Strap onto your dog a collecting
box and teach him to make collections – but not in public
thoroughfares without a special permit.'

The collecting boxes themselves were novel – one shaped like
a brick exhorted 'Be a Brick – fill a Brick', while the other

showed a patient in bed with a message 'Never Pass Me By'. Sufficient bricks were filled and the boxes seldom passed by. By the time the Duchess of Montrose cut the first sod of Gartcows in November 1926 the fund had reached nearly £90,000, well within sight of the target. In the autumn of 1928 the new Infirmary appeal was brought to an end by a 'Grand Bazaar' which would, it was hoped, raise the final £5,000 required. For four days great crowds flocked to the Drill Hall where stall-holders from all over the district sold their wares. When the last penny was counted the astonishing total raised was £9,600, the largest sum ever achieved by a bazaar in a Scottish provincial town. Today's equivalent figure would be close to £200,000. By the end of 1930 the new building was ready for inspection and in two weeks in December nearly 8,000 visitors did just that.

The patients moved to the new Infirmary at the beginning of 1931 and a year later Prince George officially declared the building open in front of 20,000 people. It had cost in total £120,000 – nearly £3 million by today's standards – and was opened free of debt. There were 85 beds, served by 45 nursing staff – five years later it was 200 beds and 75 nursing staff. And the astonishing growth went on and on.

The list of activities which helped to provide funds for the Infirmary gives something of the flavour of entertainment in the town in the first half of the twentieth century. A fine tradition in amateur drama developed and remains strong today, and high-quality operatic and choral societies provided an outlet for the abundant talents of the local community. The pubs which had such a hold on Victorian 'bairns' were still there in abundance of course, but now there were picture-houses all over the town and surrounding district. Like all of Scotland, Falkirk went movie-mad. The Grand Theatre with its new front on Princes Street became Falkirk's 'super cinema' at a cost of £20,000 and with seating for 2,000. Then there was the Pavilion, later called the Gaumont and then the Odeon, opposite the brewery in Newmarket Street. At the other end of the street was the Salon with its double seats in the back row, and round the corner in Melville Street, the Cinema, housed in the 'tin kirk'– the old Baptist Church – where a rainy day meant that the patrons heard nothing of the soundtrack. Finally, the Picture House in Bank Street which, as we have seen, began life as a church. Outside the town centre there was the Bainsford Casino, the Ritz in Camelon, the La Scala in Grangemouth, the Picture Palace in Stenhousemuir, the Picture House in Brightons and the Star and the Hippodrome in Bo'ness. The Roxy Theatre in Silver Row which had for a time operated under the name the Electric Theatre, continued to bring the cream of Scottish variety to the town until television killed off that particular art form in the 1960s. Dancing was tremendously popular, with Doak's Dancing Academy – 'Ladies one shilling, Gentlemen one-and-six', the Burlington in Cow Wynd, and Mathieson's New Ballroom in the High Street where Saturday night patrons danced to the Manhattan Band. Boxing matches filled the Town Hall and the new Ice Rink which opened in 1934 offered curling, skating and ice hockey to large and enthusiastic crowds. For a time the Falkirk Lions were among the best supported and most successful teams in Scotland but football continued to be the most popular spectator sport with 20,000 not an unusual Saturday gate at Brockville. Although the Falkirk Bairns brought home the Scottish Cup twice, in 1912 and in 1957, the old hands will tell you that the greatest ever teams were those of the late twenties and thirties when the famous Syd Puddefoot among other stars thrilled the crowds and kept the team close to the top of the professional game in Scotland.

The decades after the first war brought mixed fortunes to the burgh's tramway system. Regular motorbus services challenged the monopoly and the Tramway Company responded by acquiring buses of its own to cover routes away from its established lines. A programme of track reconstruction with all the dislocation and expense involved began in 1921 and the circular route was not completed for eight years. Soon after, ten new single-decker trams had been introduced and much of the business lost during the rebuilding phase was regained. Despite that, the death knell was already sounding. Cut-throat competition from bus companies and takeovers and mergers were the order of the day and in 1935 the shareholders were bought out by the Scottish Motor Traction Company, SMT. By the summer of the following year the brand new trams were sold, the track lifted and the whole system consigned to a premature place in the history books. On 21 July 1936 the last of the trams carried a floral wreath. Many mourned their passing and still do – seventy years later. It would however be a disservice to the bus companies, and to the Alexander family in particular, to paint them as the executioners of a well-loved Falkirk institution and nothing more. The achievement of Walter Alexander, one of the great men of Falkirk business, in creating a huge national company from small beginnings was something of which Falkirk folk should be proud. Young Walter, who worked as a foundry fitter, started out selling and repairing bicycles in Camelon in 1902 to exploit what was a fast-growing market. After a decade of growth he had accumulated enough capital to take the next step which brought to birth the Alexander's Motor Service which ran buses to parts untouched by the trams like Bonnybridge and Denny. By 1924 he was building buses as well as running local services and holiday tours, and the firm was firmly established in Brown Street, Camelon. Many others followed, like Blaylocks and Dunsires in Bainsford, Masons in Camelon, Penders of Rumford, Shields of Laurieston, Gordons of Bo'ness, but by the late 1930s almost all had been swallowed up by Alexander's. The story of the national mergers and takeovers involving the tramway companies, the railways and the buses is very complicated and has been told very well by specialist writers like Alan Brotchie in his *Tramways of Falkirk*. Suffice here to say that from the tangle Alexander's emerged as part of SMT, but running a huge national bus operation from their headquarters in Falkirk. The famous Bluebird symbol appeared in 1934 as bus design reached new levels of comfort and appearance. By then the Alexander name was on the side of over 1,000 buses nationwide. At last things were looking up for the bairns of Falkirk and for the rest of the nation, but all that was about to change once again.

The outbreak of war in 1939 for the second time in a generation provoked none of the wild enthusiasm of the first great conflict. The new threat of the bomber aircraft demonstrated in the 1930s Spanish Civil War led to grim predictions of massive bombing raids on all centres of population, especially industrial areas like Falkirk district. The ports and foundries, and the new Grangemouth airfield, were obvious targets and most early preparation was directed at defending against this new terror from the sky. A year before the outbreak of hostilities the Town Council in Falkirk, stung by repeated criticism of their tardiness, laid plans for public shelters in the parks sufficient for 10 per cent of the population. Gas masks were issued and, with the actual declaration of war, the population were ordered to carry them everywhere they went. Blackouts were introduced immediately and street lamps extinguished. The authorities dealt harshly with those who failed to cover up as John Walker reports in *Target Falkirk* (2001):

> On the first Monday in November 1939 Falkirk Sheriff Court heard the cases of 18 cyclists, 8 householders, 2 shopkeepers and an open air trader for breaches of the blackout. The cyclists were all charged with having inadequately screened and dimmed front and rear lights. They were fined five shillings with the alternative of five days in prison.

The other offenders received even harsher treatment. Children from Glasgow began to arrive in numbers at Grahamston Station on their way to Muiravonside, Polmont and other villages. The cinemas and theatres closed and at Brockville Park the players were advised to find jobs – 'no play, no pay' was the motto. Volunteers dug up tons of sand in Bell's Meadow which went to fill the bags now stacked round key buildings and the building of shelters accelerated, including the public one in New Market Street gardens. People with private property were expected to construct their own and schools were only allowed to open if they had adequate shelters in place. Despite the long advance warning, this took some time to achieve. A variety of structures began appearing in playgrounds, courtyards and back

59. Digging a shelter in Falkirk Town centre

gardens from half buried Anderson shelters with their familiar semicircular corrugated iron roofs to larger and more sophisticated brick buildings.

Six months before the war Falkirk and District Royal Infirmary had been designated one of twelve centres in Scotland for the emergency treatment of air-raid casualties and now with hostilities under way all convalescent patients were sent home and preparations made for the expected attacks. Blackouts were constructed for ward windows and brick screens erected to protect operating theatres from blast damage. One ward had its windows bricked up and was equipped as a Resuscitation Centre to offer immediate aid to fire and blast victims and twelve huts were erected as special wards for the expected rush of civilian and military casualties. But the bombers stayed away and the slow realisation that they would not be coming in the immediate future began to change the approach. Football was back on again within a few weeks, the schools were open and the population settled back into a home-front routine reminiscent of 1914–18. This time men were conscripted into the fighting services right away and women were involved for the first time. Falkirk Council had passed a resolution back in May condemning conscription which they saw as against the best traditions of British society, but like everybody else they had to buckle down and get on with the task in hand. Large numbers of Falkirk men and women received their papers and left for training centres throughout the land. Church halls and some school premises were again taken over by the military and those who stayed did what was asked of them – men who were in protected occupations in munitions or mining or essential services, or who were too old to serve, joined the Home Guard, or ARP, or special Fire Services. And once again the church groups began the fund-raising, sewing bees, jumble sales and basket teas which produced thousands of parcels for Falkirk men in the services.

As the War progressed and the immediate fear of bombing receded, the new nightmare was that the Germans would invade and occupy the country. In Falkirk the local press warned 'Herr Hitler' that his stormtroopers could expect a pretty tough reception if they made the mistake of marching in

60. The Shieldhill Home Guard

the Callendar Road. The people of the town were urged to put their savings into Defence and War Bonds and support War Weapons Weeks, like the one which took place in February 1941 when military units, ARP, Home Guard and youth organisations paraded through the town to the Burgh Buildings where Lord Rosebery took the salute. Even after the success of the Battle of Britain the belief persisted that the enemy were biding their time and that a great blitz followed by an invasion was on the cards. As part of the defence Falkirk people were urged to contribute to a fund to purchase a Spitfire to be known as the 'Falkirk Bairn'. Eventually over £10,000 was subscribed and the plane was presented to the Royal Air Force in 1941. It was actually the second locally funded warplane following 'The Abbotshaugh Falkirk Bairn' paid for by the timber company owner, Frank Muirhead, earlier the same year.

By then the local population were playing host to a growing number of Polish officers who had come to Scotland in the aftermath of the collapse of France. Many local buildings were taken over to provide suitable accommodation including South Bantaskine House, Kinnaird House, Carron School, the old Trade School, Kilns House and parts of Callendar House. People remember the handsome, well-groomed officers as they marched each Sunday to St Francis Xavier's Church in Hope Street and more than a few wartime romances were the result of their presence in the community. Most left in 1944 but after the war many Poles were settled here where work was available in mine and foundry and they and their families went on to become a well-known and respected part of the local scene. It was a reminder, if any was needed, that this community, like most of the rest of central Scotland, is an amalgam of many peoples who came here, often in difficulty, to seek sanctuary or opportunity and, after some hard years, made their vital contribution to what we are today. The Irish and Italians in the nineteenth and early twentieth centuries fleeing famine or strife, and the Hungarians in the 1950s, all worked hard in difficult circumstances to make their way and to become in time Bairns, Mariners, Portonians or Bo'nessians and our society was much the better for their being here.

The war ground on, years of digging for victory, of dried eggs and powdered milk, blackouts, air raid shelters and gas masks, ration books and clothing coupons and mince made from oatmeal. It was a world which for all its hardship had a profound influence on the lives of the people of Falkirk who lived through it. When it was over they celebrated in great style and the troops were welcomed home with special events throughout the district. The Town Council, no doubt feeling the financial pinch, were less expansive than their predecessors had been in 1919. Each returning serviceman or woman received a letter from the Honorary Secretary of the Welcome Home and Commemoration Fund which said that his committee 'have been endeavouring to arrange a suitable form of entertainment' but that this had proved impossible because of 'catering and other difficulties'. It concluded: 'I enclose a card of felicitation and a gift of £1 which it is hoped you will accept as a token of the Citizens' appreciation of the service rendered by you.'

And that was that. Across the district war memorials in town and village now bore the names of those who did not return to collect their pound, a total of 876 men and women . And once again the burgh's loss was mourned at the cenotaph – 'On the sea, in earth's distant places and in the air nearly 220 men and women of Falkirk died for their country in the cause of righteousness'.

CHAPTER 13

All Change

The second half of the twentieth century rivalled the equivalent period of the previous century for the intensity of the clearing and rebuilding which so much changed the look of Falkirk district. Unfortunately for many, the architects and the materials they chose to employ, combined to produce new townscapes of unrelieved dullness which is only now giving way to design and planning in keeping with the feel of the old villages and towns. Once the inevitable material shortages of the postwar period were overcome the Council turned its attention once more to the housing situation. By 1947 the population of Falkirk burgh was given as 32,000 and there were around 10,000 houses with a third of them described as overcrowded and nearly 2,000 unfit for human habitation. Worse still, 3,431 people were on the waiting list for a council house, and plans were approved which would provide 2,000 new houses of three apartments or bigger. Soon land at Cobblebrae in Carron, East Carmuirs in Camelon and Windsor Road was acquired and construction work started. In addition the pre-war Bog Road scheme continued.

But this time the housing boom was no lifeline for the foundries – technology and taste had changed and new materials filled the kitchens and bathrooms of the huge housing schemes. It was the age of formica and aluminium, plastic pipes and baths and the love affair with cast iron was well and truly over. The slow decline in demand and output evident before the war began to accelerate. Camelon and Callendar Abbots were the first to go in the 1950s, followed by Etna, Carmuirs, Forth and Clyde and R. and A. Main in the 1960s, Cockburns

in the 1970s, and finally the two giants Carron and Falkirk Iron
Company in the early 1980s. The last one in the town,
Grahamston, closed in 1994 and of the 30 odd foundries in
east Stirlingshire in 1940 only a handful were still operating 50
years later. With them went highly successful firms like Towers,
which manufactured refractory bricks, and a host of smaller
companies in engineering whose living depended on the success
of the iron moulders.

But amid all these bad news stories came blessed relief, if only
for a brief but wonderful moment in 1957. In the great scheme of
things a football team winning a trophy may not mean much,
but try telling that to those of us who stood on the slopes of
Hampden Park on Wednesday 25 April when those Bairns of
Brockville defeated Kilmarnock 2–1 after extra time to collect
the Scottish Cup for only the second time in the club's long
history. The open-topped bus which carried our heroes through
the town that night was greeted by thousands of ecstatic men,
women and children for whom the troubles of post-war life
seemed a bit more manageable from then on. Slater, Parker and
Rae, Wright, Irvine and Prentice, Murray, Grierson, Merchant,
Moran and O'Hara. We will never forget you as long as we live!

61. Falkirk Football Club: Scottish Cup Winners, 1957

The decline in employment continued though it was offset to some extent by the arrival of new industry. Back in 1944, for example, the government ministry responsible for producing aircraft had erected an aluminium rolling mill on a site north of the Forth and Clyde canal in Bainsford. Two years later, with the peace assured, the plant was taken over by the British Aluminium Company and in the years that followed production of plate, sheet and strip increased dramatically in response to the demand for the new material from architects, engineers and interior designers. Massive investment in new manufacturing equipment made the plant one of the most important in the kingdom and by the mid sixties over 2,500 men and women were employed on the sixty-acre site. Former ironworkers and their families found new security in the modern surroundings of the plant, and on the land of Langlees to the north a huge new housing estate developed.

The phenomenal growth of the petro-chemical complex at Grangemouth, which will be described in the next chapter, the expansion of Alexander's coach building works in Camelon and the development of a host of other enterprises including printing and bookbinding, saved the town from potential disaster. Many suffered in the process of change but somehow Falkirk as a community survived the trauma which the collapse of the staple industry had threatened. Two long established businesses in the town centre were also on the move in that period. James Aitken's brewery eventually fell foul of the takeovers and mergers of the 1960s and after a short period as part of Caledonian United, later Tennent Caledonian Breweries, production was run down and brewing ceased in 1966. Four years later the famous chimney came down and the huge site was developed as the present supermarket and a carpark.

On the other side of the west-end junction at Burnfoot, Scotland's other national drink, Barr's Irn Bru, was proving so popular that no further expansion was possible. In May 1971 the old site was abandoned and a large modern factory costing half a million pounds was opened at Hopedale in Camelon near Lock 16, where it continued to manufacture for some years before final closure and transfer to Cumbernauld in the 1990s. The old place at Burnfoot is now a roundabout.

Carparks and roundabouts – it was indicative of the new age of the car which came to dominate the planners' thinking in the decades since the war. When the last of Falkirk's old and outmoded houses were pulled down in the 60s and 70s – in the Garrison, Glasgow Buildings and the Howgate – car parks appeared in their place. The ancient Silver Row disappeared under a new commercial developments called the Callendar Centre which was hailed as a modern marvel but which most people disliked from day one. Many of the old stores on the south-west of the High Street were replaced by modern façades so utterly bereft of style that one wondered what fate the developers had in mind for the old town. Large department stores with long frontages spelled the end for many familiar closes and wynds – Burns Court, Swords and Bells Wynds, vanished forever and Falkirk, smarter no doubt, was the poorer for their disappearance.

The new Town Hall and Municipal Buildings at the bottom of Tanners' Brae, though ultra modern in design and further evidence of the 'tyranny of the right angle', had the virtue of standing well away from the old town centre in a setting which helped to ease the pain! And there is no doubt that the steady growth in municipal power this century meant that such new facilities were essential. The same applied to the Post Office which was, by the 1970s, too small – a new building across the road next to Grahamston Station replaced the familiar Victorian building in Vicar Street, which has mercifully survived the bulldozers. But there were some fine examples of modern planning and development to set alongside the disasters. When Callendar House and grounds were acquired by the Town Council from the Forbes family in the early 1960s the area was developed as a public park, with a number of high rise buildings set along the line of the Callendar Road. There can be few developments of this type in central Scotland in such a beautiful setting and they remain a model for all the others. The jewel of Callendar House itself was left to rot by a generation more concerned with solving immediate problems than protecting their inheritance. It was understandable – unforgivable, but understandable.

New school buildings were provided throughout the town, offering up-to-date facilities in keeping with developments in education – Bantaskine, Easter Carmuirs, St Francis, St Andrews and Langlees Primaries and St Mungo's Secondary, later High School, in Bainsford were opened from the 1950s onwards and in 1961 Falkirk High School moved from Rennie Street after 63 years to new buildings in Bantaskine. The old building continued to serve for another four decades as Woodlands Secondary, later High School.

But it was the education of those beyond school age which attracted the biggest investments in the period. Falkirk had campaigned for a new university in East Stirlingshire in the early 1960s and for a time it looked likely to come to Callendar Park. But there were 'wheels within wheels' and, amid the political in-fighting and special pleading, the town lost out once again to Stirling. In September 1964 came the compensation – a new college in the estate as part of a nationwide expansion of

62. The new Falkirk Technical College, opened in 1961. It is now the Falkirk campus of Forth Valley College.

teacher training. At one stage Callendar Park College of Education had many hundreds of students but regrettably it did not survive the cutbacks of the 1980s and closed its doors after less than twenty years. The site was cleared and no trace of the building now remains. A much more permanent development was the million-pound Falkirk Technical College on the Grangemouth Road. Four centres in the Falkirk area had trained apprentices for the engineering, foundry, mining and building trades since the war and in the 1950s the Education Authority decided on the bold plan of building an integrated Further Education Centre on one site. The college opened for business in 1962 and by the end of the decade it had nearly 5,000 students and 140 staff. At first the students were mainly male craft apprentices on day release courses but as the century progressed and the employment world changed the business of education and training changed with it. The typical student in the 1990s was as likely to be female as male, full-time as part-time, over 30 as under 20 and studying social care, art and design or computing as engineering or building trades.

When local government was reorganised in 1975 Falkirk, Grangemouth and Denny town councils were absorbed into a new Falkirk District Council within Central Region. In addition the district now included Bo'ness, Carriden and Blackness which were historically linked to Linlithgow and lay in West Lothian. The creators of this two-tier system thought it likely to improve efficiency but for many it was little more than an opportunity to pass the blame for future failures on to someone else. Stirling, where the powerful Regional Council was based, resumed its centuries old status as the hate symbol for Falkirk folk, though in truth Falkirk councillors exercised considerable influence at Viewforth. The first regional convener, for example, was James Anderson, a highly respected and popular councillor whose presence in Stirling reassured many suspicious bairns! Similarly, people in Denny, Grangemouth and Bo'ness thought Falkirk would care little for their concerns and resented the dissolution of their own councils and the downgrading which it represented.

The decades or so since these reforms have seen the people of the whole Falkirk area on a roller-coaster ride through decline and depression to the renewal and revived self-confidence which is evident in the area today. The collapse of traditional industry continued unabated through the 1980s and, like communities throughout Britain, the spectre of high unemployment, especially among the young, was a regular visitor. Successive economic crises at national level meant spending cuts in a whole range of essential services and there was little cash available to maintain the fabric of streets and buildings. Few developers were prepared to invest in new enterprises and, as derelict foundry buildings all over the district crumbled, the very heart of the old town itself began to fall apart. Empty buildings covered in tattered posters, abandoned shops, dirty and unmended streets and the graffiti of idle hands – that was the Falkirk of the 1980s. The people hated it but there was a resigned recognition that nothing much could be done. Municipal pride seemed at an all-time low and yet there were bright spots which held out promise for a better future. For example, a team of superb horticulturalists and gardeners brightened the approaches to the town and further beautified the magnificent parks by their skill and vision. Falkirk against all the odds was several times a prize-winner in the Scotland and Britain in Bloom competitions and this contributed in no small measure to combating the notion that the old town was finished. But difficulties there were in abundance and it was many years before the worst were overcome. Business confidence was at a low ebb and shoppers flocked to the grand new Thistle Centre in Stirling while Falkirk's long promised response at the Howgate became the When? gate to all but a few optimistic bairns.

New employment opportunities were desperately needed especially after the double blow in the early 1980s which had brought about the closure of Falkirk Iron Company and then, worst of all, Carron Company. The people found it difficult to believe that this colossus which had underwritten the prosperity of Falkirk for generations could possibly have failed, and many angry questions were asked by the astonished workers and their families. When the dust settled the giant was down and out and many more folk in the Falkirk district joined the growing dole queues. But recovery, or at least a kind of recovery did come again as the economic wheel turned for the district at last.

By the mid 80s the empty factory spaces and new modern units began to fill up with small business enterprises and the petrochemical complex at Grangemouth continued its remarkable expansion under the impetus of North Sea oil exploitation. A group of businessmen and local politicians with Provost Dennis Goldie at their head began a 'Think Falkirk' campaign and old animosities were buried in a communal attempt to reverse the decline. A multi-million pound programme to

63. The pedestrianised High Street after the restoration project

restore the town centre was unveiled and at long last the Howgate became the 'Nowgate'. The old entrance at Roberts Wynd gave way to a handsome new gateway into ultra-modern and very spacious arcades of shops which soon began to attract back the business lost to the town in the years of decline. Outside, the High Street was pedestrianised and restored to a mock Victorian splendour and the narrow Wooer Street with its small shops and cafés revived an area which had for too long lain rotting and abandoned. At the east end of the High Street the ghastly Callendar Centre fell below the demolishers' hammer to the universal delight of the townspeople. In its place came, though not without the predictable long delays and near financial disaster on the way, another new shopping area called Callendar Square. Its architecture is by popular consent more in harmony with the Edwardian and Victorian legacy of the old town and, in this multicultural age, what if the corner tower looks more like a Cairo minaret than a Scots baronial bastion?

Elsewhere the designers abandoned the hostile lines of their predecessors and produced buildings which blended into the

64. The old Howgate, lost beneath the new shopping centre

65. The Callendar Square shopping centre at the east end of the High Street

existing townscape. Municipal planners demanded higher standards, insisting for example on the retention of the front elevations of High Street buildings even when the premises behind them were to be demolished. The result of all this is a pleasant, even a beautiful town, much admired by visitors, where people wanted to shop, and dine, be entertained or even stay. Once more, as in the early centuries, and again in Victoria's time, Falkirk became the market centre of the district, serving a wide area and a larger and more affluent population. And there was no shortage of new places for these welcome incomers to settle. House building seemed a never-ending activity in 1990s Falkirk although it was no longer like the great municipal schemes which dominated the town in the years before and after the war. The last of these was the huge Hallglen development in the 1970s. Hundreds of new houses were built on the slopes of the ancient glen in that modern style which was to fall from favour so soon afterwards. After that, central government tightened the financial screw and this, coupled with the policy of selling council houses to sitting tenants, changed the face of new housing throughout the district.

The enforced relaxation of regulations on the use of empty sites for private development led to a rush of speculative building and on every corner, or so it seemed, a new 'mews' or 'court' appeared looking for all the world like something from the deep south of England. There were larger schemes too – exclusive and expensive developments filled the old foundry sites and finally a new village, Newcarron, rose up on the abandoned lands of Carron Company. Acres of small and quite closely packed private houses with neither kirk or school, shop nor hall – a great collection of people to be sure, but a village? Where the hammers of Mungal foundry once rent the air the new sounds of today are hedge-trimmers and lawn-mowers! Progress? Well maybe, but the old bairns who pass by would be forgiven if they shake their heads and wonder. Still, no one can deny the imagination which has gone into some of the new developments. The old St Modan's Church in Cochrane Street for example was converted into flats while retaining most of the character of the original building. And not far away in the Pleasance the site of the Roman fort excavations was also developed with taste and style with a new Scout Hall as well as houses and flats.

For students of local history the late 1980s brought the best news of all, with the restoration of Callendar House and the transfer of the Museum from Orchard Street. Callendar Park itself became the focus for many popular community events like the regular Family Days, Highland Games and Spring Flings which attract thousands of people to the beautiful parkland setting. Indeed the District Council's entertainment department which managed many of these activities has done a great deal over the years to increase local participation in the arts and entertainment. For many this meant attendance at a huge range of shows in the Falkirk Town Hall and throughout the district, but for others, especially young people, it offered the opportunity to participate in the much admired Children's and Youth Theatres. No praise is high enough for David Cunningham, and later Craig Murray, who masterminded these initiatives over many years and brought such distinction to the Falkirk area and so much pleasure to the population. Falkirk had always produced amateur music and drama groups of the very highest quality and this tradition continues today, supported by the long-standing Arts and Civic Council, a powerful promoter of all kinds of activities, including the annual Falkirk Festival, a showcase for the talents of dozens of clubs and societies in the district.

In 1994, after nearly twenty years of squabbling, the two-tier system of local government was abandoned and the present Falkirk Council emerged. There were few tears from the population at the change, just a resigned acceptance that things might just get better and that if they didn't then we now had only ourselves to blame. The old town and its surrounding district prepared to face the new Millennium in better heart than one might have expected given the economic disasters of the previous two decades.

CHAPTER 14

The Towns

The Falkirk district of today includes a number of thriving communities with histories every bit as fascinating as the old town itself. Of these, three are certainly 'towns' since all had municipal constitutions for at least a century until the reform of local government in the 1970s. *Bo'ness* is described here along with Kinneil, Carriden and Blackness, *Denny* with Dunipace and, first of all, *Grangemouth*, as befits the newest but largest of the settlements.

Grangemouth

Although it was the cutting of the Great Canal from 1768 onwards which brought to birth a completely new community at the mouth of the Carron, the land had a long history reaching back to the creation of the baronies of Abbotskerse and West Kerse described in Chapter 2. Tradition, supported by evidence on the ground in Zetland Park and recorded on nineteenth-century maps, identifies the 'abbots grange' – farm buildings and grain stores perhaps – linked to the Canons of Holyrood who acquired their barony in the thirteenth century. West Kerse was purchased by Sir Lawrence Dundas in 1752 and it was he who inspired the canal project and was 'the first to cut the grass' as an old rhyme has it. Reporting a decade later the Minister of Falkirk described the initiative of Sir Lawrence regarding the 'propriety of building a village and quay' at the east end of the canal: 'The place which he fixed upon for this purpose was the angle which is formed by the junction of the river Carron and the canal. They were begun to be built in the

66. The houses in Canal Street, Grangemouth, which faced the Forth and Clyde Canal not far from its eastern harbour terminus on the River Carron

year 1777; the village is now of considerable extent and is called Grangemouth.'

At first the area around the end of the canal was called Sealock but later it became Grange Burn Mouth from the proximity of a stream of that name which at that time meandered over the flat lands to join the Carron close to the village. Conversion to Grangemouth followed in the 1780s by which time it had a population of nearly four hundred. The provision of harbour facilities and the direct link to the rapidly expanding town of Glasgow via the canal brought swift success to the port and it soon displaced Carronshore as the principal landing place on the river. Trading vessels from all over Europe landed cargoes of grain, flax, hemp, iron and timber which were transferred in the new basins to canal lighters which carried them to factories and farms across the breadth of Scotland. In return went the coal of Lanarkshire as well as manufactured goods from foundry and mill and even the products of the new American states. In 1810 the village had a Customs House of its own at last and no longer had to pay duties to its ancient rival

Bo'ness a few miles away along the Forth. As early as the 1790s canal boats and sea-going sloops were being built in the village and the hulls for William Symington's experimental steam craft, including of course the *Charlotte Dundas* from Alexander Hart's yard, soon followed. The patron provided a dry-dock in 1811 and the business expanded in line with the remarkable growth of the port itself. By the late 1830s, demand had reached record levels with 750 vessels each year arriving and leaving and over 3,000 passing through to the canal. Facilities were inadequate and a great improvement scheme was started involving the redirection of the Grange Burn to take it away from the harbour area to a new meeting with the Carron a mile away to the east. A new dock, known today as the 'old dock' was built, the river Carron deepened and the major timber basin enlarged. This work was completed by '200 artificers and labourers' in 1843, by which time the population of the village had grown to over 1,500. Even more rapid growth followed the new developments and, less than twenty years later, yet another, the Junction Dock, was completed. These additions

67. Postcard view of the Old Town with the Town Hall in Bridge Street

firmly established Grangemouth as Scotland's principal timber import centre and soon the storage, saw-milling and distribution of redwoods and pines from the Baltic and Canada became Grangemouth's most important activity and the foundation of much of its prosperity.

Long before these mid-century developments the people of Grangemouth had petitioned their Dundas patrons regarding the two special needs of every aspiring Scottish community of the period, namely a church and a school. As early as 1817 over £750 was collected towards the provision of a church, but nearly twenty years passed before a building was erected with the support of the presbytery, the minister of Falkirk and Lord Dundas, grandson of the founder. In 1837 he, 'from due regard for the spiritual instruction of the district, erected a substantial and commodious church' and, when the minister and the majority of the congregation left the established church six years later to join the new Free Church, the patron, by this time Earl of Zetland, allowed the building to be transferred to the new church since it had never been legally conveyed to the Church of Scotland. This caused a mighty ecclesiastical and legal furore but when the dust settled it was still with the Free

68. Charing Cross, Grangemouth, showing the short-lived Parish Church in the distance on the left-hand side

Church, possibly their first building in Scotland? In later years this became the West Church, demolished in 1986. The Church of Scotland congregation, or what was left of it, reverted to Falkirk's control and it was not until 1866 that they had a building in the parish, across the canal in Zetland Place. By then the old town had another congregation with the establishment of a preaching station by the Falkirk Erskine UP Church. In 1859 the congregation moved into a new building in Grange Street.

Education was another of the priorities, and here we are told that as early as 1797, 'Lord Dundas gives to a schoolmaster in Grangemouth, a house to dwell in, a schoolroom and 5 pounds a year'. This was probably in Burnet Street but by 1808 the school was on a new site in Middle Street on the banks of the Carron. In 1827 this was replaced by a new building with schoolrooms for both boys and girls, a library, houses for the teachers and 'extensive playgrounds', which makes it quite a contrast to the dingy overcrowded buildings serving the more populous parts of the district. By 1840 it had over 100 pupils and there were also several small 'venture' schools operated by private individuals for fees including a 'Ladies Seminary' and one grandly titled 'Grangemouth Academy'. Again it was the personal patronage of the Dundas family which ensured that the village was ahead of their rivals. This was very much in keeping with their whole approach to the design and construction of Grangemouth itself which was laid out quite deliberately in a grid pattern with streets forty feet wide and substantial dwellings built in regular fashion. The same principles were applied when the inevitable expansion of the town followed the dock extensions in the mid century. By then Grangemouth had spilled out over the canal and a whole new town was emerging on the unoccupied land to the east. But there was to be no uncontrolled sprawl as so often happened elsewhere. Careful planning again ensured that the streets were wide and well laid out and that they were filled with houses of quality, each with its own garden. For 1861 this was astonishingly far-sighted and the splendour of Grangemouth's 'new town' today owes much to the vision and, of course, the massive wealth of the founding

69. Charing Cross, looking east, past the Commercial Bank building and the new Town Hall

fathers. At a time when it is fashionable, and frequently justifiable, to pillory the wealthy patrons of the Victorian era for their limited concern for the well-being of their communities it is refreshing to report such an outstanding example of good sense and public spirit. It was more than this of course. Grangemouth was growing in economic power and keeping the community relatively contented with their lot was a key part of exploiting the opportunities which were coming along with every year that passed.

The railway arrived in 1860 and six years later the Caledonian Railway Company purchased the canal and the dockyard and began a major investment programme which increased the volume of business passing through the docks. Capacity was severely stretched and in 1882 the large new 20-acre Carron Dock was opened, but even that was insufficient. Ten years later work began on the an even bigger Grange Dock which opened for business in 1906 and for the first time allowed direct access to the Forth. By then the population of Grangemouth was over 8,000 and growing fast. Although the employment opportunities which drew these people to the area were mainly centred on the docks and the timber trade which passed through them, there were other enterprises like the Grangemouth Coal Company which had operated north of the Carron near Newton Mains in Bothkennar Parish since 1830, extracting clay and ironstone as well as coal. By the mid century the firm had extended their activities to include a brick and tile works and a terra cotta pottery which produced artistic works of very high quality to the design of the English master John Wornell. A number of pieces were exhibited at the Great Exhibition of 1851 and at other major events, and these included remarkable life-size figures of Queen Victoria and Prince Albert, presently on display in the National Museum of Scotland. By the 1890s the firm was employing nearly 400 workers, mainly in coal mining, but it did not suvive long into the new century and had closed before the outbreak of World War I.

In 1872 responsibility for municipal affairs in Grangemouth had passed from the Dundas family to a new burgh council, and soon the marks of civic pride began appearing all over the prosperous town. A magnificent public park was opened in 1882, named after the Earl of Zetland, and two years later he laid the foundation stone of the new Town Hall to replace the one in the old town. In 1888 the handsome Victoria Public Library was erected with the help of Andrew Carnegie's vast

70. Zetland Park with the Grange School in the centre

fortune. Fine new buildings graced the elegant streets with Bo'ness Road, Charing Cross, Abbots Road, and Talbot Street among the most attractive. Here the well-to-do merchants and traders built high-quality homes while ensuring that the working population in Marshall and Lumley Streets were better served than their opposite numbers elsewhere. In 1875 Dundas School opened to serve the new town and twenty years later it was joined by the beautiful Grange School, facing the gates of the new park which offered higher level education for the first time. Fifty years before the school roll had been 170, but by 1900 there were 843 children attending Dundas, 373 at Grange and 342 at Zetland in the old town. A new infant school followed in 1903 in Abbots Road and six years later the handsome new High School which brought about a reorganisation of elementary education in the new town with boys attending Dundas and girls going to Grange, which reverted to primary classes only. Zetland remained mixed but in a fine new building opened in 1912 on the same site in the old town. The building is still there today though it is no longer used as a school.

The church too was expanding to meet the needs of the growing population. The Free Church in the old town was first to act in 1884 with a fine new building at Charing Cross, close to the Parish Church. For some reason Grangemouth churchgoers were particularly prone to in-fighting which led the Dundas congregation to break away from the Grange in 1893 and Kerse from the Parish Church in 1897. It was good news for the builders because new churches were built to house the breakaway groups, Dundas in 1894 and Kerse five years later. Grange itself moved from the old town to a new building in Park Street in 1903 and the Parish Church was forced to relocate to a new building in Ronaldshay Crescent in 1911. Five new architect-designed churches in just 27 years is an astonishing record and testifies not only to the role of the church in late Victorian Grangemouth but underlines the economic strength of the community. By 1900 the union between the United Presbyterian Church and the Free Church meant the town now had four United Free congregations and two attached to the established Church of Scotland. The Catholic people had opened what was called a chapel-school in 1897 but it was thirty years before the present Sacred Heart church building was opened near Zetland Park.

The outbreak of war in 1914 brought immediate problems to the town. As already noted in Chapter 12 the port was closed to non-military shipping within weeks and many of the import and export companies moved their operations and most of their employees to ports at the mouth of the Forth, especially Leith. Unemployment was high among dock workers whose security of employment was not great at the best of times and nearly 600 men enlisted in the services in the first few months of hostilities. There was a limited amount of work in converting fishing boats to minesweepers and later, as war losses mounted, naval sloops were built for the Admiralty. As local men departed military personnel arrived in large numbers to billets in the town, and schools, church halls and even the library were pressed into service. The docks were used mainly for refuelling ships using storage facilities established before the war. At first the bulk fuel was delivered by oil tankers, many from America, sailing round the coast and into the Forth estuary. But this was obviously a very dangerous undertaking and it was decided to attempt a cross-country delivery using canal scows converted to floating tankers filled at Bowling on the Clyde and hauled to Grange-mouth. This worked well enough but was too slow for the powers-that-be and in 1918 a pipeline was constructed below the towpath along the 35-mile canal which began pumping oil just a few days before the armistice in November 1918. None-theless it continued to operate in the inter-war years and was in fact replaced at the beginning of the Second World War by an improved version. Large storage tanks had been constructed at Grangemouth and no doubt helped make the town the obvious place for future developments in the oil industry. Military control came to an end in April 1919 and the town began the slow process of recovery though the Forth and Clyde canal was never the same commercial force as it had been before the war. In 1924 a war memorial bearing the names of 276 Grangemouth men was unveiled by General Sir George Ian

Hamilton in Zetland Park. Costing £2,478, it was the most expensive in the Falkirk area and by far the most controversial, with the sculpted German eagle clamped in the jaws of the British lion on top of the cenotaph. It was, for some, not in keeping with a spirit of reconciliation but it remained unchanged.

The story of the years after the war is dominated by the phenomenal growth of the chemical industry which dated back to 1897 when the Scottish Co-operative Wholesale Society established a large factory making soap and glycerine. This was followed in 1906 by the Anglo-American Oil Company, and later Ross's Chemicals of Falkirk constructed the oil storage tanks in the docks which had served well during the war. In 1919 James Morton's pioneering Scottish Dyes, which eventually became part of the ICI's giant dyestuffs division, began production on an 80-acre site in Earl's Road. From the huge factory which developed near the Earl of Zetland's Kerse House, came a succession of famous and money-earning dyes, like the Caledon and Monastral blues and greens, which secured the future for many a Grangemouth family. Finally in 1924 Scottish Oils opened the first plant to refine crude oil from the Persian Gulf, and from these small beginnings the massive Grangemouth petro-chemical complex has grown to dominate all other activities in the area. It would be impossible to do justice in the space available to this particular part of Grangemouth's fascinating story; suffice to say that what became the British Petroleum refinery, processing oil brought in through a new overland pipeline from the tanker terminal at Finnart on Loch Long, attracted an array of giant chemical companies to the area anxious to convert the feedstock from the BP into the products demanded by modern societies all over the world. Since the mid 1970s the crude oil has come from deep below the waters of the North Sea and there have been a number of major new developments in the processing and manufacturing facilities.

In February 1939 Scottish Aviation Limited announced plans to provide central Scotland with what would be the largest airport in the country. Five hundred acres of farm land

71. Grangemouth Airport with the terminal building and hangars in 1939

were purchased in the Grangemouth area by the firm which had secured a government contract to train pilots in preparation for the war that everyone seemed to expect. They had also decided that there was a real opportunity to develop a commercial airport serving both Glasgow and Edinburgh and within two months of starting work the new grass runways were in use for a commercial flight on the Shetland to London route. The first ticket was sold to Provost Robert Peddie for £9 10 shillings and he flew south in a six-seater de Havilland Dragon Rapide. By June the airport was almost ready with 2,000 feet of runway, a fine terminal building and control tower and two large hangars. It had cost £160,000 and was officially opened by Air Marshal Viscount Trenchard, the 'Father of the RAF' on 1st July. Of course, the outbreak of war a few months later changed everything once again. At first the airport was designated as a fighter station but by the end of 1940 it had been given the role of training Spitfire pilots in the special flying and fighting skills then required. Over sixty young men, from Britain and all parts of the Commonwealth, as well as from

Poland and Czechoslovakia, died while practising the daring
manoeuvres demanded in those incredible times. Many are
buried in a special part of Grandsable Cemetery, a tangible
reminder of the high price we ask our young people to pay
when the world goes awry.

The arrival of hundreds of RAF men and women had a
major effect on the town which was, as a major port, already
partly under military control. Again the schools, church halls
and public buildings were pressed into service as billets and the
Portonians settled down to the same round of fund-raising,
rationing and making the best of it as people everywhere. The
difference in Grangemouth was that the airfield and docks were
an obvious target for German bombers and the fear of attack
was never far away. In the end there were no direct attacks
though some bombs were dumped near the town by planes
returning from raids on west-coast towns. Once again the
shipbuilding facilities of the Dockyard Company were pressed
into national service maintaining Dutch submarines, constructing corvettes for the Royal Navy and Empire ships for the
Ministry of Supply. Elsewhere the ICI medicinals division
produced antimalarial drugs as well as antibiotics and anti-
septics which played a very significant part in alleviating illness
and injury among the forces in the field.

The end of the war brought the usual round of celebration as
John Walker reports in *Target Falkirk*:

> In Grangemouth over 700 people including the Council and
> Magistrates, attended a service of thanksgiving at Charing
> Cross church. Later in the evening the town was described as
> 'haywire' as large crowds gathered at Charing Cross. There
> was dancing and fireworks, and as darkness fell huge bonfires
> were lit all around the town and the Municipal Chambers
> were floodlit.

At the war memorial the names of 136 men and women were
added to the roll of the fallen and the community set about a
return to normality. The Air Ministry retained control of the
airfield into the 1950s, by which time the expansion of the

refinery made its civil use untenable. It was gradually abandoned leaving nothing now but the two hangar buildings used
as warehouses. The runways have vanished and industry has
expanded to fill the space along with new houses, the Charlotte
Dundas shopping centre, schools and recreational facilities like
the fine sports stadium. The houses went some way to meeting
the post-war demand for new accommodation resulting from
the continuous growth in population and the demolition, in the
1960s, of much of the Old Town beside the canal. As new
chemical works arrived other traditional parts of the local
economy began to change. In 1967 the docks were taken over
by the Forth Ports Authority and the introduction of contain-
erisation meant a huge reduction in manpower. Shipbuilding
continued until 1974 but, after a period of doing repair work
only, the yard closed in 1983. Astonishingly the railway station
was closed in 1968 though trains still link the docks to the
network. It seems an incredible decision to end passenger traffic
when industry in the town was expanding rapidly and more
and more people from outside the area were drawn to the town
by the job opportunities. However history teaches us that if we
look for common sense in the decisions of the powers-that-be we
will often be sorely disappointed.

On a more positive note the 1960s brought a host of new
primary schools and in 1971 a new Grangemouth High in
Tinto Drive. This allowed for an interesting educational experiment watched by authorities across the country. This was
the three-tier system with two 'middle schools', Moray and
Abbotsgrange (the former High School), catering for children
beween the ages of 10 and 14. It was judged a success by most
educationalists but other authorities were reluctant to make
such a fundamental change and the idea withered on the vine.
It was abandoned in Grangemouth in 1987 after thirteen years.
A new sports stadium was opened in 1966 and it has attracted a
number of national events over the years, and six years later a
modern swimming pool in Abbots Road replaced the familiar
outdoor pool in Zetland Park. The nearby sports complex
followed in 1975.

Modern Grangemouth, which generates so much of the

area's wealth, should be the best appointed and most affluent part of the district, and its people the most contented and self-confident. But that does not seem to be the case. The loss of separate status in 1975 and the moving of power to Falkirk have continued to rankle Portonians, many of whom believe that their town, with its large and growing population, deserved a bigger share of the cake and a higher priority as far as community projects were concerned. Whatever the truth there is no doubt that a feeling of disappointment remains and the most recent reform of local government has not done much to redress the balance. Indeed the prosperity delivered by the chemical industry has been threatened in recent years by mergers and closures which have transformed the ICI into a number of separate companies; even the giant BP has been the subject of some speculation as the global economy seeks the most efficient and cheapest suppliers wherever they are based in the world. Nonetheless these great enterprises and many smaller high technology ventures are still the best hope for the future of manufacturing in Falkirk district. Many of the villages of East Stirlingshire look to Grangemouth to provide their people with relatively well-paid and secure employment and to a large extent the future prosperity of the whole Falkirk area is tied to that of the town.

Bo'ness

Long before the town of Bo'ness was established on the River Forth, the medieval village of Kinneil to the west was the main centre of population. It lay on the line of the Antonine Wall and some have suggested that the main street of the village was either the old military way or perhaps even the stone base of the wall itself. A little to the west of the village stood the Roman fortlet of Kinneil which was was identified and excavated in the 1980s. A number of the features have been left exposed and there are information boards which show the fortlet as it would have appeared in the second century when it was built as part of the Antonine frontier. Much of the history of the Kinneil and Bo'ness area is preserved in the excellent little museum housed in a converted stable building which lies close to Kinneil House. Until the seventeenth century the village was clustered round this building which was one of the most important homes of the Hamilton family who had acquired the land four hundred years earlier. A favourite local legend tells us that one Gilbert Hamilton was gifted the lands by Robert the Bruce because he killed the 'great lieutennand of Yngland upon Kynnale Muir' around about the time of Bannockburn. It is a great story backed up by the proverbial big flat stone which once lay on the muir and covered the 'great lieutennand' himself! Of course it disappeared a long time ago and, anyway, scholars tell us that the original Hamilton was in place quite a few years before Bruce came to the throne and that he was in fact a supporter of the English and King Edward I. Whatever the truth, we know that the Hamiltons remained the most influential family in the Bo'ness area until well into the nineteenth century.

Kinneil House itself began life as a large fortified tower-house dating from around 1500. In the mid sixteenth century a 'palace' was built next to the tower to provide more elegant living quarters for the family which was rising to even higher prominence in the land – James, the 2nd Earl of Arran, was the Regent of Scotland during the early childhood of Mary, Queen

72. Kinneil House, Bo'ness

of Scots. The building contains several murals on religious subjects thought to be amongst the finest surviving examples of such Renaissance art in Scotland. The first Duke of Hamilton was executed in 1649 for supporting King Charles I against Cromwell along with James Livingston, Earl of Callendar, and the house was occupied for a period by the Cromwellian General Lillbourne. His wife Alice was so fed up living in the big house alone while her husband was off doing what generals do that she jumped to her death from the top floor. Bo'ness children used to learn the rhyme which went something like 'Lady Alice Lillbourne, Died in the Gil Burn'. The locals will tell you that she is still to be seen in the vicinity of the house from time to time though mainly on a Saturday night after the pubs close. A decade or so later, under the influence of the Duchess Anne, the house was changed for the last time when two pavilions were created, one of which linked the old tower to the 'palace'. Plans to add a second 'palace' on the other side to create a symmetrical group were later abandoned. In the late eighteenth century, Dr John Roebuck, of Carron fame, stayed in the house and it was he who brought the engineer James Watt to Kinneil in 1769, where he worked on his improved steam engine in the little workshop behind the house which still stands, though in a ruinous condition. Roebuck had hoped that Watt's development of a separate condenser would so improve existing engines that the flood-prone colliery at Kinneil which he owned could be made viable. He was right, but unfortunately Carron Company were unable to manufacture the equipment to Watt's demanding standards, and eventually Roebuck, in severe financial difficulties, sold his share in the invention to Matthew Boulton of Birmingham. Off went Watt to England and with him the idea that was to transform industry and accelerate the revolution which had already started at Carron. The famous Scottish philosopher Dugald Stewart was another resident of Kinneil House in the period following Roebuck's departure. Sadly the building stands empty and the central tower block, though it looks good on the outside, is nothing more than an empty shell. It deserves a much better fate and could yet play a part in the revival of historic Kinneil.

Behind the house on the other side of the Gil Burn are the empty fields where the village once stood. The ruins of the twelfth-century church survive with only the west gable with a double belfry left standing. One of the bells bearing a dedication to St Catherine is on display in the museum. The church was in use until 1669 and was burned by Hanoverian redcoat soldiers who stayed there during the 1745 rising. There are several flat gravestones though the markings are almost indecipherable. One exception bears a carved anchor indicating the maritime links which eventually led the population to leave the village for the new settlement on the 'ness' in the seventeenth century.

From the late 1500s at least, ships were landing goods at the point where the later harbour of Bo'ness stood. During the next century the population grew steadily as the village of Kinneil declined in size and importance and Bo'ness soon became the major centre. The celebrated Sea Box Society, which still exists, dates from 1634. It involved captains putting a percentage of their earnings into a chest for disbursement to those of their number who lost ships, or for other charitable works. Around 1638 some of this money helped pay for a new church on Corbiehall, the building which eventually became the Star Cinema. It soon became more important than Kinneil, becoming a separate parish a decade later and absorbing Kinneil in 1669. A year before this, the Duchess Anne Hamilton had used her influence at court to have the town raised to the legal status of a burgh and this helped to accelerate its growth and success.

A mile or so to the east on high ground overlooking the river stands Carriden House which, like Kinneil House, had a church, graveyard and small community clustered around its castle walls. It was the centre of a parish that included the settlements of Grangepans and Bridgeness on the Bo'ness side and Blackness with its formidable royal castle to the east. Carriden House was built around 1601 for John Hamilton of Lettrick but later became the home of Alexander Myln, Provost of Linlithgow, who began a process of extension and change which continued almost unabated for the best part of two centuries. Its most famous resident was Admiral Sir George

Hope who was at Trafalgar with Nelson and whose interesting grave with its anchor chain is in the 'new' churchyard at the bottom of Carriden Brae. By the middle of the eighteenth century the church near the house was replaced by the present picturesque ruin in the new graveyard and it was itself replaced by the present Carriden Parish Church designed by Peter Macgregor Chalmers in 1909. Dr John Roebuck is also buried in Carriden and there is a memorial to another local hero, Colonel James Gardiner, who died at Prestonpans in 1745. There is no longer a settlement called Carriden and only the names of the house, church, glen and brae remain to remind us of an important part of the area's history. Blackness on the other hand has remained a distinctive settlement with its famous castle a considerable attraction for tourists. Kinneil House is a ruin and Carriden House a private dwelling, but Blackness Castle, with its ship shape and bloody history is one of Falkirk district's most valuable assets.

The castle dates from the mid fifteenth century when the local barony was owned by Sir George Crichton, Earl of Caithness and Admiral of Scotland. He was also Sheriff of Linlithgow, and Blackness was the official port of the Royal Burgh. The main purpose of the castle was to protect the village and its important harbour. Maybe it was Crichton's naval connection, or the shape of the promontory, that led to the castle's distinctive ship-shape. Either way the result is a remarkable building with a curtain wall running all the way round like a ship's hull and towers to 'stem and stern', with a third set as the 'main mast' in the middle. A few years after it was built, King James II took it into his ownership as crown property and it has remained in the hands of crown and state ever since. In the sixteenth and seventeenth centuries it was used as a state prison with many political prisoners held there during the various religious wars. It was besieged many times during the Mary Queen of Scots and Cromwellian periods and was prison to many of the Covenanters in the late seventeenth century. In the nineteenth century it was used as an army barracks and later as an important ammunition store. The castle's dramatic appearance has caught the eye of several film producers over the years and parts of *Ivanhoe*, *The Bruce*, *Macbeth* and *Hamlet* were filmed there. The sheltered village harbour was a busy and important port dating from the medieval period, with Linlithgow merchants trading with Holland and the Baltic until it was overtaken by Bo'ness in the eighteenth century. Thereafter it declined rapidly, lost its customs house to its new rival and with it its national importance.

In Bo'ness the west pier was built around 1700 with the east added in 1733, and to pay for their upkeep the price of beer in the town was increased by two pence in 1744. By then the town was said to be Scotland's third most important port. This east pier was extended in 1787 by which time there were twenty-five Bo'ness-owned ships sailing from the harbour and fortunes were made by the canny skippers and traders. Despite the threat from the new town of Grangemouth from 1800 on, it continued to prosper. Today, clustered in the area of the old west pier are several buildings with links to the town's mercantile history. In Scotland's Close, which was once the main street of the town leading to the pier there is the 'tobacco warehouse' built in 1772, which may have been used to store tobacco from the American colonies on its way as a re-export from Scotland to Europe. It is now used as part of the library as is the old West Pier Tavern which bears a marriage lintel with the date 1711. The nearby five-storey granary building, now converted into flats, is of slightly later date and, as the name implies, was used to store grain from the import trade. There are several other buildings of note in the vicinity like the Tolbooth, the circular Hippodrome Theatre designed by Matthew Steele in 1911 and said to be the first purpose built cinema in Scotland, the recently restored seventeenth-century Dymock's Buildings, the Anchor Tavern and the *Bo'ness Journal* building with its fine 'candle-snuffer' roof. One building which did not survive was the original Town Hall, built sometime in the eighteenth century, which stood near the harbour and looked like a square castle with a tall clock tower. Undermining put paid to it in two instalments. In the 1890s the main building began to sink and was demolished. The clock tower survived for another 60 odd years and was the most distinctive landmark in the

73. Old Bo'ness, with the clock-tower of the original Town Hall

old town. Unfortunately it met the same fate and was brought down to be replaced by the simple clock which stands in Market Street.

As well as shipping, the Bo'ness and Carriden area, boasted a number of industries like coal mining, saltmaking, shipbuilding, pottery manufacture and iron founding. The whole area is completely undermined and there were hundreds of coal shafts with fascinating names like Tinkler's Sink, Dylon's and Well o' Spa, with great quantities of coal being removed for at least seven centuries. Much of this was exported to Europe from the harbours at Bo'ness and Bridgeness. The great boom came with the industrial revolution in the eighteenth century and continued right up to the mid twentieth and the black smoke from the large number of collieries gave the town a grim black appearance which made the visiting Robert Burns remark that it was a 'dirty, ugly place'. Seventy years later another visitor was equally scathing and added for good measure that 'the poorer lieges have the same wretchedly "reekit" appearance as the town itself.' And yet what statistics there are seem to suggest that the population, 'reekit' or no, were healthier and longer-lived than working folk in other parts of the district. The explanation for this, at least according to the local minister in 1796, was not difficult to find: 'The shore is washed by the Forth, twice every 24 hours, when, from the influx and reflux of the river, a great evaporation of vegetable effluvia must impregnate the atmosphere; which, combined with the vapours from the salt-pans in the immediate neighbourhood, will correct any septic quality in the air.' Hopefully his theology was better than his science. Or maybe he was on to the ozone effect?

Another early industry, mentioned by the reverend gentleman and preserved in the names Grangepans and Panbrae, was saltmaking. The shores of the Forth on both sides were lined with saltpans and from the early 1500s at least there was a good export trade from the Bo'ness area. At its height there were sixteen pans employing thirty salters and for a period salt was a main source of income for the town. We are told, for example, that a ton of salt was carted every week to Falkirk for use as a preservative for meat and fish. The industry survived for a remarkably long period with the last pan closing as late as 1889.

As one might expect, there were several shipbuilders in Bo'ness from quite an early period and two of the ships sent to Darien in the famous failed expedition in the 1690s were fitted out in the town. In the mid eighteenth century quite a large number of men were engaged in the trade but it was never as significant as at Grangemouth and shipbreaking was to play a greater part in the twentieth century, with huge liners finding their last resting place beached on the shore at Bridgeness to be taken apart by the hammermen at P. & W. McLellan's yard.

In the late 1700s whale-fishing started but the results were mixed. At one stage there were at least eight whaling ships sailing from the harbour and on their return to the town after months in the Arctic seas, the blubber, already cut up into large pieces, was carted to the oil works at the top of the Wynd to be boiled into the oil that lit the lamps and greased the machinery. One relic of the trade is a harpoon bearing the name 'William Cumings, Blacksmith, Bo'ness 1853' found sticking in a whale caught by the famous Dundee whaler the *Terra Nova*. However the trade did not survive long and by the mid eighteenth century only one ship was still sailing from the harbour. Fifty years later the town became the centre of a huge new trade importing vast quantities of pit props from Scandinavia. Soon giant stacks of props lined the foreshore from Carriden to Kinneil, so much so that the area was called by some, *Pitpropolus*! George Stewart, later the Provost of Bo'ness, is credited with starting the business which, of course, made him very rich indeed. In 1910 a strike by workers provoked the employers to bring in so called 'blackleg' or non-union labour and this in its turn led to a pitched fight – the 'Battle of Slag Hill' – as the striking men and women chased the terrified recruits among the mountains of pit props and delivered summary justice to those unfortunate enough to be caught. The business survived until the introduction of hydraulic props after the First World War.

Inevitably the proximity of Falkirk meant that there were iron foundries in the town. In fact there were seven at different times all along the coast, most dating from the mid nineteenth century. The last one to survive, Ballantines, is still in operation, and is now the only one of its kind in the whole of Falkirk district.

Dr John Roebuck, who seemed to be involved in just about every new venture going, opened the first pottery in the late eighteenth century and at one time there were several operating in the area. The most famous of these, the Bridgeness Pottery of Charles McNay, closed in the 1950s and Bo'ness pottery is now quite collectable though it has not yet attained the value of the celebrated Dunmore ware described in the next chapter.

The profit from these enterprises brought considerable benefit to the area, with many fine houses and buildings appearing in the nineteenth and twentieth centuries on the terraced streets above the original settlement. The new Parish Church on Pan Brae dates from 1888 and the handsome Town Hall and Carnegie Library in Glebe Park were completed in 1900. Fine new churches and schools were, as we noted in Falkirk and Grangemouth, one of the principal ways in which our wealthy Victorian ancestors underlined their status and that of their community. Bo'ness merchants were no different and soon old and inadequate buildings were replaced by fine examples of the

74. Corbiehall, looking past the original Parish Church to the new one on
Pan Brae

architects' and builders' crafts. The United Presbyterian congregation, whose first church in the town stood at the top of
Providence Brae, moved in 1883 to the beautiful Craigmailen
Church in Jane Terrace with its stone crown reminiscent of St
Giles' Cathedral. This became a United Free Church in 1900,
but when the final reunion with the Church of Scotland took
place in 1929, Craigmailen was one of only a handful of
congregations in Scotland to stay outside. It is still a UF chuch
today. The original 1844 Free Church in Boundary Street was
replaced in 1905 by what is now St Andrew's Church of
Scotland in Grange Terrace. The old building served first as
a reading room for working men and then the Bo'ness United
Social Club. It was demolished in 2006. Sometimes the abandoned buildings served the needs of new denominations like the
Episcopalians who took over the old Parish Church in Corbiehall in 1889. Twenty years later they moved to a new building,
in Cadzow Crescent, the present St Catherines. The Catholic
congregation purchased the former UP church in Providence
Brae in 1883 and six years later added a new building creating
St Mary of the Assumption Church and Hall and, for a period,
a school. They remained there for eighty years before moving to

the ultra-modern building in Dean Road designed by the celebrated firm of Gillespie, Kidd and Coia. It proved a bit too experimental and after many structural problems it was finally demolished around 1988. An act of 'religious vandalism' says historian Richard Jaques, though most members of the congregation seem happier with the simple replacement.

Provision for education was also improving. As far back as 1796 when the population of the parish was around 3,000 there were five schools with 80 pupils attending the main parish school in Bo'ness. Fifty years later the number had increased to ten, though most seem to have been the private 'venture' schools with small numbers of pupils. The most significant development in education was the foundation in 1869 of Anderson's Academy, the forerunner of the present Bo'ness Academy. John Anderson was an very wealthy local merchant and man of business who was anxious to promote the education of young Bo'nessians beyond the elementary level. The first school was a plain and simple affair in Providence Brae but by 1900 it was housed in a handsome classical building in Stewart Avenue which survives as Bo'ness Public School. Thirty years later and further expansion meant a move to another new building, this time in Academy Road. In the decades after the Second World War several buildings were added and the whole became a bit of a guddle which was replaced by a large modern school which opened in October 2000. Another new school building of note in the period was the fine building completed for Grange Primary in 1905 near the site of the old Grange, home of the Caddell family.

The first half of the twentieth century saw a steady growth in population but industries like mining, iron-founding and the potteries faced the same kind of contraction as elsewhere. During the First World War the port, like Grangemouth, was closed to shipping for the duration and it never really recovered. The town also suffered the loss of 400 men whose names are recorded on the War Memorial in Stewart Avenue which was unveiled in 1924. Things were even worse in the depressing inter-war years, and following further disruption during the Second World War, which cost another 136 Bo'ness

75. Kinneil Colliery, once the most modern of the Scottish coalfields.

lives, the docks were closed in 1959. For a time the modernisation of the colliery at Kinneil promised something of a revival. In the 1960s it was said to be one of the most up to date in Scotland and in 1981 there were over 1,000 men employed there. Five years later it was gone and the two industries, shipping and mining, that had dominated the region for 700 years and had made Bo'ness, vanished forever.

Since then much of the land between Kinneil and Carriden has disappeared under new housing, shopping and industrial developments. The town also expanded further south, covering the high land above the 'ness' to the east and west of the road to Linlithgow. Inevitably the 1980s and 1990s were a period of high unemployment and economic difficulty for the population, and there was a general air of hopelessness which comes when the staple employment disappears, taking with it not only money and security but pride and purpose. But like Falkirk in the aftermath of the collapse of the iron industry, things have started to change for the better. For example, recent developments in tourism offer great opportunities for the future. At Birkhill Clay Mine, for example, visitors enter the deep caverns to see for themselves the 300 million-year-old fossils and learn something of the processes of mining fireclay which was an important part of the area's industrial history. The Bo'ness and Kinneil Railway, operated by the Scottish Railway Preservation Society, houses Scotland's largest collection of historic locomotives, rolling stock and railway architecture, much of it brought from other parts of Scotland. Each year it attracts thousands of visitors to the town, and they are able to take a steam train the three miles or so along the shore to Birkhill. A more recent attraction is the Bo'ness Motor Museum which has has an interesting mix of classic cars and motoring memorabilia. At the time of writing there is a major refurbishment programme under way in the town and the old docks and harbour are being restored as a marina. Prospects are better than they have been for many a long year and property prices are on the rise. Bo'ness is the place to be, and quite a few Edinburgh folk are moving from the crowded city to a town that is among the most historic and interesting in the land.

One of the most cherished of the local traditions is Fair Day in June which has its origins in annual parades of the miners and carters of the town. Now it has the usual queen, pages, maids of honour, magnificent decorated arches and houses and a grand parade with a 'coronation' in the Glebe Park where up to 20,000 Bo'nessians thunder out 'Our Festal Day' before retiring to drink the weekend away in traditional style. Unmissable!

Denny and Dunipace

In 1877 the villages of Denny and Dunipace were brought together to form a single burgh and remained linked until they were absorbed into Falkirk District in 1975. However, for many

76. The Hills of Dunipace, a graveyard (*Photograph by Geoff Bailey*)

centuries they were quite separate communities lying on opposite banks of the River Carron.

The original settlement of Dunipace lay near the intriguing mounds known as the 'Hills of Dunipace' which survive near the modern cemetery. About a mile west along the river in the area still known as Kirkland stood the little chapel of 'Donypas' dedicated to St Alexander. A few yards away are the remains of a well which has been variously described over the centuries as 'St Alchanter's' or St Alexander's Well, said to have special healing powers. Along with 'Lethbert', the chapel of Dunipace was part of the medieval parish of St Ninian's through which it was attached to the Augustinian Abbey of Cambuskenneth. At the end of the thirteenth century, as noted in Chapter 3, tradition tells us that the priest here was the uncle of William Wallace and the importance of the place is further underlined by the fact that in June 1329 the body of King Robert the Bruce rested here overnight on its way to Dunfermline Abbey for burial. At this period the more prominent of the two remaining Hills of Dunipace may have had a 'motte' or castle on top with a 'bailey' or enclosure ditch attached. At some time in the late sixteenth or early seventeenth centuries a new church was built nearby, close to where the old graveyard with its circular surrounding wall stands today.

Civil power in the fourteenth century was represented by the de Morham family who were succeeded in time by the Douglases and then the Sinclairs, Earls of Orkney, one of whom built Herbertshire Castle in the early 1400s. The castle stood a mile or so to the west overlooking the river-crossing that links modern Dunipace to Denny and it remained in Sinclair hands for two hundred years. These were powerful and important families with all to play for in one of the most turbulent and bloody periods in Scotland's history and there can be little doubt that the Denny and Dunipace area and the castle itself featured in the lawlessness and intrigue of the times. We know too that the celebrated Hospitaller Knights, whose main place in Scotland was at Torphichen, held some of the lands of Dryburgh, a connection preserved in the name Temple-Denny which at one time encompassed almost a third of Denny parish. The current obsession with the Templars and their links to the Sinclairs of Orkney through their chapel at Rosslyn has so far failed to focus on the Herbertshire connection but the afficionados of conspiracy will no doubt be on to it soon enough! Sadly there is not a scrap of evidence to link Denny to the Templars beyond the name.

At a later period it seems that the Stewart Kings used the Dunipace area for hunting and falconry and on those occasions Herbertshire Castle would no doubt have become a royal residence for the duration. The Livingstons were the next owners in the early seventeenth century but by 1632 it was sold on to the Stirling family who were in possession until William Forbes of Callendar acquired the lands and castle in 1835. It was for a time a Forbes dower house until damaged by fire in 1914. It was demolished in 1959.

After the 1560 Reformation Dunipace was a separate parish until 1616, when it was once again united with Larbert. Despite many attempts to separate them they remained linked until 1962. For some years Dunipace was the most important part, but this situation gradually changed and, as Larbert expanded, services at Dunipace declined and then ceased altogether and the church was more or less abandoned. Not far away stood an important seventeenth-century house known as the 'Place of Dunipace', only the stair tower of which survives as a ruined doocot. The Primroses were the principal family at the time of the Jacobite rising in 1745 and the head of the house, Sir Archibald, was executed for aiding and abetting the Prince. The later mansion of Dunipace House on the same site was demolished in the 1940s.

Until 1601 Denny was a small village within the parish of Falkirk, but in that year it was established as a parish in its own right, though where the church stood or when it was built is not known. The present Parish Church at the cross was built in 1813. Although the disjunction does suggest that the population was increasing at this time the fact remains that both Denny and Dunipace were very small settlements and it

77. Denny Cross and Parish Church around 1900

was not until the first half of the nineteenth century that industrialisation brought rapid growth. There were however a number of corn mills on the Carron and the majority of the scattered population in both parishes were engaged in agricultural work of one kind or another. Flax was an important crop and the expansion of linen production in the eighteenth century was the trigger which began the process of change. In 1783 Herbertshire printfield began the process of calico printing followed in 1800 by an even larger undertaking at Denovan, both in Dunipace. Textiles imported from the east and decorated with beautiful coloured prints were in high demand and the Dunipace printers were able to reproduce these with great success. By 1836 these two were employing nearly 1,000 workers and many families were drawn to the area, some from Paisley, where the printing skills were already well developed. Much of the workforce lived on the Denny side of the river, a situation encouraged by the construction of a stone bridge over the Carron in 1825 carrying a road linking Airth and Denny parishes. But there were also many new workers in Dunipace and to house these incomers the work's owner built houses further west, opposite the village of Denny at the north end of the important and ancient Denny bridge, which was itself rebuilt in 1828. Known at first as Milltown of Dunipace the new community soon displaced the original village which declined and eventually disappeared. The church which had lain abandoned for decades was replaced by a new building at Denovan about midway between the old and new villages and the old building was demolished in 1835. Only the old kirkyard with its collection of ancient gravestones remains. The new 'Denovan' church served until the modern era when the congregation joined with the former Free Church, by then called Dunipace North. It stands near the Denny-Dunipace bridge and is now the Parish Church of Dunipace. It dates from 1890. Denovan Church was closed in 1988 and has recently been converted into a private house.

At the same time as calico printing was transforming the local economy, entrepreneurs had been mining blackband ironstone to feed the new industry in Falkirk, and when cheap imports from Spain effectively killed off the market in the early nineteenth century they turned their attention to chemicals, coal mining, textiles, iron founding and brickmaking. This expansion was given a further boost by the arrival of the Caledonian railway in 1859 which improved communication with markets beyond the local area.

Important as it was in bringing industrial processes to a rural area, calico printing lasted only around fifty years before new methods of dyeing and a change of fashion brought about decline and closure. Once again the local reaction was to switch to other activities or other markets. For example, the chemical works at Custonhall in Stripeside, which had supplied dyes to the calico printers, turned instead to making lacquers and enamels for the iron foundries. The so-called 'steam coal' mined in Denny was particularly good for use in shipping and output expanded throughout the century. By 1896 the three local mines Herbertshire, Quarter and Carronrig were employing over 500 men. In the 1850s there were three mills driven by water power producing woollen shawls and tartans and 'linsey-woolsey stuffs' and employing 200 men and women. Four foundries were established in the late Victorian era, the largest, Cruikshanks, specialising in engineering components for the Clyde shipyards. All of these played a part in saving industrial Denny, but by far the longest lasting and most important was paper making. The mills using the soft water of the Carron created an industry which employed hundreds of men and women and made Denny one of the country's most important paper-making centres.

The earliest venture was Herbertshire Mill, established in 1788, making small amounts of paper by hand. Difficulties with the power supply meant poor results but the construction of a new lade in 1802 was a major step towards expansion and success. Around 1810 part of Carrongrove woollen mill was given over to paper making, and although both mills changed hands several times output continued to increase as machines replaced manufacture by hand. Herbertshire Mill specialised in high-quality writing paper, much of which was exported to London, while Carrongrove made mill board and coarse paper.

By the middle of the nineteenth century they were employing nearly 100 men, women and boys between them and villages at Stoneywood and Fankerton grew up to provide housing for this expanding workforce. With the explosion in publication of books and newspapers, demand for Denny paper increased dramatically and new mills appeared along the length of the river. John Luke, whose father operated a successful paper-works at Crook of Devon, leased an old bleach mill at Heads-wood in 1869 and converted it for paper-making. This was named Denny Paper Works and later his own sons followed suit on the Dunipace side by opening the Anchor Mill and the Vale Paper Works. All three were eventually brought together as the Vale Paper Company in 1894. By then the owners of Herbert-shire had purchased Stoneywood Woollen Mill and converted it for paper-making so that by the end of the century there were half a dozen mills in operation. The early twentieth century brought consolidation with the purchase of Herbertshire by Carrongrove in 1906 and its closure two years later. The others continued to prosper through to the modern era with Heads-wood and the Vale, which had in 1936 become part of the Associated Paper group, surviving until 1974 and Stoneywood closing its doors ten years later. That left Carrongrove which had became part of Inveresk Paper in 1924. In 2000 the company published a very handsome history of its 200 years and the general manager concluded by saying the 'we can look back with pride to what our forefathers established and look forward with confidence to Carrongrove Mill continuing as an active contributor to the Scottish economy. Whether this will be for another two hundred years, we can only guess.' Five years later it was gone and paper-making came to an end in Denny. Now the 'For Sale' notice has gone up on the factory gate with the hope that some new industrial use might be found. The record elsewhere is not good and it seems likely that the old chimney will soon hit the ground and the riverside, for so long a hive of industry, will welcome the busy private house builders who are always ready to fill another empty space. Let us hope that if and when this happens the Carrongrove man-sion house used as the company office and dating from the mid nineteenth century will survive. There remains one other link with the paper industry which will survive. Just across the road from Carrongrove stands Randolph Hill, a very handsome mansion built for the owner of the mill. In 1981 it was purchased by a trust and converted into Strathcarron Hospice which for the last two decades has offered palliative care to those with terminal illness or degenerative disease. By any standard Strathcarron has been an outstanding success and the affection and regard with which it is held by the people of the whole of central Scotland is underlined by the amazing fund-raising campaign which has supported this vital work for all of these years and still provides more than £2 million annually. We are very fortunate indeed to have such a place staffed by people who really understand what caring means and who bring love and dignity to so many at their moment of greatest need.

Back in Victorian Denny industrial opportunities were many and varied and a good example of the sharp-eyed entrepreneur in action was the Anchor Brickworks which John Stein opened in 1896. Stein, whose major fire-brick operations in Bonnybridge will be described later, noticed that there was a large bing of waste left over from the ironstone mining near the Anchor Burn. He realised that this mixture of fire clay and ganister could be used to make common bricks and so secured a lease on the land and access to the bing. Within a year tens of thousands of bricks were leaving the works each week and special brick-making machinery and steam engines were in operation. Bricks cost ten shillings per thousand to make and Stein sold them for twenty! In 1921 they were used in the building of Gleneagles Hotel. Stein's estimate that the bing would last for twenty years was conservative and the works survived until 1931.

Economic success in the nineteenth century brought investment in new public buildings, including as usual, new churches. Like most Victorian towns Denny had three Presbyterian congregations formed from earlier breakaways from the established church. If anything the people of the area seemed even more determined than others to oppose the national church

78. Denny Town House

and had supported in large numbers the first secession in the 1730s. By the middle of the nineteenth century this had produced two United Presbyterian churches, one at Dennyloanhead, of which more later, and one in the town centre. Broompark Church was opened in 1797 and reconstructed a century later in its present square form. In 1843 the long-serving minister of Denny parish, John Dempster, led a substantial number of his congregation to a malt barn at East Boreland to form Denny Free Church. Their first new building opened soon after the Disruption and was said to have been built by the congregation, who carted stone from Thorndyke Quarry. They remained there until 1900 when the present Westpark Church was opened as one of the first United Free churches in Scotland. The Broompark congregation joined with them in 1963, by which time they were all once again Church of Scotland, and their building was converted into a community hall. From 1859 the growing Catholic community held services in a little schoolroom and later in a new chapel-school. By 1870 the first priest was appointed and twenty years later the present large St Alexander's Church was opened for worship. This dedication to St Alexander – whoever he was – echoed the thousand-year-old local link and it is said to be the only church named after this saint in Scotland.

It is difficult to talk with any certainty about early education in Denny and Dunipace. There were parochial schools in both in the seventeenth century along with the usual crop of private ventures. Kirk session records confirm that there were school-rooms and teachers in both from the mid 1600s, though in Denny it seems that the local heritors were very reluctant to pay up the legal salary or indeed any salary at all to the poor man appointed to look after the local bairns. Three years after the Education Act of 1872 a fine new public school with its distinctive spire was built in Duke Street and in 1890 a new building next door was opened to provide secondary education. This building later served as Denny High School until replaced by the modern school south of the town at Glowrorum in 1959. It is itself scheduled for replacement in the near future.

The coal, iron and paper industries survived well into the twentieth century, but the years after the Second World War brought the same kind of decline to Denny and Dunipace as to the rest of Falkirk district. In the 1950s only Herbertshire No. 3, or 'station pit' as it was called, was still working, but most of its 300 miners travelled each day from Bo'ness. It closed in 1959. The last foundry, Cruikshanks, survived because it specialised in engineering components but the collapse of the shipyards and the general decline in demand brought closure in 1985. As we have already seen, the paper mill at Carrongrove survived longest and for a time was the last best hope for the local economy. It was still prospering at the dawn of the new Millennium but not for long afterwards. Foreign competition and changing demand brought closure in 2005. Coal, iron and paper, the three pillars that supported thousands of families, all gone within the space of fifty years. The town that emerged from the calamity is, like many of its neighbours, now a dormitory with little local employment available. In the 1960s much of the centre was demolished and replaced by a modern development of flats and shops along one side of

Stirling Road and Duke Street. Like similar developments in Falkirk and Camelon these 'modern' buildings were never popular and today it has a run-down and neglected appearance. At the time of writing there are plans to refurbish this area completely. Let us hope that whatever appears is in keeping with the surviving buildings and reflective of the history of the town.

CHAPTER 15

The Villages

As well as these three towns there are many smaller settlements all over east Stirlingshire which have grown-up over the centuries into substantial villages and their history is every bit as fascinating as that of Falkirk itself.

Camelon

Of all the villages, Camelon has most exercised the imaginative power of antiquaries and local historians over the years. A mighty Roman harbour, a great Pictish city with twelve brass gates, battles galore involving Pict and Scot, Angle and Briton and, of course, the Camelot and round table of King Arthur himself – all have had their champions and such theories continue to appear regularly even in this more sceptical age. Alas for romance, the evidence for such past glory is scant or non-existent and this is not the place to reinforce such fancy. The truth is interesting enough by any standard.

We have already encountered the great fort built by the Romans during their brief but eventful occupation in the second century. The military road which crossed the Antonine Wall at Watling Lodge passed the fort before crossing the Carron at Larbert – it is certainly possible that the river was navigable as far as Camelon during the Roman period and may well have been used as the point of entry and departure for men and materials during the years of occupation and campaigning. But whether there was a harbour or not the north road was important enough to demand a heavily garrisoned fort in its defence and if Roman positions were indeed attacked by tribal enemies then Camelon would have been an obvious target.

When the Romans withdrew from the area for the last time the place we now know as Camelon disappeared from the record for close on 1,500 years. Only with the coming of the new age of iron and the cutting of the Great Canal in the eighteenth century does the village emerge from the darkness and have an existence which we can identify and describe with any certainty. The stretch of the canal from Bainsford through the farmland of Camelon was completed in the early 1770s and soon attracted manufacturers and traders who recognised the benefits of a swift and dependable transport system. The Lock 16 area, and the junction point where the road from Falkirk dipped under the canal, quickly became growth points and there were no doubt storehouses, loading basins and stables serving the growing canal traffic from quite an early stage. By the beginning of the nineteenth century the village population was reported to be close to 600 and growing with a considerable number engaged in the manufacture of nails.

79. The two canals were linked by a series of locks and pools which provided the children of Camelon with outdoor swimming facilities! The King's Bridge carried the railway over the Union Canal, but the locks, pools and bridge have long since disappeared.

It is William Cadell, son of Carron's founder and himself the
first manager of the works, who is credited with the establishment of the earliest nailmaking concern in Camelon. In 1790,
more than twenty years after he gave up a direct interest in the
works at Carron, Cadell brought a group of skilled nailmakers
from England to begin manufacturing in the village. The
Cadells had bought out Carron's interest in this particular
activity in the 1770s and had already established workshops in
Bannockburn and Laurieston as well as places much further
afield. In Camelon the trade expanded steadily and young men
were drawn to the area and apprenticed to masters who taught
them the secrets of a hard, heavy and ill-rewarded trade.
Houses, workshops, tools and nailrods were supplied by Cadell
to the men and boys, often as young as 9 or 10 years old, who
slaved for twelve or more hours each day to turn out the
thousands of nails required to earn a living wage:

> round the central fire hammered away four nailers . . . no
> rest, no breathing space for them. From hour to hour the
> bent back and steady quick stroke, for the naile must strike
> when the iron was hot and he had to pay for heating the iron.
> In the morning they hied to the warehouse for their bundles
> of rods which were converted into nails ranging in length
> from ½ inch to 12 inches.

Four nailers' rows or squares appeared in Camelon – the Wee
Square, at the west end; Fairbairn's Square, owned by George
Fairbairn, a leading nailmaster of the early nineteenth century;
George Square, close to Lock 16 on the canal; and Gunn's
Square in the same vicinity. Living conditions were extremely
poor and the nailers and their families developed a reputation
for hard living and hard drinking and, of course, radical action
which has already been discussed in an earlier chapter. One
observer in 1840 thought things were improving: 'The morals of
the nailmakers have been improved within the last few years. In
particular drunkenness and habits of improvidence are greatly
on the decrease.'
By then a visit of the dreaded cholera in 1833 had brought

many deaths to the nailers' rows with Mr Fairbairn paying £40 to assist with the burial cost 'which has been repaid from the earnings of survivors'. After this, a penny-a-week death fund was established to offer the vulnerable nailers some protection, but not long afterwards the development of mechanical nail-making effectively robbed them of their livelihoods.

The completion of the Union Canal in 1822 confirmed Camelon's status as the fulcrum of the new communication system and soon new inns, workshops, storage facilities and houses appeared along the banks and basins of Port Downie. By 1831 the population was over 800, rising within a decade to 1,340. Sometime around 1840 two brothers from Airth, James and Andrew Ross, began building boats in a yard near Lock 16; after only five years Andrew was dead and young James, having discovered the value of pitch as a commodity in the boatyard, moved into chemical manufacture at Limewharf just a few hundred yards west of Port Downie. Crude tar from various gas-works was shipped to Camelon where it was con-verted into naphtha, pitch and refined tar. Business boomed and James Ross directed the expanding company for thirty years until 1878, when Robert Sutherland and Robert Orr assumed control. New products multiplied – sulphate of am-monia, benzine, creosote and toluene, a key ingredient in the manufacture of TNT explosives – and prosperity followed. The firm did well during the years of war but in 1929, the same year as the sore-pressed iron foundries were forming the Allied, the Lime Wharf Chemical Works became part of Scottish Tar Distillers. It survived until a disastrous fire in 1973 destroyed the works and soon afterwards almost all production on the site came to an end.

By the end of the Victorian era a number of chemical companies had followed James Ross into business in Camelon and were employing hundreds of men in the manufacture of sulphuric acid, iodine and dozens of other compounds by then in high demand in the rapidly expanding Scottish economy. The Hurlet Works (1851), Camelon Chemical Works (1878) and Crosses (1900) flourished briefly but never attained the prosperity of Lime Wharf, though they did help bring the infant chemical industry to the Falkirk district where it would reach its full flowering in the Grangemouth developments of the twentieth century.

From the start the people of Camelon village looked for the services which confirmed their status as a new community. As part of Falkirk Parish they depended on the minister there for their spiritual needs and on the heritors for the provision of education. In 1786 a rented house, paid for by subscription among the villagers, was converted to a schoolroom and five years later a 'thatched but and ben' was built on land feued from Forbes of Callendar. Thus in 1797 the minister of Falkirk could report that 'in the village of Camelon there is a dwelling house and schoolroom for the encouragement of a schoolmaster, but no salary'. The establishment of the 'School and Well Committee' in 1799 to maintain what were seen as the community's principal or only assets, was another example of the villagers' willingness to band together to fight for the common good of all, a tendency which has marked the people of Camelon in all the years since then. The Committee appointed seven 'stint-masters' from their number and while they found it as difficult as their opposite numbers in Falkirk to raise the sums

80. Camelon Main Street at Rosebank Distillery

due, the school did continue to grow and the teacher's salary was usually paid. Sometimes though, their poverty was to his disadvantage, as in 1847 when the Committee resolved that 'all the panes of glass awanting in the school to be replaced by the teacher', later clarified as 'such glass as is broken in school hours'. A new school building was provided in 1874 but it proved to be too small, and a much larger building, the present Carmuirs primary, was opened by the Parochial Board in 1901.

The explosion of iron founding in the district in the second half of the nineteenth century had a major impact on Camelon and again the Forth and Clyde canal had a great deal to do with the choice of site. The first was established in 1845 near Lock 16 and was known variously as Port Downie or Camelon Iron Works. It survived until the 1950s. It was followed by the Union (1854–1879), the Forth and Clyde (1870–1963), R. & A. Main's Gothic Works (1899–1964), Grange (1900–1960s), Carmuirs (1899–1968) and Dorrator, founded in 1898, which survived until 1994. At their height, in the years before the First World War, the Camelon foundries employed over 1,300 men, manufacturing the familiar range of domestic and industrial ironware including grates, stoves, pipes, cookers, gates, fences and mantelpieces.

The rapid growth in the population increased demands for a church in Camelon and, with the support of the minister of Falkirk, William Begg, and William Forbes of Callendar, who provided a site free of charge, a new building was erected at the west end of the village to the design of Edinburgh architect David Rhind. It was opened in August 1840 and a few weeks later William Branks from Lanarkshire became the first minister. After the great Disruption in 1843 the charge was vacant for six years as the established church struggled to find ministers for the hundreds of deserted congregations throughout the land. In 1849 John Oswald was inducted as the second minister, and due to his perseverance Camelon was erected into a parish in its own right in 1853. In 1889 a Free Church, later named the Irving Church, was opened in Dorrator Road, followed in 1905 by Trinity United Free Church in Baird Street. This was closed in 1973 and is now the home of the

Plymouth Brethern while more recently Irving and the Parish
Church have joined to create one Church of Scotland congregation in the village. The Catholic community built their
first church at the Hedges in 1923 and this was replaced in 1960
by the modern building on Glasgow Road, designed by Gillespie, Kidd and Coia. It is Camelon's only 'A' listed building
and one of only four churches in the Falkirk district to attain
this grading.

The life of Victorian communities was very often tied to that
of their parish church and the long ministry of the Revd John
Scott (1867–1918) in many ways symbolised the true coming of
age of Camelon. He was a leading figure not only in Camelon
but in the wider Falkirk district and it was during his time that
the village, with a population of nearly 6,000, and the town
joined together in 1900 when Camelon became part of the
burgh. Since then, the 'mariners' as the sons and daughters of
the village call themselves, have played a very full part in the
life of the larger community and no fewer than nine out of
twenty-four Provosts of Falkirk have come from the village.
The population continued to grow in the new century and
hundreds of new houses were built by the council both before
and after the Second World War. The centre of the village
suffered badly from the 'improvements' of the 1960s and sadly,
many old buildings were lost.

More recent times have brought the same kind of closure and
decline to Camelon as to other parts of the district. The
chemical works were the first to go, followed by the foundries,
and even the 'modern' industries, which offered hope for a
while, eventually shut up shop and vanished. The Wrangler
clothing factory, for example, closed in 1999 with the loss of
over 450 jobs, mainly for women. Sadly the building remains
empty and proposals for a new use have come to nothing so far.
The reopening of a new Camelon railway station in 1994,
though very welcome, seemed to underline the fact that work
now lies somewhere else on the rail route and not in the village.

Still, the list of institutions which serve the area from a base in
Camelon is long and impressive. There are firms like Alexander's, both bus-building and driving, and Dunn and Wilsons,

the Mariner leisure centre, the new Sheriff Court, Falkirk Golf Club and, of course, the cemetery and crematorium! The *Falkirk Herald* is printed in the village and there is a fine new centre for those who suffer from sensory deprivation recently opened near the Roman Bar. The restoration of the canal link, and especially the Falkirk Wheel, hold out some prospect of jobs in tourism and may also offer Camelon a new focus for other kinds of development. However it will not come quickly and the mariners will need plenty of patience in the years ahead.

Bonnybridge

The village of Bonnybridge lies three miles west of Camelon on the line of the Antonine Wall, the Edinburgh–Glasgow railway line, the Forth and Clyde Canal and the pre-motorway main road from Falkirk to Glasgow. Until the mid twentieth century it was a major industrial centre but with the slow decline and eventual closure of the foundries and brickworks it seemed to lose its sense of purpose. The village had a depressed air and a run-down appearance and the rest of the Falkirk district appeared to take little interest in what happened there. Enter stage left (or right) the redoubtable Billy Buchanan whose eccentric approach to local politics catapulted him to local and even national attention. And with him, the village which is his pride and joy. More than anyone else he reminded the community of their own history which spans two thousand years and can be found, albeit in fragments, in every corner of the village.

Bonnybridge lies on both sides of the River Bonny which once separated two feudal baronies, Seabegs to the south, where the earliest settlement was called Bonnywater and South Herbertshire to the north, where it was called Water of Bonny! Not until the end of the seventeenth century does the name Bonnybridge appear, which suggests that the first bridge between the two places dates to around that time. On the Seabegs side we can still see the remains of both the Roman wall at Seabegs Wood and the fort of Roughcastle as well as a twelfth-century 'motte' which survives today as an elevated mound in the grounds of Antonine Primary School. It probably had a wooden fortified structure on top and would have been home to one of the early feudal barons of Seabegs, perhaps Alexander Straiton whose family were in possession of the barony at that time. There are a number of early records of 'St Helen's Chapel' nearby, and not far away, though separated in the modern era by the canal, was the ancient burial ground called by the locals the 'Chapel Yard'. It was in use until 1900 and was not removed until the construction of the present Community Centre in the 1970s. There is a tradition that the stones from the ruined chapel were used to construct Bonny Mill on the site now occupied by a garage close to the canal pend. This mill was the baronial corn mill of Seabegs which the local farmers were obliged to use.

Bonnybridge lay within the great medieval parish of Falkirk but in 1601, forty years after the Reformation, a new Parish of Denny was created to include the part of the village north of the Bonny. The other side remained with Falkirk, a strange situation which continued into the modern era. From then on the two parishes were responsible for education, poor relief and 'discipline' on their own side of the water. What an incentive to go for a cross-river stroll before committing some Sabbath offence or worse! There does not appear to have been a school of any kind until the early decades of the eighteenth century when, following a bequest, a schoolmaster was appointed to teach poor children in 'Water of Bonny'. However it does not seem to have been too successful and the session had great difficulty in making the schoolmaster perform his duties to their satisfaction.

When the transport revolution of the eighteenth and early nineteenth centuries reached Bonnybridge it changed the village forever. The east–west path through the valley first brought the new turnpike road from Edinburgh to Glasgow with its toll house and bar at Bonnybridge Toll. Then came the Great Canal in the 1770s lying south of the Bonny on the Seabegs side and finally, further south still, in the 1840s the Edinburgh–Glasgow Railway and the Perth–Carlisle line with an important junction at the railway village of Greenhill. In their wake they brought warehouses and yards, houses and inns and people galore seeking employment opportunities. From then on all the important industrial development was concentrated on the south side of the village and there it remained throughout the boom years of the nineteenth century until the decline and closure of the late twentieth. The only road between the new industrial centre and the rest of the village was the so-called 'radical pend' associated in legend at least with the Battle of Bonnymuir already described. This tunnel beneath the canal is the oldest one in Scotland still in use, dating to the 1780s, and though it developed a reputation as a dank, dirty and dangerous place it was not replaced by a bridge until 1899.

Whisky distilling and chemicals were two of the earliest industrial ventures but the most significant arrival came in 1854 when James Smith returned from the United States with the intention of selling American cast-iron stoves, which were lighter and more efficient than the standard British design. He soon discovered that it was even more profitable to make the

81. A postcard view of industrial Bonnybridge around 1908. On the back someone has written 'Having a beautiful day here'.

Industrial Bonnybridge. (Eclipse over all)   Published by Wm. Welsh, Springfield Studio, Bonnybridge

stoves in Scotland and contracted with several foundries in the Falkirk area to produce the parts. He teamed up with Stephen Wellstood, another Scot who had spent time in the USA, to form what was destined to became one of the most famous partnerships in the Scottish iron industry. They acquired premises in Glasgow which they called the Columbian Stove Works where the parts were assembled and marketed throughout Britain. The foundry which served their interests best was the Union at Lock 16 in Camelon and they eventually persuaded the managing partner there, George Ure, to join them in a new foundry in Bonnybridge on the site of an old abandoned chemical works. The new partnership, called Ure and Company, opened the works which was named the Columbian Stove Works *Foundry* to distinguish it from the assembly works in Glasgow. Under Ure's experienced hand the firm flourished and, as well as continuing to manufacture a wide range of stoves, they were successful in winning a valuable contract from the Singer Sewing Machine Company. This proved so profitable that in 1872 the partners decided to split the company into two parts with Ure moving to a nearby site for the new Bonnybridge Foundry, leaving the original works to concentrate on the making of stoves. Both continued to prosper though they were reunited in 1890 under the Smith and Wellstood name. By then iron founding was by far the most important industry in Bonnybridge and remained so for much of the twentieth century. As well as Smith and Wellstood there was the Broomside Foundry, known to one and all as the 'Puzzle' for some unknown reason; Lane and Girvan's Caledonian Foundry; and Mitchell and Russel's Chattan Stove Works.

Related to iron production was of course the manufacture of refractory bricks, and this was another early industrial activity in the village. There was fireclay in plenty in association with the coal measures and a number of firms like the Bonnybridge Brick and Tile Works, Griffiths' Bonnybridge Silica and Fireclay Company, Dougall's Bonnyside Brickworks and Stein's Milnquarter Fireclay Mine and Brickworks survived until the modern era when, like the foundries they served, declining demand brought takeover and eventual closure. A mile west of the village, also on the industrial south side of the canal the new village of Allandale was created by Steins – and named after the son of the founder – to house the workforce from his new Castlecary Brickworks. The two lines of well-built red sandstone cottages, now part of a conservation area, are a handsome reminder of a lost era.

As the population of Victorian Bonnybridge increased much of the money earned by masters and workers alike went to provide the usual crop of new churches, schools and other public buildings. A new Parish Church opened in 1877 with the support of the ironmaster George Ure, and twenty years later a church missionary was appointed to work in the industrial heart of High Bonnybridge. The Free Church was also active in the area and by 1908 they had acquired a church building which was itself replaced in 1934 by St Helen's Church of Scotland. The building is now a Baptist Church. In 1910 the growing Catholic population were meeting in a hall in the old Broomhill paper mill under the name St Joseph's Mission and by 1925 the handsome church of St Joseph was opened with a new Catholic school next door. The public school in Main Street was opened in 1876 with an additional building added in 1891 and these served until the present school building was opened in the 1960s.

In keeping with the prevailing view that drink was the root of all evil, a Temperance Hall was built in Bridge Street in 1882. What deterrent it was to the thirsty ironworkers is not known, but it did at least serve the village as a meeting place for twenty years until the fine new Public Hall was opened at the turn of the century, supported by a 'penny rate' for its upkeep. Sadly the building was allowed to fall into disrepair and was demolished in the late 1960s.

On the north side of the Bonny to the west of the village a number of settlements lie along the line of the main road to Kilsyth and Glasgow. These have more or less merged into one continuous 'village', though the individual parts are still recognisable, at least by the folk who live there. And each in its separate way has something to add to the story of the Bonnybridge area. The first is Dennyloanhead, standing as the name

82. The ill-fated Bonnybridge Public Hall

implies where the 'loan' south from Denny meets the main road. The church here, now converted to private houses, was the earliest and strongest congregation of the Erskine break-away in the 1730s. The Railway Inn is a reminder that all these villages were once linked by the Bonnybridge–Kilsyth railway line built in the 1840s to carry coal from the pits operating in the hillfoots just to the north where most of the local people worked. In the late 1970s over 250 acres of land between the main road and the Bonny Water were given over to large-scale whisky bonds, a throwback to the distilling days of the nine-teenth century of which, more later. Today they are the Bonnybridge Bond of the international Diageo Company.

Longcroft is the next settlement to the west with its fine Masonic Arms and War Memorial, then Haggs, which takes its name from the former peat 'haggs' in the area and is certainly not a reflection on the merits of the local womenfolk, as one 'historian' told me some years ago! Haggs Parish Church was built in 1840 to the design of the Glasgow architect David Rhind and is almost identical in design to his other local church, Camelon St Johns. Finally we have the village of Banknock which incorporates Bankier, a place-name of great antiquity derived from a prehistoric earthwork in the vicinity.

The distillery which was established here in 1828 drew its water from the Doups Burn and occupied a very large area near Wyndford. A detailed description of the site in the late 1800s reports two large maltings 'lighted by no less than twenty-four windows', a huge barley store with a 36-foot square kiln, still house, mash house, tun room, warehouse, engine room, co-operages, smithy and its own gas-manufacturing plant. Over 200,000 gallons of malt whisky were produced, each year, described by the writer as 'a thoroughly wholesome beverage' though what the Temperance Hall committee thought of it is not recorded. It survived in production until the 1920s when it became a bonded warehouse, a function which continued until the 1960s at least. Large and important as it was, the distillery was dwarfed in significance in the Banknock area by the local coal mines which provided most of the income and employment. From here coal was shipped along the canal to Edinburgh and Glasgow and the mines provided employment for ninety workers and three steam engines in the mid nineteenth century. The coal masters here were the same Wilsons who owned and operated South Bantaskine, and William Wilson of Banknock had the same patrician attitude to his workers as his brother John in Falkirk. One account says he was 'well known as a liberal patron and intelligent connoisseur of art, and also as a leading antiquary'. In his collection were works by Turner, Millais and Lanseer! Little surprise that his Falkirk niece, Helen Wilson, became an artist of distinction herself. By 1900 there were over 200 men employed in the Banknock pits, many of them Irish immigrants who used the school as a chapel for the best part of fifty years. Their families had to wait until 1974 before they had their own Catholic Church, St Luke's, but by then the jobs that had drawn them here were long gone. Like much of the Scottish coalfield the main pits at Banknock declined and closed in the 1930s. Attempts were made to provide alternative employment and one reasonably successful venture was the Cannerton Brickworks, opened in 1932, using pit waste to produce building bricks and employing nearly 100 workers in the 1960s.

By then, of course, the days of economic success in the Bonnybridge area were long gone. Such a high dependence

on heavy industry meant that the closures when they came
dealt the local population a particularly severe blow and the
village struggled to find a purpose in a new high-tech world.
And yet today the name Bonnybridge is as likely to be known in
Tokyo or San Francisco as is Glasgow or Edinburgh. Sometime
in the 1990s a trickle of reports, eye-witness statements and
extravagant claims grew to a veritable flood as Bonnybridge
became the unchallenged centre for spotting Unidentified
Flying Objects. No amount of scorn poured by the sceptical
on the UFO hunters has deterred them, and at the time of
writing, the village, now twinned with the famous Roswell in
New Mexico, has plans for a high tech UFO study centre and a
Disney-style space theme park. Driven forward almost single-
handedly by Councillor Billy Buchanan these projects, if they
are completed, will be located along the road linking Bonnybridge to Lochgreen, known nowadays as the 'flightpath'. As a
scorn-pourer-in-chief I should be worried by all this collective
delusion, but if it brings attention and jobs to the village, and a
smile to the faces of people everywhere, then let us make the
most of it. Certainly the village is on the up and up. A huge
number of new private houses have been built on the north side
of the canal in recent years and at present the same is happening to the brown field sites at Milnquarter and Greenhill on the
south side. Bonnybridge may now be no more than a dormitory
village but it is one in remarkably good heart considering all
that it has suffered over decades of decline.

Larbert and Stenhousemuir

The origin of the villages of Larbert and Stenhousemuir lies
somewhere in those dark ages when the nation of Scotland was
beginning to emerge from the amalgam of Pict and Scot, Angle
and Briton. We know that the crossing point of the Carron
River was important to the Romans and that the road they
constructed from Watling Lodge on the Antonine Wall at
Camelon crossed the river by a bridge located somewhere near
the present Larbert Old Parish Church. Traces of this road
were still identifiable in the Torwood as late as the eighteenth

century and the high and dry land above the road and river crossing probably housed a settlement of some kind from the earliest days. At some stage a Christian community was established in the area with a chapel which, like its counterpart in Falkirk, was handed over by the Bishop of St Andrews to the Augustinian Canons as a gift in the year 1160. This time it was the priests of Cambuskenneth rather than Holyrood who received the 'chapels of Donypas and Lethbert', a present they retained for almost four hundred years. Incredible as it seems, this ancient linkage between Larbert and Dunipace survived until 1962 despite the strains of both Reformation and industrial revolution which elsewhere tore apart the religious and social fabric of the nation. And despite the mutual suspicion and open hostility between the two 'united parishes' which surfaced from time to time over the centuries. Of the chapel itself we know only that around 1500 a new plain building appeared on the site of the present kirkyard and that either before or in the immediate aftermath of the Reformation it fell into disrepair. Beyond that we have little information about the Larbert area before the sixteenth century but we can be sure that the turbulent relations between powerful feudal families which were the norm throughout lowland Scotland did not pass by the Larbert area. The Foresters of Garden who from the 1400s were the keepers of the valuable and strategically important royal forest of Torwood, the Bruces of Airth Castle, later Stenhouse and Kinnaird, and the Livingstons of Callendar shared the territory between them, at times in harmonious alliance and at others through bitter feud and conflict with much blood shed on both sides. On the slopes of the ancient wood not far from the broch already described stand the remains of Torwood Castle, the last surviving symbol of Forester power. It was built in 1566 for Sir Alexander Forester and its size and construction confirm the status of its lord and the dangerous times in which he and his family lived. Another of the powers in the local area lived a few miles east in the splendid baronial building called Stenhouse, the early seventeenth century home of the Bruce family. It stood to the north of the Carron ironworks in the vicinity of the present Lodge Drive,

83. The mansion of Stenhouse, home of the Bruce family. Demolished in the 1960s.

just yards from the site of Arthur's O'on demolished in 1743. The house passed from the Bruce family to John Bell Sherriff of Carronvale in 1888 and thirty years later his grandson sold it to Carron Company which converted it into flats to house key workers. It continued in this way until the 1960s when it was demolished despite being a listed building. The Bruces also owned Kinnaird House and the present building is the third to stand on the same site – it was two of the Kinnaird Bruces who figured most prominently in the subsequent story of Larbert and Stenhousemuir.

Robert Bruce was both lawyer and churchman who had succeeded to the pulpit of John Knox himself in St Giles by 1590. At first his relations with King James VI were very close and some observers regarded him as the most powerful man in the Kingdom. Later, on a point of principle, these two determined and dogmatic men disagreed so profoundly that Bruce found himself in exile abroad and then, after some years, confined to a three-mile area around his Kinnaird home. From this base he continued to defend what he saw as the fundamentals of the protestant reformation and hundreds of people flocked to the parish to hear him preach. He restored the broken-down church at Larbert and until his death in 1631 continued to attract the attention of Scotland to the little country parish. He was without doubt one of the most famous men of his generation and as 'Bruce the Covenanter' is still remembered as one of the founding fathers of the Church of Scotland. He is buried in Larbert Kirkyard as is his illustrious descendant James Bruce who attained international fame as the great 'Abyssinian Traveller' a century later.

James Bruce was an intrepid adventurer who crossed the swamps, forests and deserts of Africa in the process discovering the source of the Blue Nile. His own account of these travels was thought by some to be so incredible that he was accused of fabricating the whole amazing tale. But enough people were convinced and Bruce became a living legend enjoying the favour of both royalty and Government alike. Standing over six feet, four inches tall and with a mastery of thirteen languages, it is not surprising that he impressed all the people he met – in 1773 Dr Johnson's friend Fanny Burney said that 'Mr Bruce's grand air, gigantic height and forbidding brow awed everyone into silence – he is the tallest man you ever saw . . . *gratis.*' Even today when men walk on the moon or sail single-handedly across the world's oceans, Bruce's two-hundred year old account remains an enthralling read. But despite the survival instinct which protected him in various foreign scrapes, he died at Kinnaird falling down the stone steps while helping a lady to her carriage!

It was during James Bruce's time at Kinnaird that the greatest change in the local area came about. Before the arrival of the Carron ironworks in 1759 the scattered population were mainly engaged in agriculture with the occasional interesting exception. One of these was identified back in the late 1950s when workers were removing sand in the vicinity of the mansion of Stenhouse. They stumbled on the remains of a considerable pottery with the remnants of at least eight kilns for making pitchers and general pots from local clay which have been dated to the early 1500s. The scale of production suggests more than a local market and it is likely that the products were carried by the Carron and Forth to all parts of central Scotland and possibly beyond. If so, then the little harbour at Quarrolshore, later named Carronshore by the Company, which had a well-established export trade in coal to the Continent, might well have been the port of departure. By the early eighteenth century there was a boat-building yard and several ropeworks, a semi-official 'customs house' called the King's Cellar . . . and the usual successful smuggling trade! With the support of Thomas Dundas, the local laird, the port was beginning to challenge the supremacy of Airth and had already established itself as the staple port for the town of Falkirk, displacing the Pow at Abbotshaugh which had served since the medieval period. By the mid eighteenth century there were thirty or more dwelling houses along with the usual range of shops, inns and warehouses, but this steady growth was as nothing compared to what was to follow with the opening of the ironworks in 1759. The huge demand for raw materials and the need for an outlet for their products led Samuel Garbett, one of the founding partners of Carron Company, to establish a private shipping company in 1763, managed by his son-in-law, Charles Gascoigne. The firm soon monopolised trade in and out of Carronshore at the expense of other operators, which caused considerable ill feeling, but such was the power of the Company that Garbett and Gascoigne had their own way. Two years later Gascoigne secured the lease of the harbour and began the construction of a new wharf, with cranes, warehouses, stores, smithies and a graving dock for building and repairing their fleet of ships. Downstream the River Carron was straightened to allow larger ships to reach the harbour and waggonways were laid beween Carronshore and the works to carry finished products for onward shipping to the world-wide Carron markets. As trade expanded the Company brought in more and more workers and settled them in new houses at the north end of the village, so that by the 1780s the population was over 700. And for the leading man there was a fine new house as well.

Gascoigne decided that the site overlooking the great loop in the river was an ideal place to live and had the grandiose and very expensive Carron House built close to the new Carron Wharf around 1770. It did not survive long after his hasty departure for Russia, being almost destroyed by fire in the early nineteenth century, and today it survives as a ruin incorporating a rebuilt house on a much smaller scale. Although Garbett's shipping company collapsed the port continued to prosper despite the building of the Forth and Clyde Canal and the emergence of Grangemouth from the 1770s. However this did not last and by the mid nineteenth century the Carron Company had transferred its business to the new port and Carronshore went into decline.

Elsewhere in Falkirk district, the impact of Carron was similar and this has already been discussed in Chapter 8 and need not be repeated here. Suffice to say that it was the Larbert area which bore the immediate brunt of the great enterprise and was inevitably changed beyond recognition. The centre of gravity of the parish moved eastwards and Stenhousemuir began to grow in size and importance and the social tensions began to show. In 1762, just three years after the arrival of the Company, the kirk session of Larbert recorded that there was 'a report going round of Robert Turnbull, Innkeeper at Quaroleshore, his endeavouring to seduce some young girls into the Company of some rude people belonging to the Carron Company.'

As the years passed more and more of the offenders called to answer for their misdemeanours were described as hands or wrights or even sailors working for the company. But these minor moral lapses were as nothing compared to the widespread poverty and suffering which followed the rapid expansion of iron founding and coal mining in the area. At Quarrol and Kinnaird for example, the Dundas and Bruce lairds took advantage of Carron's high demands to secure their fortunes at the expense of the wretched colliers tied to their backbreaking labours. It was a problem that neither church nor state seemed willing or able to tackle – in Larbert, as in every other part of Scotland, as industrialisation increased the profits of the few,

84. Larbert Old Parish Church, built in 1820 to replace an earlier building which stood in the graveyard shown here

whose great wealth stood in sharp contrast with the misery of those who laboured at their pits and furnaces. Instead, the money went to build or improve fine mansions for both entrepreneurs and ancient local families and, in 1820, to a fine new church at Larbert, designed by David Hamilton of Falkirk Steeple fame, which has continued to grace the parish for the best part of two centuries. As with Carron Company, the establishment of the great Falkirk Trysts at Stenhousemuir in 1785 has already been discussed in an earlier chapter and there is little more to add here except to stress the further dislocation which such enormous events must have had on a small parish and the additional work and money which they brought into the area.

When the Church of Scotland began to break up in the eighteenth century a number of seceders from Larbert and Stenhousemuir found their way to the new Erskine Church in Falkirk. No new congregation was formed in Larbert for another century until the 1843 Disruption led the Revd John Bonar, the evangelically minded parish minister, to quit his church and manse and lead a large part of his congregation into the new Free Church. That first Sabbath he preached in a tent borrowed from the Falkirk Relief Church which was pitched on the site in Stenhousemuir where the first Free Church was built the following year. It was a plain and simple building costing just £700 and it served the congregation until 1900 when its successor, the present Larbert East Church of Scotland was built on the same site.

The Original Seceders, by now the United Presbyterians, were keen to extend their own mission to the new industrial areas and this led to the opening of Carron Church in 1878 and the establishment of a Larbert UP congregation twenty years later at Burnhead, now Larbert West. By the time they had a new church building, the union at national level meant that the parish now had three United Free churches. The established church was very slow to recognise that it was a long way from the people, but finally, in 1900, a new building was planned in Stenhousemuir, ostensibly as a memorial to the fifty years' service of the Revd John McLaren. Designed by the celebrated architect, John James Burnet, the McLaren Memorial Church, later called Stenhouse Church, and now Stenhouse and Carron, was opened for worship in 1900.

The early history of education in Larbert mirrors the experience of most rural parishes in the days following the Reformation. At some stage the national church's demand that a school be provided in every parish was answered in Larbert by the establishment of classes for children in the church building itself. Later there was an inadequate schoolhouse built on the site of the present church halls and the kirk session records, which survive from 1699, report early difficulties with the heritors in providing enough money for both school and master. There was trouble too with the teachers, and at least two were dismissed for immorality or being 'slothful, negligent and drunk to the detriment of the children's learning'. By the middle of the eighteenth century the parochial school, legally maintained by the heritors, had moved to Stenhousemuir, while the kirk session supported a second school in Larbert village. The money for this came from funds gathered at the church door on Sundays or from the fines levied on Larbert offenders whose regular appearances for fornication, Sabbath breaking and drunkenness ensured no shortage of cash for a worthy cause. By the 1790s there were additional schools at Kinnaird colliery and Carronshore, and nearly 200 children in a rapidly expanding parish of 4,000 people were attending for at least part of the week. Half a century later the numbers were more than doubled, but the minister of the parish was less than happy about the support given by some of the parents who withdrew their children at an early age because 'colliers, moulders and others are enabled to turn their children's labour to profitable account at the age of twelve years.'

It was just one more facet of the new industrial world into which the people of Larbert and Stenhousemuir were catapulted from the beginning of the nineteenth century. Developments mirrored those taking place elsewhere in Falkirk district with agricultural reform followed by improvements in communications. The arrival of the Scottish Central Railway in 1848 and the village's subsequent importance as a junction – the 'Constantinople of the Scottish railways' said one observer – provided the impetus for a wide range of new industries which appeared as the century progressed.

In the late 1830s one Thomas Jones had established a timber business in Camelon where he eventually became mine host at the Union Inn. His son James worked for a time in Fairbairn's nail-works and in 1864 established his own nail-making business at Port Downie, extending it to include the production of other ironware. He formed a partnership with his brother-in-law, James Forbes, whose brother Peter joined with Major Robert Dobbie and others to create Dobbie, Forbes and Company in 1872, with premises in Larbert. Three years later James Jones opened a sawmill on a site next door to the new foundry. And under the careful hand of the 'grand old man', the firm expanded to become one of Scotland's leading timber merchants, with over forty different premises across the country. Everything from simple window frames by the tens of thousands to the timbers of Captain Scott's ship *Discovery* came from the Jones yard and a century and a half later the company continues to thrive.

James Jones had not completely severed his connection with the iron industry and in 1888 he formed a partnership with Dermont Campbell, the Dobbie Forbes cashier, in a foundry that bore their names until its recent closure. By then, of course, iron mania had swept through the whole of the Falkirk district. The village's first venture already mentioned was the Larbert Iron and Stove Works of Dobbie-Forbes which was by then employing over 200 hands. The firm are probably best remembered in the village for the handsome public hall which Major Robert Dobbie of Beechmount presented to the people in 1900, partly as as a memorial to those lost in the wars in South Africa. The company became part of the Allied group, later Glynwed, in 1934 and, like Jones and Campbell, survived until recent years, when the decline which had closed all the Falkirk foundries finally caught up with them. The same fate befell the last iron foundry to open its doors. As late as 1927 when other ironfounders in the district were preparing to band together for survival, Robert Taylor started Muirhall Foundry, a completely new venture in the village. Judicious management and regular modernisation ensured its survival against the tide of closure until it succumbed in 2005.

Not all the new enterprises were iron-based. In order to supplement the earnings of her husband Andrew, an aerated water and confectionery salesman, a Mrs McCowan began to sell toffee from the window of her house in Stenhousemuir. It was soon more popular than the lemonade and the family took to working full-time in the sweetie business. Together, Andrew and his son Robert turned Highland Cream Toffee and the famous cow into a huge national institution and established a factory in the Tryst Road. It continues today as part of a national group, but retains its own unique identity and is still part of the fabric of village life, despite recent scares.

Another development which in its own particular way put Larbert on the national map was the Scottish National Institution for the Education of Imbecile Children established at a cost of £13,000 in the 1860s on more land bought from the Stenhouse estate. At around the same time on a nearby site the £20,000 Stirling District Lunatic Asylum opened its doors and for more than a century the two provided through changing times for those unfortunate enough to suffer from mental handicap or illness. These were enormous undertakings, with huge numbers of patients living in great Victorian baronial style buildings as was the fashion of the times. The word 'Royal' was added during the First World War and the RSNH was born. 'Larbert Asylum' became Bellsdyke Hospital as a new age wrestled with the difficulties of providing adequate care and security without creating a world of isolation and despair cut off from and misunderstood by the community beyond the high walls. The modern world continues to search for a solution and, at the time of writing, the 'care in the community' initiative has brought about a significant reduction in the number of patients in both hospitals, though not without a feeling that many are less well served by the new system than the one that is now all but consigned to the history books. The buildings are being demolished or sold and a modern industrial 'park' has appeared on the Bellsdyke Road along with many new houses. More are promised!

Back in Victorian Larbert the new captains of industry, like Dobbie and Jones, built superb villas in the village, many of which have survived to serve the community in different capacities. Kinnaird, rebuilt for the third time in the 1890s, Torwoodhall, Beechmount, Carronvale and Carrongrange among others remain as a small reminder to today's villagers of the splendour of their local heritage as well as the sweat and struggle of the working men whose hard labour paid for most of the grandeur.

The passing of the Education Act in 1872 brought pressure in Larbert for better school provision, not least because the three existing buildings, the Parochial School in Muirhead Road, by then called Larbert Public School, the Free Church School, known as Stenhousemuir Public School and the Village School were old, small and quite inadequate for education in the modern era. This is not the place to recount the in-fighting and wrangling that dominated the discussions before a final decision was taken to build the fine new Larbert Central School which opened in 1886 at a cost of nearly £8,000. Suffice to say that there were many harsh words exchanged by the leading

men in the community and the *Falkirk Herald* had a field day.
The new building provided both primary and secondary
education and in 1948 became Larbert High School. The
two public schools were closed but the village school survived
and was provided with its own new building in 1891.

In the last decades of the nineteenth century the annual
cattle trysts slowly declined in importance, so that by 1900 they
were effectively dead. Long before the final cow was presented
for sale much of the huge area between Bellsdyke Road and the
Main Street was given over to other activities. In 1881, for
example, it became the Ochilview home of Stenhousemuir
Football Club, known to all as the 'Warriors', a team which
survives today and still generates a loyalty as fierce as that
found in Falkirk. One claim to fame is that the very first
floodlights in Scottish football history shone in Stenhousemuir
in 1951; sadly the teams' performances have never grabbed the
headlines in the same way. Even before the arrival of the
Warriors, Stenhousemuir Cricket Club had settled in their
Tryst Road ground and in 1885 a group of local golfing
enthusiasts met in the Plough Hotel to form Larbert Tryst
Golf Club, the first one in Falkirk district. Elsewhere in the
village, bowling was the preferred choice of many: the first club
opened in 1867 and several more were formed in the decades
which followed.

The arrival of the trams in 1905 helped draw Larbert and
Stenhousemuir closer to the other parts in the district, and
especially to Falkirk, with its array of shops and entertain-
ments, and there were more than a few who feared for the
independence of their village. They had good reason to fear,
since the burgh councillors, fresh from their success in annexing
Camelon had turned their eyes to Carron, Carronshore,
Larbert and Stenhousemuir as the next target. The 1912
proposal to remove the villages from Stirling County and
absorb them into Falkirk was resisted by a group of influential
men supported by Carron Company, conscious no doubt that
the bugh rates were higher than the county ones. This 'no'
campaign, led by James Jones, the Larbert ironmaster, won
widespread support and when the battle was over he was

presented with a very handsome illuminated address in thanks
for his part in the victory.

   The twentieth century story of Larbert and Stenhousemuir
mirrors that of most of the district: deprivation and loss in two
world wars marked by the names of 282 men from 1914–18 and
80 men and nursing sister Agnes Young from 1939–45, en-
graved on the memorial at the Dobbie Hall; slow decline and
closure of the main industries, realignment of streets, demolition of old buildings and 1960s replacements that are themselves facing the wrecker's ball in the near future. The old
Larbert High School has gone, replaced by the ultra-modern
building across the road. Beside it is Carrongrange, a new
special school replacing the long-serving Dawson Park in
Bainsford. Of the five Church of Scotland congregations which
were finally reunited in 1929, only Carron is gone, closed in
1963. How long the other four will retain their independence is
a matter for speculation. In 1935 a new Catholic Church, Our
Lady of Lourdes and St Bernadette, opened for worship in the
Main Street and there is also a new Baptist church opened in
2000 on the site of their previous building, the former Larbert
Village School.

   The population rise has continued and the number of new
houses to the north of the village has alarmed those who wonder
if the infrastructure of schools, roads and vital services will
manage to cope. There is an upside to this of course. The new
arrivals, often young people with families, bring with them
energy and vitality and are often the ones most willing to fight
to keep community activities alive and thriving. They have a
fine tradition to build on and a proud history to live up to.

Airth and Dunmore

The villages of Airth and Dunmore lie north of Falkirk on the
River Forth. Airth Castle stands at the south end of a plateau,
rising some sixty feet above the carse lands, and the original
village, now long disappeared, lay north of the castle, high
above the flood plain of the river. In 1128 the church and
church lands were given by King David I to the Augustinian

Canons of Holyrood Abbey and it appears that the village was raised to the status of a Royal Burgh around the end of the twelfth century, though this seems to have lapsed some time thereafter. Descriptions of the medieval settlement suggest that it consisted of the castle, church and one long and several short streets in a grid pattern. At this time the resident family appear to have been the original 'de Erths' who in 1240 are said to have held lands in Elphinstone and Plean as well as Airth.

However Airth is most often associated with the Bruce family who make their first appearance in 1452 when Alexander Bruce of Stenhouse feued some land from Holyrood. Thirty years later the castle was badly damaged following the Battle of Sauchieburn in 1488 and was replaced by the present structure by Alexander's grandson, Robert Bruce of Airth. During the reign of James IV (1488–1513) the pow of Airth which had long been an important harbour was chosen as the site of the royal dockyards in which the great wooden ships of the Scottish navy were refitted using large quantities of oak carted down from the Royal forest of Torwood. These included the *Margaret* and the *James* and possibly also the most famous, the *Great Michael*.

85. Airth Castle from a nineteenth-century engraving

The extraction of coal and the making of salt as well as agriculture and fisheries brought a measure of prosperity to the village and in 1597 it was made a burgh of barony. The mercat cross, described as 'the heidless croce', which stood until recently in 'high' Airth probably dates from this time. Twenty years later financial difficulties meant that the castle and lands were sold by the Bruces to the Livingstons and then in 1632 to the Mentieth family. A year later Willam Graham of Mentieth was created Earl of Airth, a title which survived only until 1694 by which time the estates had long since returned to Bruce hands. A judicious marriage by Alexander Bruce allowed him to acquire the estate which his father had been forced to sell. In 1717, two years after the failed Jacobite rising, Alexander's daughter, having backed the wrong side, was forced to sell again and the Bruce estates passed into the hands of James Graham, Judge-Admiral of Scotland with whose family they remained for over two centuries.

The earliest surviving part of the present Airth Castle, the south-west tower, dates from the late fifteenth century. However, there were probably at least two previous buildings. During the Wars of Independence, if we are to believe Blind Harry, William Wallace attacked the castle of Airth and rescued his uncle, the priest of Dunipace. Following the Bruce takeover of the estates in the mid fifteenth century the castle seems to have been rebuilt only to be destroyed thirty years later following Sauchieburn. The tower was extended eastwards in the mid 1500s and in 1581 a new east wing made it L-shaped. It remained like this until the early nineteenth century, when the architect David Hamilton created a new block by filling in the angle of the L with a mock gothic castellated structure which is the familiar face of the present hotel.

The ruined parish church of Airth close to the castle has elements which date to the twelfth century but the bulk of the surviving and rapidly decaying structure is much later. There are three aisles, Airth (*c.*1480), Elphinstone (1593) and Bruce (1614) and a square tower which was built in the mid seventeenth century as part of a reconstruction of the nave etc. At one time the tower had a slated pyramid-shaped roof. There are several interesting grave inscriptions inside the church and many grave markers in the extensive graveyard. These include three cast-iron mortsafes dating from the body-snatching days and inscribed AIRTH 1831, AIRTH 1832 and AIRTH 1837.

Towards the end of the seventeenth century the population began the move from the village on the hill to the lower ground next to the river. At that period the harbour was much closer to the foot of the hill than it now appears, following the extensive land reclamation of the eighteenth and nineteenth centuries. A new mercat cross dated 1697 was placed in what was now the high street of the burgh and with a thriving trade especially in coal, the port flourished. In the 1720s Mr Johnstone of Kirkland said that the village had 'a weekly market . . . [and] two yearly fairs, there's building a tollbooth and fleshmarket. There are several good houses already built and others building.' There are still many fine houses in the village from the eighteenth century and earlier, though a number have been lost in more recent times by poor stewardship of these precious assets. The failed rising of 1745 dealt a heavy blow to the burgh which was the scene of an exchange between the Jacobite artillery mounted at Airth and Dunmore and government ships in the

86. The new Mercat Cross in the High Street

Forth. The outcome was the subsequent destruction by the navy of many of the ships anchored in and around the harbour of Airth which effectively killed off the mercantile trade and allowed Carronshore and later Grangemouth to take over the business. The driving through of the turnpike road from Falkirk to Stirling in 1817 destroyed the layout of the town, bypassing as it did the High Street and ignoring the established street pattern. The outcome of all this was that Airth became a place to drive through or sail past and its decline as a prosperous centre in its own right accelerated.

A new church was built to the design of William Stirling in 1820 and the original church was abandoned to the elements. The Erskine seceders had a church to the east of the High Street as early as 1809 and after the Disruption the Free Church built another on the east side of the Main Street in the 1840s. Both are now demolished following the reunion of their congregations with the Parish Church. The earliest reference to education in the parish comes in 1661 by which time the school seems to have been in existence for some years, since the session records report that repairs to the seats and windows were to be paid for out of the fines levied on the local 'fornicators'! In that year the heritors provided a new school building but later records suggest that some of them, especially those who arrived afterwards, were reluctant to pay their legal share of the costs involved. In 1683 the session itself had to make good the difference by funding quite a high level of provision including a schoolhouse, a master's house, and even a house for an assistant teacher which were ready two years later. At the same time the elders made strenuous efforts to force parents to send their children to school instead of keeping them at work on the land – a problem which was to continue for much of the next century. In his excellent account of *Education in Stirlingshire from the Reformation to the Act of 1872*, Andrew Bain recalls the efforts of the far-sighted minister of Airth at the end of the seventeenth century, the Revd Paul Gellie, successfully urging his session to make regular visits to the school, to compliment and reward the best pupils with prizes of books for further study. This enthusiasm did not last however, and by the 1840s the Presbytery of Stirling describes the school at Airth as being in a deplorable condition presided over by a master who was 'careless and incompetent'. By this time it was probably housed in the building at the top of The Path which is now an attractive private house called Rosebank. A new school was built in 1906 in Elphinstone Crescent to the design of James Strang and this year celebrates its centenary.

The second important historical settlement in the area is Dunmore, a name which was introduced in the middle of the eighteenth century by the Murray family. For many centuries the estates, fortified tower house and settlement were called Elphinstone from the family which had been in residence since sometime prior to 1338. In that year John of Elphinstone of the famous East Lothian family is present in the area, the husband of 'Marjorie of Airth' who was the daughter of 'William of Airth'. Their son Alexander inherited their title to the estates and the family continued to acquire land in the area, so that by 1503 the holdings were erected into the Barony of Elphinstone and the family were close to the royal court of James IV. The then family head, another Alexander, became the first Lord Elphinstone and fought and died beside the King at Flodden in 1513.

In 1754 John Murray, Viscount Fincastle, heir to the Earldom of Dunmore, purchased the lands of Elphinstone for £16,000 and soon after changed the name to Dunmore, a place in Perthshire associated with his family who were related to the Murrays of Blair Castle. Two years later he succeeded his father as 4th Earl of Dunmore. The principal building on the estate, Elphinstone tower, is now a ruin under severe threat of collapse through weathering and neglect. It was built around 1510 for Sir John Elphinstone and was much altered and enhanced over the years. At one time it had an added extension shown in some early nineteenth century drawings, but this appears to have been demolished sometime after 1836, making room for the construction of St Andrew's Episcopal Church which was completed in 1845. Around the same time the lower part of the tower was converted into a family mausoleum, though modern vandalism prompted the removal of the incumbents to safer resting places. The church itself survived into the modern era but was finally demolished in 1976. For educational purposes Dunmore was part of Airth Parish but the Murrays provided a school for their own area throughout the nineteenth century. In 1875 a fine new building was opened in the model village, now called Moray Cottage. It merged with the public school in Airth in 1917.

One of the main reasons for the new family's investment in the estates was the presence of significant quantities of coal which had been exploited for decades by the Elphinstone family. In his short history of Airth, Steve McGrail quotes one Thomas Tucker who visited the area in 1655 and observed that 'Elphinstone . . . A small toune where there is a pretty store of greate coale shipped far beyond the seas. And though there be never a vessel belonging to this place, yet the Dutch mostly and others choose to lade there because of the goodnesse of the coale and its measure.'

There is a tradition that one of the first beam or 'Newcomen' steam engines erected in Scotland was in place at Dunmore in 1720. New investment from the Murrays increased output and for the next century the Dunmore mines produced steady income for the family and employment for a growing number of colliers drawn to the district. Eventually the pits were exhausted and closed in 1811. Throughout this period agriculture remained the principal activity, assisted by the systematic removal of many feet of peat from the moss of Dunmore. By the 1770s there were thirty families, the celebrated 'moss lairds', settled there on low rentals and clearing the land, which then became highly productive. The other activity associated with Dunmore is, of course, the famous pottery which came to national prominence after Peter Gardner assumed control in 1866. The business had been started at the end of the eighteenth century by his grandfather who was described as a farmer-potter and carried on by his son John who was in charge for forty years. Throughout these decades the product was simple undecorated crockery and tiles using local clays, but Peter Gardner introduced many changes which created an art pottery using imported clays from England to produced majolica ware with special translucent glazes. The patronage of the Earl and Countess of Dunmore with their high society and royal connections put Dunmore on the ceramics map and the London dealers began importing the frogs, toads and teapots which began to decorate the parlours of the great and good. Peter Gardner died in 1902 and the pottery did not survive the loss of his genius. For a time his successors reverted to plainer wares but the firm did not survive beyond the First World War. Today Dunmore Pottery is highly collectable and there are many fine examples in the People's Palace in Glasgow and in the Falkirk Museum at Callendar House.

Back in 1820 the 5th Earl of Dunmore commissioned the architect William Wilkins to build Dunmore Park, a magnificent mansion very similar to Dalmeny House completed a few years previously. It was occupied by the family from 1822 until their departure in 1911 and remained as a private home until 1961. After a short spell as a girls' school from then until 1964 it was abandoned. Although substantial parts of the building were demolished much remains to remind us of its grandeur and of our criminal neglect of our heritage. At the time of writing a new proposal to restore the building for housing is being considered by the planners. It is not the first, of course, but indications are that it will go ahead. We can only hope.

Without doubt the building which has attracted most attention is the Pineapple, a huge representation of the fruit placed above a garden pavilion by John Murray sometime between 1761 (the date which appears on the garden doorway below the fruit) and 1777 when the Earl returned from spells in America as Governor of New York and Virginia colonies. He returned with much wealth and more than a little vanity, and the pineapple, a symbol in the colonies of welcome, may have been his ostentatious celebration of his return to his home. Pineapples were certainly grown here and many of the great houses including Holyroodhouse were among the recipients of what was then a rare delicacy. The Pineapple was restored by the Landmark Trust in 1973 for the National Trust of Scotland and is now a holiday home as well as a much visited and photographed folly.

Before the arrival of the Dunmores the settlement on the River Forth which housed the workers on the salt pans, and later coal-miners, was called Elphinstone Pans. In the mid nineteenth century Catherine Herbert, widow of the 6th Earl, thought it a miserable and unpleasant place and set about replacing the three rows of miners' cottages with an 'English' village with two ranges of arts-and-crafts-style houses on either side of a village green. Over the next few years the present picturesque settlement with school, well, smithy and a number

87. The Dunmore Pineapple (*Photograph by Ronnie Blackadder*)

of vernacular houses was constructed. Most of the work was completed by 1879 when the well was dedicated with the message: 'The School and the Village of Dunmore together with this well built by Catherine Herbert Countess of Dunmore were completed A.D. 1879.' The village is a little gem of a place and many people driving past from Grangemouth to Stirling miss it altogether. The houses are highly prized and expensive as befits one of the prettiest parts of the whole Falkirk district.

For Airth and Dunmore the twentieth century brought a continued decline in employment in basic industries like agriculture and coal-mining, though a new pit in 1912 more or less created the village of Letham with 250 houses built to house the miners and their families. The only other mine operating in the vicinity was a mile or so away at Carronhall. The William or 'Garibaldi', opened in the 1860s, was the biggest of the pits owned and operated by Carron Company, employing 340 men at the turn of the century. The 1920s were a very difficult period for the miners, with lockouts and bitter and ultimately unsuccessful strikes which left the local pits damaged by water and probably shortened the working lives of both men and mines. Letham closed in the 1930s and Carronhall in 1945.

There were still 28 farms operating in the parish in the mid twentieth century though mechanisation meant that jobs were few. Today most of the population travel to work each day in Stirling, Grangemouth and Falkirk and in the last few years the land on which the original burgh of Airth stood on the top of the hill has been developed for housing with a large number of high quality and very expensive houses commanding fine views across the river Forth.

Polmont and Brightons

When the great land holdings of Abbotskerse were broken up after the Reformation the area we know today as Polmont, Brightons and much of the Braes area came into the hands of the Earls, later the Dukes of Hamilton. Indeed, as noted

already, when discussing the Falkirk Trysts, the present Duke
and his predecessors have Lord Polmont as a subsidiary title.
The pasturage and mineral wealth of the area was exploited in
the Hamilton interest for nearly two centuries before the local
residents were strong and numerous enough to persuade the
church authorities to separate them from Falkirk in 1724 and
create a new parish of Polmont. At the time, and for decades
thereafter, the village was little more than a collection of
cottages on the escarpment which sweeps down to the carselands of the River Forth. Here a new church was built in 1731
and probably a school of some kind, close by the mills and
smiddy, which served the farmers of the parish. During the
nineteenth century, long before the bridges at Queensferry
and Kincardine spanned the Forth, all traffic from east to
west and north passed along a road just to the south of
Polmont village. The Laird of Whyteside, who was the feudal
superior of the land, agreed to allow building to take place
along the line of the road, provided the new settlement was
called Bennetstown – the family name! It soon became the

88. Polmont's first church. The ruins remain in the churchyard.

commercial heart of the village with small workshops, houses, schools, stores and inns.

A mile or so to the south, the settlement of Brightons had grown up around a famous sandstone quarry which was in operation as early as the seventeenth century. From here stone was carried by the Union canal to help build Edinburgh's New Town in the 1830s and Falkirk's fine new public buildings twenty years later. The canal encouraged the development of industry and this was given further impetus by the arrival of the Edinburgh to Glasgow railway in 1842. The halt near Brightons was given the name Polmont Station, and slowly but surely the original village, by then known as Old Polmont, Bennetstown, Brightons and Polmont Station began to merge into one coherent settlement.

The wealth generated by industrial success brought to Polmont the usual crop of fine mansion houses and elegant estates. There was Millfield, built by John Millar, chief engineer of the North British Railway Company, and later the home of the Stein family whose fortune came from the manufacture of refractory bricks for the expanding iron industry of the Falkirk district. And there were Polmont Park and Polmont House,

89. Millfield House, one of the finest of the Polmont mansions. It was demolished in the 1960s.

mansions dating back to the late eighteenth century, and Polmont Bank, which served as a nursing home and a hotel. All four were demolished to make way for the post-war housing and commercial developments which have so changed the character of the old village. Others like Parkhill the home of the Gray-Buchanan family, survived, and after a spell as a restaurant it was converted into flats.

The growth of the village was such that by 1844 the original church was too small, 'damp, ill arranged and most inadequate' according to the minister, and the present twin-spired building was erected in its place. The old church, now a picturesque ruin covered in ivy, stands in the kirkyard which, like that of Larbert, is a wonderful place to escape, for a little while, from the bustle of our modern world and find the peace and quiet of the past centuries. What a pity that the ancient graves of Falkirk Old Parish Church were cleared away in the 1960s as part of a misguided attempt to tidy up the town centre. Many of the early stones that once recorded the names of deceased parishoners now lie forgotten under the roadway to the crematorium. In loving memory indeed.

What provision was made for education in the early years of the new parish of Polmont is uncertain, but by 1789 a building was provided by the heritors along with a new master, Thomas Girdwood, who remained in post for well over half a century and served as clerk to the heritors for an incredible sixty-two years. Towards the end of his time, in the 1850s, a new school was erected at a cost of £365, but by that time there were several other establishments offering education of one kind or another. The community centre on the main street was originally a school for ladies, financed by the proprietors of Polmont Park, and there were other girls' schools at Ivybank, and in the Back Row where Miss McPherson taught sewing. Perhaps the most famous educational establishment in the parish was Blairlodge Academy opened in 1843 by Robert Cunningham, a Church of Scotland minister, who also played a significant part in the Free Church breakaway in Polmont in the same year. The new school was for boy boarders and flourished under an innovative and dynamic headmaster, J. Cooke-Gray, who took over in 1874. Modelled on the English public school system it attracted the sons of some of Scotland's wealthiest families, and inevitably, cricket and rugby were the principal sporting activities of the three hundred pupils. But there was an admirable practical strain to the curriculum and an emphasis on science which was unusual for the period. At the turn of the century Blairlodge was the largest school of its kind in Scotland and was the first to use electric lighting on such a large scale: it had nearly 900 bulbs at the time when the people of Falkirk were being shown electric light as a novelty in a church bazaar. The pupils who left Blairlodge entered the privileged world of the Colonial Service, Oxford or Cambridge or the upper echelons of the commercial world. After the death of Cooke-Gray in 1902 the school experienced financial difficulties, and when it was forced to close in 1908 by an outbreak of an infectious disease, possibly measles, it never reopened. The buildings were purchased by the Prison Commissioners in 1911 and shortly afterwards opened as Scotland's first Borstal. It is now of course Polmont Young Offenders Institution.

Polmont today is a dormitory village with many new houses standing in what were once the grounds of the lost mansions. The people travel to the petrochemical complex at Grangemouth or commute daily to Glasgow and Edinburgh to work, and village life and community spirit are difficult to generate and sustain. But then Polmont is no different in this regard from many other parts of a district much changed by the demands of a very different and sometimes difficult world where a job across the road from home is now very rare and a job for life almost non-existent.

Laurieston, Redding and Westquarter

Laurieston, which lies just a mile east of Falkirk on the main road to Edinburgh, owes its origin to the famous Napier family of Merchiston in Edinburgh whose main claim to fame was that one of them invented logarithms and so seriously damaged the well-being of schoolboys for centuries. With a new turnpike road in prospect the importance of the area was increasing when the family acquired some of the farm land of Langton which was then almost empty of people and buildings, and in 1756 began the process of creating a carefully planned model village which they called New Merchiston. They did not stay for long after this, selling the land just six years later to the celebrated Sir Lawrence Dundas of West Kerse, the man responsible for the Forth and Clyde canal. At the time there was little more than a central market square with a few buildings along the main road. However, under its dynamic new owner building work increased and the village grew in size and importance. Soon its name changed to reflect the new arrival, first to Lawrencetown and Laurieston.

As early as 1761, before the change of ownership, an expert nail-maker called John Raybould was brought from England by William Cadell of Carron Company and settled in the village to help establish what was to become the first industrial activity. Within six years there were ten men and thirteen boys engaged in the trade and 'Marchiston', as the records called it, was outstripping Camelon in output. Incidentally Raybould himself was not to profit much by his endeavours – he was executed in 1768 for forging banknotes, thus continuing the tradition of bad behaviour which seems to have been a particular trait among the nailer fraternity!

Over the next few decades village life expanded to suit all tastes with an annual fair, which seemed to consist mainly of drinking and gambling on the one hand, and on the other, an unusual congregation of independent Presbyterians called MacMillanites. By 1821, with the population over 800, a village hall was built and there was a thriving society for gardeners with their own land in the village. At first, most people tended to work in agriculture or at land-related activities like weaving, brewing and distilling – Camelon's Rosebank distillery began life in Laurieston – but there were many coal-miners employed at Laurieston pit as well as the nailers. The population doubled by the 1870s and in 1899 an iron foundry, McKillops was established at Thornbridge. Five years later it was taken over by the Glasgow firm of McDowell and Steven. It survived until 1934. In 1896 a new church was erected at a

90. The dedication of the Laurieston War Memorial in 1920

cost of £1,000 which eventually became the Parish Church. It merged with the old MacMillanite congregation (by then the West Church of Scotland) in 1945 and with Redding and Westquarter in 1980. From 1909 until 1924 the village was linked to the Falkirk tramway system and this no doubt encouraged the villagers to use the shopping and other facilities of their bigger neighbour to the detriment of their own. Nowadays the village, like so many others in the area, is a dormitory with most of the working population travelling to Grangemouth, Falkirk or beyond.

Half a mile to the south-east of Laurieston on rising ground is the village of Redding with the lands of Westquarter lying more or less between the two. When the name Redding first appears in written records in the sixteenth century it refers to an area of land which formed a part of the great barony of Abbotskerse. Following the Reformation the lands passed into the hands of the Hamilton family and in 1672 an Act of the Scottish Parliament records that the Duke and Duchess have 'pertaining to them herittiblie ane little toun called the Redding situat in ane muirish place'. They were given permission to hold weekly markets and annual fairs and collect the tolls and duties and this may have given rise to the first trysts which, as we have seen, were to eclipse all others in Scotland in the following century. This no doubt contributed to the growth of the village but it was the huge expansion in coal mining in the eighteenth and nineteenth centuries which was of the greatest significance for Redding and indeed for most of the other villages in the Braes area.

As we noted earlier the hungry furnaces of Carron ironworks brought prosperity to the coal owners of Redding and elsewhere and miserable working conditions to the growing number of men, women and children, collier serfs, who served them. The colliery emerged badly from investigations into working conditions and the village was the centre of strikes and strife throughout the nineteenth century.

From these battles came the formation of the famous Sir William Wallace Grand Lodge of Scotland Free Colliers established in Redding in 1863 and still going strong today long after the last lump of coal was lifted from the land beneath their homes. Each year they march round the Braes area with bands and flags as a reminder to the watching population of the struggles their forefathers faced in those grim Victorian days. But the marching tradition of the Redding colliers goes back much further than the struggles of the 1850s. At the same time as the Scottish colliers were finally freed from their legal serfdom in the 1790s people had rediscovered the story of William Wallace and it seems likely that around the 500th anniversary of the 1298 battle of Falkirk the local miners began what would become an annual march from colliery to colliery, ending up at Wallacestone where tradition had placed Wallace on the day of the battle. Here they reaffirmed their status as free men and evoked the spirit of the hero to ensure that they remained so. In 1810 they raised the necessary funds to erect the present 10-foot memorial column on the site.

Fifty years later, in 1863, following the battles with their employers described in an earlier chapter, the Redding colliers led by James Simpson constituted themselves as the first lodge of Free Colliers pledged to take up the struggle. They were, he claimed, the natural successors of those ancient brotherhoods whose traditions had been kept alive in Redding and the villages of east Stirlingshire. It was an idea whose time had come. Within nine months there were lodges in Slamannan and Bo'ness, each bearing the name of a Scottish hero from those legendary days – John de Graeme and Robert Bruce – and the movement had spread to the Lanarkshire and Ayrshire coalfields. By the end of the following year there were sixty-five lodges in a network covering the whole Scottish coalfield and uniting miners by the thousand. Some areas like Stirlingshire and Lanarkshire were more enthusiastic than Fife and Midlothian but no area was without its lodge. In Redding the original Wallace marches now became an annual 'demonstration' – a title that remains in use today.

However, elsewhere things did not progress so well. For some years the lodges carried on the fight, but the industry was changing and the influx of large numbers of Irish workers brought division within the colliers' ranks. Many lodges withered away and by the end of the century only the original Redding lodge survived. It continued to demonstrate and when its original role changed and the coal mines closed it continued as a living testimony to the sacrifices of the past. And so it has remained. On the first Saturday of August each year close on a hundred men of all ages, many dressed in tail coats and top hats and linking pinkies with their neighbours, walk for over ten miles through Redding, Shieldhill, Westquarter and Laurieston to the monument at Wallacestone as their forefathers have done for over 200 years.

In the village of Redding by the 1850s the population was nearly 600 and the colliery remained at the top of the local league of coal producers. At the end of the century it was the biggest in the Falkirk district, including the Bo'ness mines which were at that time part of Linlithgowshire. There were

369 underground workers and 91 on the surface compared to Kinneil with 310 and 96 which was the next largest.

As early as 1835 church services were being conducted in a colliery schoolroom by a probationer from the Church of Scotland, but the community had to wait until 1907 for a parish church of its own. In that year the present Redding and Westquarter building was opened and it was later supplemented by services in a hall in Westquarter. Today it serves both communities. The reference to the schoolroom in 1835 is a reminder that with the Polmont Parochial School a long way away and the colliers notoriously reluctant to lose the services of their children during the day, the colliery organised what education there was, though what quantity or quality existed is a matter of conjecture.

It was, however, the tragic events of 1923 that won the village an unwanted place in Scottish mining history. The Redding disaster was one of the worst in the long story of the Scottish coalfield and a devastating event in the life of the whole community. At 5.00 am on Tuesday, 25 September, an inrush of water flooded much of No. 23 pit and by the time the rescue and recovery operation was completed in December the bodies of 40 men had been recovered.

Redding No. 23 pit was operated by the Nimmo family of Westquarter House on a lease from the Duke of Hamilton. The main shaft was on the north bank of the Union Canal to the west of Redding village and the coal was being worked in a southerly direction towards a dyke of hard rock created by an ancient geological fault which separated No. 23 from old abandoned coal workings. These were filled with water but it was believed that the dyke was thick enough to prevent any dangerous inrush. However it transpired that on the abandoned side of the dyke a sump, or chamber had been cut deep into the dyke, making it significantly thinner at that point. This was opposite the Dublin section where coal was being stripped from the dyke. It was at this point that water entered and flooded the pit. There were 66 men trapped in the pit at the time of the disaster and a huge rescue operation was mounted involving pit-rescue teams from all over the Falkirk district and beyond. After five hours 21 men were rescued as they emerged through a old shaft to the south-east called the Gutter Hole. Huge crowds of anxious relatives gathered near the pit-head and teams of divers arrived to examine the flooded workings. On 4th October five men were recovered alive and well, but they were the last.

Over the next days and weeks the bodies of the other men were brought to the surface. Most had been drowned in the first moments of the disaster but eleven had survived for up to 14 days in a dry section of the pit which the rescuers had assumed was full of water. Several of the men had left messages for their families, at first full of optimism that rescue was near, but later despairing of their own futures and those of their families. It is impossible to remain unmoved on reading these scribbled notes from father to son and husband to wife when hope of rescue was gone. The last body was recovered from the main part of the pit in early December, the fortieth man on the fortieth day of the rescue operation. Amazingly, work began again in January 1924.

Within days of the disaster a fund had been established by the Provost of Falkirk and the *Falkirk Herald* and within a year had raised over £60,000, well over £1million at today's values. An official inquiry concluded that the management should not have allowed work to proceed when they were unsure of the conditions and noted that some miners had commented in advance on the unusual amount of water seeping into the pit but that the warnings had been ignored or not conveyed to the management!

Redding No. 23 Pit was finally closed in 1958 and 22 years later a memorial stone was unveiled near Redding Cross with the names of the forty men who lost their lives. In the last few years this stone has been beautifully refurbished with mining scenes etched on a black granite stone. Much of the credit for both the original and new stones must go to Jim Anderson, former Convener of Central Regional Council, and to the members of the Free Colliers whose annual demonstration includes the laying of a wreath at the Redding Memorial.

Today the village is bereft of public buildings of any age or historical importance other than the church already mentioned, but at nearby Reddingmuirhead there are three which remind us of the life and times of earlier generations. The oldest is the Methodist Church which opened for worship in 1873 and is still in use today, and next door, the attractive school building which served the children of the Redding colliers from 1875 until 1910 when it was converted for use as a community centre. Across the road is the co-operative society building of redbrick trimmed with sandstone, known inevitably as the Red House. It dates from the early years of the twentieth century and although today it houses a number of small shops it still bears the clasped hands symbol of the Co-op movement which reflects the solidarity that bound the people of Redding together in times of distress, of which there were many.

On the north side of Redding is its twin village of West-quarter, a name which first appears in the written record in the mid sixteenth century when it is described, not surprisingly, as 'the fourth part of the lands of Redding commonly called Westquarter'. It had already been in the possession of the Livingston family for 150 years by then and remained there until the early twentieth century. The family were closely related to the Livingstons of Callendar and were often involved in the same historic events as their Falkirk cousins. For example, in the mid seventeenth century Sir William Livingston of Westquarter served with his cousin James Livingston of Callendar in the Civil War and was punished by the Kirk Session of Falkirk for his part in the attempt to save King Charles from Cromwell. He is described in the record as 'Sir William Levingstone of Wastquarter, lieutenant-colonel and governor of the toune of Carlyl'.

In 1701 the estate passed to the Livingstons of Bedlormie (a village in West Lothian) and for a few years in the eighteenth century it was in the hands of the Drummonds and then the Napiers before returning to Livingston hands in 1769. Thereafter the family are styled of Bedlormie and Westquarter. The Livingstons, Earls of Callendar, lost their titles and land after the 1715 Jacobite rising and in 1784 Sir Alexander Livingston of Bedlormie and Westquarter tried to claim the Callendar earldom. Although legal opinion was on his side he did not proceed with the claim. The death of his son Thomas in 1853 brought the male line, and the claim, to an end. The first house of which we have any knowledge was built in the early seventeenth century and displayed 1626 and 1648 date stones. The house was described by one observer in the nineteenth century as 'beyond comparison the most picturesque residence in the eastern district of Stirlingshire' though another more local visitor thought it 'an exceedingly rude piece of architecture . . . not improved in appearance either by its plebian coat of faded yellow'! It was demolished in 1884 and the only survivor from the early period is a handsome lectern style doocot bearing the date 1647 and the initials WL for Sir William Livingston and HL for Dame Helenore Livingston his wife. In 1884 a new baronial style mansion was built for Thomas Fenton Livingston, and it survived until the radical redevelopment of the estate in the 1930s. In 1909 the house and estates passed out of Livingston hands and into the ownership of James Nimmo, a Glasgow coal merchant who settled in the

91. Westquarter School: the 'jewel in the crown' of the model village
(*Photographs by Ronnie Blackadder*)

area and whose family firm began working the local coal measures. The Nimmos leased and worked Redding Pit No 23, the site of the disaster of 1923.

In 1934 the mansion was sold for demolition and the estate was purchased by Stirling County Council which created a model village to house the mining families of the village of Standburn where the existing homes were thought to be unfit for human habitation. Over 450 houses were built for a planned population of around 3,000 and there were to be shops and recreational facilities as well as a school. The whole scheme was designed by the architect John A.W. Grant and used the natural features of the glen to create an arts-and-crafts-style 'garden city' environment. The school, designed by the same architect, was recently described by architectural historian Richard Jaques as 'a true child of the Modern Movement . . . It was a huge step forward from the usual rather grim schools . . . the jewel in Westquarter's crown.'

While coal continued to dominate in both Redding and Westquarter there was another industrial development which brought high employment to both communities from the 1870s onwards. This was the factory of Alfred Nobel which lay on the banks of the Union canal in Redding. Here a mainly female workforce made detonators for both military and civilian use until the 1960s when the factory finally closed. There was already a Westquarter Chemical Works making sulphuric acid operated by three partners incuding a George McRoberts, and in 1876 he became Nobel's partner in the new venture. A small factory was established beside the existing works and six workers were engaged to produce the detonators using fulminate of mercury. Incidentally, a century later, when the Union Canal was being refurbished as part of the Millennium Link project, tons of poisonous mercury deposited in the canal during the lifetime of the works had to be removed at huge cost in time and money. Though they may have been careless as far as this aspect was concerned the opposite was true with regard to the danger of explosions. Huts were separated by high grassy banks so that accidental explosion would send the wooden huts – and the workers – up in the air and prevent the whole factory from destruction. Discipline was severe and workers were searched every day lest a stray detonator might find its way out of the gate, and to prevent contamination of the explosive material the whole works was scrubbed down every week with soap and water. With the invention of the electric fuse another valuable product line was introduced and Nobel's thrived . The original 4-acre site was extended to 10 with part on the opposite side of the canal, and by the outbreak of war in 1914 it occupied 15 acres and employed 450. Demand during the war was huge and a further 350 workers were employed to help keep the army supplied with the necessary explosives for all manner of bombs and shells. Between the wars there was a predictable decline with much of the equipment at Westquarter dismantled and moved to Ardeer in Renfrewshire. By this time the factory was part of the ICI's Nobel Division. The new war in 1939 brought a return to huge military requirements with an astonishing 1,700 workers engaged on a three shift pattern required to meet the demand. The firm continued in business after the war, producing for a growing export market, but never ever reached the levels of output or employment again. The plant closed in 1969.

The post war history of Westquarter is somewhat mixed, with a period when there was a good deal of vandalism and neglect. In the 1980s the community made strenuous efforts to counteract this, and today the genius of those who designed the model village is still evident in the houses, school and general layout, which includes the beautiful glen through which the Westquarter Burn flows and which maintains some of the characteristics of the the original estate.

Shieldhill and California

Two other villages in the Braes area which are worthy of note are California and Shieldhill which grew up as homes for the expanding mining community in the nineteenth century. But while California has little history beyond the coal boom, Shieldhill is of earlier origin. The land on which both stand was once the common muir of the barony of Polmont and was used to pasture cattle in the summer months away from the land under crops; consequently the name Shieldhill may come from 'shieling'. In the eighteenth century the Falkirk trysts were held on the muir and the fields on the south side of the main street were the site of the 'tented village' which serviced the drovers and their customers. As at Slamannan coal-mining was an early activity which blossomed into an industry with the arrival of Carron which took over ownership and control of the Shieldhill mines. Coke was manufactured on site and carted with the coal the six miles northwards to the ironworks. The village was home to the miners and their families and remained the same until the decline and closure of the 1950s. The present church, now named Blackbraes and Shieldhill Parish Church was built in 1864 as a Free Church to the design of the celebrated Falkirk minister the Revd Lewis Hay Irving. Shieldhill has a modern primary school and, like most of the Braes, has many new houses for its growing population who work in Falkirk, Grangemouth and further afield. The village of California began as a cluster of miners' rows in the middle of the nineteenth century and one imagines that the name was introduced by the miners whose black gold reminded them of the American gold rush of 1849. The settlement grew up near the old village of Blackbraes and when a mission church was built in 1865 it took that name, as did the primary school which, in the modern era, served as a further education centre. Both are long since demolished. California might well have gone the same way as Blackbraes but somehow it survived the closure of the pits and is now a highly desirable place to stay, with a school built in 1916 and many fine new houses.

Maddiston

Muiravonside parish was formally disjoined from Falkirk in 1641, though the area, which included both the Livingston castle of Almond and the ruined pre-Reformation Priory of Manuel, had been 'semi-independent' for half a century. The arrival in 1838 of the Slamannan Railway line at Causewayend on the Union Canal brought a hive of activity as cargoes were stored, loaded and transferred between barge and rail wagon. The rural tranquillity gave way to a mass of rail lines, stores and quays which were further extended in 1855 when the Falkirk lawyer James Russel opened the Almond Ironworks nearby. This short lived but highly profitable venture involved the manufacture of pig iron in three blast furnaces, but by 1879 it was closed and a decade later the buildings were demolished. Despite these developments the principal settlement in the parish was, and remains, the village of Maddiston which is recorded as early as 1424. A century later part of 'Mawdestoun' was in the hands of a man called John Knollis, described as a burgess of Linlithgow. Coal-mining was an early occupation and hewers, coalheughs and 'sinkis' appear in several charters from the beginning of the sixteenth century. A report of 1723 says that 'The village of Maduston stands . . . half a mile southwest from the Kirk – here are good coal pits'. The demand from Carron Company brought the familiar rapid expansion in production and for a time there was also iron-ore mining in the area. The Parish Church of Muiravonside was a mile away to the east, and it was 1904 before the village had its own place of worship with the opening of the Cairneymount Church high up at the south end of the village. It is a handsome building designed by James Strang of Falkirk but today it lies empty.

At the opposite end of Maddiston, to the north, Rumford grew as a mining community with a large Irish immigrant population. It had a separate Catholic church as early as 1891 and still has, despite closures and mergers elsewhere. Although stone quarrying was another important occupation in the Maddiston area in the nineteenth century, coal mining continued to dominate well into the modern era. When the inevitable decline came, after 1945, the expansion of the pre-war Smith family transport business helped to offset the loss of jobs as the mines closed and the farms reduced their labour forces. By the early 1960s the firm had 370 lorries on the road with 'Smith of Maddiston' emblazoned on their sides, carrying goods and the name of the village, to all corners of Britain. In 1968 Smith's became part of the United Transport group and the Maddiston base slowly

declined until today there is no trace of the once mighty undertaking beyond collectable models of Smith's lorries which still
command high prices at antique fairs!

Today Maddiston is home to a lively community of over
3,000, although most people work outside the village. The
headquarters of the Central Fire Brigade are located there
though the building hardly adds to the beauty of the surroundings. House building is the main development activity, as the
whole Braes area, born of the Forth Valley's need for coal
becomes instead a residence for its working population.

Slamannan and Avonbridge

The medieval parish of Slamannan lies six miles or so to the
south of Falkirk on a plateau 500 feet above the carse lands of
the River Forth. Of all places in the district it has provided
place-name speculators with the greatest opportunity to exercise their fertile imaginations. You can choose from a variety
of exotic derivations including a Pictish God called 'Treman-
na', the 'Mannau' home of the famous Gododdin tribe, the
Gaelic for 'Blind Man's Valley' or even a local saying that the
unyielding soil of the muir would 'slay man and mare'! Whatever the truth, and it is likely to be far more prosaic than these
four, we can be certain that the parish and the settlement
around its church, are very ancient and existed by the end of
the eleventh century when the parochial system evolved in
Scotland. The church was dedicated to St Lawrence and as late
as the end of the eighteenth century the parish was still
occasionally referred to by this name. Nearby, at the River
Avon crossing, are the remains of a fortified mound called a
motte which probably dates to the twelfth century and may
have had some kind of structure on top. This no doubt was
constructed by the leading family in what was by then the
barony of Slamannan. The Malherbs, Sandilands and Livingstons are recorded over the centuries as barons of Slamannan
and agriculture seems to have been the only activity of the
scattered population. In 1730 the parish was increased in size
by the addition of a large area north of the River Avon which

had been part of the huge parish of Falkirk. Typically this triggered the usual Scottish enthusiasm for disputation followed by prolonged litigation. This time it only took until 1940 to settle the case with a £50 payment from Falkirk to Slamannan. Two centuries and a bit – not too bad really!

The industrial revolution changed everything for Slamannan as it did for so many of the Braes communities. From the mid eighteenth century coal was being carted northwards, down the hill, to Falkirk and on to Carron ironworks, a considerable journey across rough and ready roads. Little wonder that, when the technology allowed, one of the first places to be served by a steam railway was Slamannan. From 1840, when the line opened, the local coal industry boomed and remained the major activity in the area until the early decades of the twentieth century. All over the district, pits with names like Binniehill, Bawbee, Wet Meg, Klondyke and Nappyfaulds were established, each with a rail link to the new network. The village expanded in size as more and more miners were attracted to the area with new houses, shops and inns as well as a new church built in 1810 to replace the pre-Reformation building which was in poor condition. A miners' co-operative was established and the village had gas lighting installed as early as 1855. Slamannan was awash with churches with the Methodists, Burghers and the Evangelical Union vying with each other to save the souls of the miners and their families. The great 1843 'Disruption' added another and caused a considerable stramash when the entire congregation of the Parish Church left to form a Free Church in the village. The two remained apart until 1929 and by 1948 they were once again joined as a single congregation using the old Parish Church. In the meantime the arrival of many Irish families during the mining boom to the little settlement of Limerigg further south had led to the first Catholic chapel and school in the parish but they did not survive the decline in coal production when the families moved away.

The turn of the century saw the heyday of the village life with football teams galore, bands, a Masonic lodge and numerous community activities which helped to mitigate some of the

92. The main street in Slamannan with the clock-monument Boer War memorial

effects of the desperate working and living conditions which were the lot of mining communities everywhere. Fifty-two local men died on active service in the First World War and afterwards those who returned found the employment situation much changed.

Technical problems in the mines, followed by a reduction in demand, led to a rapid fall in output and inevitable closure. Although mining did continue on a small scale, the days of secure employment in the Slamannan pits were over. There was a movement back to agriculture among the people who remained, but even here the introduction of mechanisation ensured that relatively few would find long-term employment. The railway closed down and with it went the sense of connection with the wider world. To the people of Falkirk, Slamannan seems a long way away and no doubt the people of the village feel much the same. Nowadays the village is, like so many others, a commuter dormitory, but its location and history are attractive to those who like the idea of living away from the bustle of the valley below. What they think of the recurring rumour that a future central Scotland airport might be sited nearby is not recorded . . . yet!

The other main settlement in the parish, Avonbridge, lies three miles or so to the east of Slamannan village. Its history is very different from its neighbour and it was geography rather than mineral wealth which determined its growth and importance. The bridging of the River Avon towards the end of the sixteenth century probably created small settlements on both sides of the river which hardly deserved the description 'village' and indeed the name 'Avonbridge' is not recorded before the nineteenth century. The south side is called by variations of the names Bridgend and Dalquhairn, and the bridge became a crossing place and overnight stance for drovers taking cattle south from the trysts at Falkirk. There were a number of mills in the locality and agriculture was the only significant activity until the railway age, when the village began to grow with some coal mining developing, though not on any significant scale.

There was a Burgher Church here on the north side of the river by 1804 and this was replaced by the present building in 1890, by which time it was home to a United Presbyterian congregation. They rejoined the Church of Scotland in 1929. The village had a second church built in 1869 for the Evangelical Union and it also remains as a Congregationalist church linked to Grahamston United in Falkirk. The other noteworthy building in the area is the Grey Rigg Inn with its distinctive wall mural showing a coach and horses.

In the modern era, with coal mining ended, some jobs were provided by Avonbridge brickworks which operated from the early 1950s about a mile or so to the east. Known to the locals as the 'tinplate' for some reason, it closed in 1977. Today most of the villagers who are not employed in agriculture or local services must travel to Falkirk, Grangemouth or Bathgate for work and the village is an attractive rural residential community.

CHAPTER 16

Today and Tomorrow

In March 2000 Falkirk celebrated its 400th birthday. 'Falkirk 400' was a grand bash in the town centre as the population were reminded of that first burgh charter from King James VI to Alexander Livingston of Callendar in 1600. But it was more than just an opportunity for street theatre, music and general goodwill to all bairns, including a few pints of Brian Flynn's specially brewed 'Falkirk 400' ale! It was a reminder that in the new world, whether we like it or not, heritage can be a major engine of economic recovery if it is used effectively. This recognition is one of the most significant changes in the life of the community and nothing illustrates it better than the success of the Millennium Link and especially the spectacular Falkirk Wheel.

This project, which caught the imagination of the public and brought national, even international attention to the district was the restoration of the Forth and Clyde and Union Canals which had lain unused and unloved for over three decades. This was to be one of a number of major projects across the UK to mark the Millennium and the announcement in 1994 was greeted with delight, especially by enthusiasts in the canal societies, of whom there were many. They, more than anyone, had battled for years for this day and their jubilation was understandable. But there were some who felt that the estimated £100 million should be spent on other worthy causes and their scepticism mounted as the huge civil engineering programme got under way. The disruption caused to the travelling public, especially at Camelon, Bainsford and Bonnybridge, where important roads crossed the waterway upset many a weary motorist, but as the new locks and bridges with their distinctive logo began to appear the mood changed to one of anticipation and support. In Grangemouth however, there was disappointment. Here, in the community that owed its birth in 1768 to the canal, the people found themselves by-passed by the restored link. The planners certainly had a problem since the last three miles of the canal from the original junction with the River Carron in the old town back to Abbotshaugh had been filled in in the late 1960s and replaced by Dalgrain Road and several factory buildings. Restoring the old route was deemed too expensive as was an imaginative proposal to extend the canal from Abbotshaugh via the old railway line into Grangemouth and a meeting with the River Forth through the Carron Dock. This would have brought Grangemouth fully into the scheme and held out the promise of marina-style development in the town. But the extra millions were not forthcoming and in the end British Waterways settled for the reopening of the old Carron Company cut from canal to river well to the west of the low-span Kerse Bridge which boats and barges would have to negotiate before entering the new waterway. The tidal mouth of the Carron was another potential problem and few thought the decision a sensible or a permanent one. However, it allowed the project to be completed more or less on time and on Saturday 26 May 2001 the Forth and Clyde Canal was declared officially open from east to west. There were celebrations along its length but there remained one missing piece required to complete the Millennium link.

When the Union Canal was completed in 1822 it was connected to the Forth and Clyde Canal by a series of eleven locks descending 110 feet to Port Downie near Lock 16. The declining use of the canal system in the twentieth century brought eventual closure and the removal of the link in the 1930s. One of the major challenges facing British Waterways in 1994 was 'the creation of a link between the two canals at Falkirk, providing an opportunity to build a new landmark as a symbol for the new millennium'. The idea of a rotating boat lift emerged during the planning stages and by early 1998 the main operational principles were established, though the lift itself as then envisaged looked more like a fairground wheel. It was not the twenty-first century image demanded by the promoters and soon afterwards the now familiar futuristic Falkirk Wheel emerged as the preferred solution.

Employing a boat lift like the wheel meant reducing the distance – both horizontal and vertical – between the two waterways, and this was achieved by constructing a new section of the Union Canal which extended it by just under a mile westwards. After dropping down through two new high locks the extended waterway turns north before entering a 160-yard tunnel under the Edinburgh–Glasgow railway and the Antonine Wall. It was the first canal tunnel constructed in Britain for a century. Emerging on the north-facing slope the canal is carried on a 330-yard long aqueduct resting on five huge piers, to the 114-foot diameter wheel. Two caissons within the wheel, each holding 24,000 gallons of water, carry boats up and down simultaneously between the two canals, a journey that takes

93. The Falkirk Wheel (*Photograph by Ronnie Blackadder*)

15 minutes. The various elements of the wheel were fabricated by the Butterley Engineering Company in Ripley, Derbyshire, and brought north for assembly and installation. The whole system, which alone cost some £17 million, was completed by a large basin linked to the Forth and Clyde canal, and the predictable Visitor Centre.

On 24 May 2002 the wheel was officially opened by the Queen, since when it has attracted many thousands of visitors and won several awards including being named by the Saltire Society's Civil Engineering Award Panel as the finest project in Scotland during the 25 years of their annual award. Now all that remains is for the powers-that-be, both private and public, along the length of both canals, to provide the kind of attractions and services that will draw people here where they can experience something of the history and beauty of this part of central Scotland.

But this new appreciation of the importance of our heritage did not stop the loss of important parts of it! Buildings continued to fall below the bulldozers for a whole variety of reasons, some of them genuine but many more because, as ever, money talks louder than common sense. The 100-year-old classical building in West Bridge Street, for example, built originally as the Falkirk headquarters of Stirling County Council, but latterly the Police Station, was demolished in 2001 despite undertakings to preserve the façade at least. There was no argument about the need for a new police station, nor that the listed building had suffered from years of neglect and would be costly to repair. The debate centred on whether a town with an aspiration to become an attractive place for visitors was willing to fight to preserve a handsome piece of its Edwardian inheritance or not. It was not. The same was true of the beautiful Grange School and the YMCA building in Grangemouth, the old parochial school in Stenhousemuir and many others.

And then there was the great burning schools mystery. In the 1990s the Council had announced its intention to replace Woodland's High School (the old Falkirk High in Rennie Street), Graeme High School in Callendar Road and Larbert

High School with 'purpose built for the new Millennium' schools on new sites using the so-called Private Finance Initiative method of funding. This caused something of a political row with many people concerned that their grandchildren would still be paying the bills in fifty years' time; but in the end, with some modifications, the plans went ahead and the new schools were opened in September 2000. Woodlands was replaced by the Braes High School in Reddingmuirhead, Graeme High moved a few hundred yards along the Callendar Road and Larbert High crossed to the opposite side of Stenhouse Road near Carrongrange. Although the three new schools have a semi-industrial look there is no doubt that the facilities are much better and that teachers and pupils will benefit greatly by the change. So far, so good. The abandoned sites were to be developed for housing by the consortium which had built the schools, or by others to whom they sold the rights, and applications were made in all cases to demolish the old buildings and clear the sites. The heritage enthusiasts, while recognising that most of the buildings would be lost, nonetheless made noises about saving this bit or that as a tangible reminder of the past. But before any such discussions could make progress, one by one, the buildings burst into flames and, when these died away, demolition was the only safe option. Was it copy-cat vandalism? Or vengeful ex-pupils? Or something else? You may think it, but I couldn't possibly say! What we can say with certainty is that no tangible link with over a century of educational endeavour remains.

Churches too are under threat. Throughout the district buildings continue to be 'surplus to requirements' as the decline in religious observance means smaller congregations cheek by jowl with others in the same plight. Younger readers of this history may be surprised at the amount of space given over to matters religious in the earlier pages, but hopefully the story so far will have convinced them that an understanding of the life and times of this, and every other community in Scotland, is not really possible without an appreciation of the crucial role of the Church. It was at the very heart of almost everything of significance, for good and ill, that happened in the Falkirk area from the arrival of those first missionaries 1,000 years ago. Now things are very different and churches of most denominations struggle to hold on to their members who find other ways of passing their Sundays and new outlets for their energies. Mergers have left buildings empty and several have already been demolished while others have been converted to houses and flats. It is obviously a worrying time for the church members themselves, but lovers of beautiful buildings which grace our towns and villages also watch the changing scene with anxiety. We must, however, resist the temptation to exaggerate the decline. Today in 2006 there are over fifty churches of the main denominations in Falkirk district still operating successfully as well as many well-supported evangelical groups. Thousands of people still attend services each week and the congregations play a very important part in the life of their communities, supporting all kinds of activities from Scouts and Brownies to Boys' and Girls' Brigades. Their role may be very different from the past but they remain a vital part of the fabric of our ever-expanding society.

While historic buildings continued to tumble down, houses were going up at lightning speed all over the district. Throughout the 1990s small schemes and large filled every available space within the built-up area and since then have spread outwards onto that precious green belt beyond. In the eight years from 1997 over 6,000 new houses were completed and the demand seems almost unlimited although the population of the area has increased by less than 3 per cent in the same period. This is due less to population growth than to the change in lifestyle which characterises the modern era with many one-parent families and single young folk anxious to put a toe on the property ladder. Bonnybridge, Larbert and Stenhousemuir and the villages of the Braes area in particular seemed to suffer – if that is the right word – from this phenomenon, but no part of the district was immune from the appearance of hundreds of new homes straining the already over-stretched infrastructure.

In the local educational world there were also significant changes taking place. Between 1975 and 2005 Falkirk Technical College had changed its name twice as further education evolved and the kinds of courses and students reflected the new economic world. Falkirk College of Technology was the first as technical studies went up-market, then plain Falkirk College, as the mix changed to include social care, art and design, sport and recreation as well as more traditional fare, and finally in 2005, Forth Valley College when Falkirk, which had opened a study centre in Stirling in 1998, merged with Clackmannan College to create the fifth biggest college in Scotland. At the time of writing there are over 25,000 students and 850 staff at the three locations and the range of courses, and variety of ways of studying them, reflect not only the huge changes in employment patterns but also the crucial importance of lifelong education in the modern world.

The restoration of the Scottish Parliament in May 1999 after nearly 300 years brought the Falkirk district into the national spotlight in a somewhat unexpected way. For most of the twentieth century the Labour Party were the clear choice of the people in both local and Westminster elections and this preference was cemented by several long-serving and popular MPs like Malcolm MacPherson, who held the Stirling and Falkirk Burgh seat from 1948 until 1974, and Harry Ewing, who succeeded him and then went on to represent Falkirk East until 1992. It would be difficult to exaggerate Harry's popularity in this area both during his time at Westminster and since his elevation to the Lords and retiral. Suffice to say that he was and remains an honorary Falkirk 'bairn', one of the best of men and a true friend of the people he represented. He was for a time one of the key figures in the devolution debate and was delighted by the advent of the Scottish Parliament when it came at the end of the 1990s. The mantle of long-serving local MP had fallen on Dennis Canavan who had represented West Stirlingshire from 1974, then Falkirk West from 1987. He had a reputation as a bit of a firebrand of the political left and over the years had demonstrated that for him, staying true to what you say and what you believe in, was the guiding principle of public life. It was a characteristic that people of all political persuasions admired and when he decided to leave Westminster and opt for the Scottish Parliament his victory in Falkirk was certain. But the national Labour Party blocked his adoption as a candidate because of his reputation as a frank and honest critic of government policy and in the end he was forced to stand as an independent. For a time in 1999 the media flocked to the district to watch the battle between the 'rebel' and the mighty powers-that-be and all kinds of parallels with the past were drawn, from Roman invaders repelled to Wallace's brave fight and Bonnie Prince Charlie's victory. The Falkirk folk, insulted by being told who should represent them, and mindful of their motto, gave Dennis the biggest majority of the 73 constituency MSPs – a position he retained in the second election four years later. His stand has won him many more friends and supporters and he has continued to be an outstanding consti-tuency representative, a doughty campaigner and a familiar figure at all manner of events throughout the area.

One subject close to the heart of Dennis Canavan – and most Falkirk people – was the fate of their beloved football team. While those involved in the successful Millennium Link project were basking in the well-earned praise of the local populace, a proposal which had been bubbling along for two decades or more came to the boil at last. Twice in the space of a couple of years the Brockville bairns had been denied entry into Scottish football's elite because the dear old ground was thought in-adequate for the higher echelons of the modern game. The Catch-22 which faced the club and community was that money for refurbishment could only be raised by selling Brockville to a developer. That would give them some money, but no ground to develop! This is not the place to review the political and financial contortions which followed; suffice to say that after what seemed an eternity of wrangling a fine new and expensive community stadium appeared at last at Westfield on the Grangemouth Road, and in April 2004 the 'bairns' were promoted to their rightful place in the Premier League. Fans had queued to buy bits of the old ground before the demolition contactors arrived and Brockville finally disappeared, the site re-emerging as yet another supermarket, albeit with a décor that reminded shoppers of the magic moments that once thrilled thousands there. The new ground which some locals

94. The new Falkirk Stadium at Westfield (*Photograph by Ronnie Blackadder*)

have dubbed the '*Bairnabeu*' in homage to that other great team in Madrid, has so far only two stands, but given that the team survive in the top flight then others will follow. While most locals were happy there were some dissenting voices but their annoyance was as nothing compared to the wrath which accompanied the great hospital debate.

Few topics have raised the wrath of people in the Falkirk area more than the fate of their beloved infirmary. We have already noted the fantastic community effort in the 1920s which funded the new buildings in Gartcows, and the sense of ownership generated then has remained strong despite nationalisation, rationalisation, regionalisation and the rest. Add to this the centuries-old suspicion that Stirling is forever hell bent on the destruction of all things Falkirk and you have the potent mixture which has fuelled decades of angry exchanges. Over the last ten years or so this has reached fever pitch as health chiefs put forward plans for a single, ultra-modern hospital to serve both communities. With the memory of the transfer to Stirling of the childrens' ward, and then the maternity ward,

95. Health Board Chairman, Ian Mullen, with a model of the Forth Valley Hospital due to open in 2009 (*Falkirk Herald*)

fresh in their minds, Falkirk campaigners of all political shades
and none went to war! There were public consultations, peti-
tions and inquiries and in the end the decision was to build the
new £300-million hospital on the old RSNH site in Larbert.
Such was the tension between the Stirling and Falkirk parties
that the latter thought the decision a triumph and there were
howls of objection from beyond the Forth. The war of words
continued and at the time of writing many services including
accident and emergency have been transferred to Stirling in
anticipation of the final move to the new 800-bed hospital
which is still at the design stage. In May 2006 detailed plans
were unveiled by Health Board Chairman, Ian Mullen, himself
a Falkirk man, and while there are still many reservations,
especially about the funding methods and the element of
privatisation in the proposed staffing arrangements, there
was widespread relief and pleasure that the impressive project
was at last seen to be under way. Work is due to start in 2007
and the promise is a state of the art hospital in 2009. An anxious
wait for action remains.

   Throughout the district the industrial decline continued.
The British Alcan plant in Bainsford reduced to nothing and
closed its doors in 2004, and in Grangemouth the ICI subdivided into several companies of which one has already
disappeared. Even the giant BP refinery and chemical plants
have not been immune from rumours of contraction or even
closure, but at the time of writing the future seems relatively
secure. Only one foundry, Ballantines in Bo'ness, remains and
there have even been closures among new high technology
companies. And yet, as the massive house building programmes and low unemployment statistics suggest, there is
no shortage of money in the local economy. Of course there are
new jobs, nearly 10,000 more than there were in 1997, but not
many of them are in manufacturing industry. At one time nine
out of ten people in the area worked in primary work like
agriculture and mining or in maufacturing. That figure has
fallen now to less than a third, with the rest in the service
sector and the trend is accelerating. The bairn of today is
likely to work in a shop, office or call centre and earn his or her

living as a health carer, administrator, technician or computer operator, and bright new Business Parks across the district are the current magnet for such fresh jobs as there are. The site of the old College in Callendar Park houses one such venture which brought the high-profile Child Support Agency to the town with the welcome opportunities for reasonably well-paid work, though recent action at national level suggests an uncertain future. Another example of what has happened came with the opening of a huge ASDA distribution centre in 2003 on the abandoned Alcan site in Bainsford. This created a staggering 300 new jobs. In Grangemouth the Newhouse Business Park, and Central Park on the Bellsdyke Road in Larbert were created to offer other focal points for small business growth and great efforts have been made to attract inward investment to the area. More recently the scale of the initiatives has increased significantly. 'My Future's in Falkirk' is the campaign slogan adopted by a £23-million partnership involving the Council, BP and Scottish Enterprise, to transform the local economy. The ambitious target is 4,000 new jobs and £200 million of new investment, and early indications are that things are beginning to happen. Another initiative, 'Falkirk Inspired', hopes to convince the world that this is the place to live, work, shop and be entertained, and to complete the hat-trick of slogans we have 'Big in Falkirk' a spectacular spring feast of music and outdoor entertainment which attracts huge crowds of young fans from all over the country to Callendar Park. What the ultimate outcome of all these activities will be is anybody's guess. Technology is changing so fast that it would be a brave forecaster who would attempt to predict the future even with the benefit of a thousand years of historical experience.

The Falkirk of the twenty-first century then seems to be a wealthier and more self-confident place with a growing population and an optimism scarcely justified by the events of the last fifty years or so. Over 200 years ago the town adopted as its motto, 'Touch Ane, touch a', Better Meddle wi' the Deil than the Bairns of Falkirk'. It suggests a proud and independent people ready to band together to protect their town and district. No doubt such resolution will be put to the test many times in the years ahead and the future happiness and prosperity of the area may well depend on the peoples' readiness to live up to their motto. The long and rich history of the district suggests that they will not be found wanting.

Sources and Further Reading

This account of the history of the Falkirk area is based on the work of many antiquarians and local historians, both past and present, whose scholarship has so enriched our understanding of this part of the world. Because it is aimed at the general reader I decided not to pepper the text with footnotes and detailed references but if any reader wants to follow up on any particular point I would be delighted to hear from them and will be glad to help in any way. They can contact me on ianqscott@blueyonder.co.uk or by telephone on 01324 627692. An excellent introduction to the source material held in the Callendar House archives is given in Maria Castrillo's *Researching the local history of Falkirk District* which would be a useful starting point for those interested in discovering more. The following are the sources on the main themes and periods which I have used in this book. Many are long out of print but are available in libraries but a good number are quite recent and are still on sale.

General

Statistical Accounts. Essential sources for all local historical study in Scotland are the Statistical Accounts compiled by local parish ministers and published on three occasions since the last decade of the eighteenth century. The first or *Old Statistical Account* was edited by Sir John Sinclair and published in twenty-one volumes between 1790 and 1799. Fifty years later the exercise was repeated and the *New Statistical Account of Scotland* was the result. The parishes of Stirlingshire appeared in Volume 8 published in 1845. Over a century passed before the last survey was completed as the *Third Statistical Account of Scotland* with the counties of Stirling and Clackmannan being published in Volume XVIII in 1966. These are no dry lists of figures but fascinating essays covering an enormous range of topics; taken together they tell us a great deal about the changing face of Scotland over two centuries.

Calatria, The Journal of the Falkirk Local History Society (24 volumes) 1991–2006

Corbet, L. et al *Central Scotland Land – Wildlife – People* (Forth Naturalist and Historian) 1993

Falkirk Herald 1845–2006

Gifford, J. and Walker, F. A. *The Buildings of Scotland: Stirling and Central Scotland* (Yale) 2002

Jaques, R. *Falkirk and District: an illustrated architectural guide* (Rutland Press) 2001

Kier, R. *History of Falkirk* (Falkirk Monthly Magazine) 1827

Lawson, L. *History of Falkirk* (Falkirk Town Council) 1975

Gillespie, R. *Round About Falkirk* (Maclehose) 1868

Love, J. *Antiquarian Notes and Queries* 4 volumes (Johnston) 1908–1928

Reid, J. *The Place Names of East Stirlingshire* (forthcoming)

RCAHMS, *Stirlingshire* 2 Volumes (HMSO) 1963

Stewart, J. *Falkirk, Its Origin and Growth* 1940

WEBSITE: www.falkirklocalhistorysociety.co.uk

The Romans

Bailey, G.B. *The Antonine Wall* (Falkirk Museums) 2003

Breeze, D.J. *The Antonine Wall: the north-west frontier of the Roman Empire* (Historic Scotland) 2004

Robertson, A.S. *The Antonine Wall* (Glasgow Archaeological Society) 1979

The Medieval Period to the Eighteenth Century

Armstrong, P. *Stirling Bridge and Falkirk 1297–98* (Osprey)

Bailey, G.B. *Falkirk 400* (Falkirk Museums) 2000

Bailey, G.B. *Falkirk or Paradise: the Battle of Falkirk Muir 1746* (John Donald) 1996

Fleming, J. *Ancient Castles and Mansions of Stirling Nobility* 1902

Hunter, D. (ed) *The Falkirk and Callendar Regality Court Book 1638–1715* (Stair Society) 1991

Livingston, E. *The Livingstons of Callendar and their Principal Cadets* (EUP) 1920

McLuckie, J.R. *The Old Kirkyard, Falkirk* (1879)

Nicolaisen, W.F. *Scottish Place-Names* (Batsford) 1976

The Church

Baird, A. *The Erskine Church, Falkirk 1737–1937* (Callander) 1937

Lawson, L. *The Church at Falkirk* (Falkirk Old Parish Church) 1973

Murray, C. *Records of Falkirk Parish* (2 volumes) 1988

Scott, I. and J. Ferguson, J. *Larbert Old Parish Church* (Larbert Old) 1993

Scott, I. *St Francis Xavier's Parish Falkirk 1843–1993* (St Francis) 1993

Walker, J. *St James' Parish Church, Falkirk A Short History* (St James) 1993

In addition there are several other short church histories written by members of local congregations which provide valuable information especially on more recent events.

Education

Bain, A. *Education in Stirlingshire* (ULP) 1965

Love, J. *Schools and Schoolmasters of Falkirk* (Johnston) 1898

Transport

Bailey, G. B. *Locks, Stocks and Bodies in Barrels* (Falkirk Libraries) 2000

Bowman, A.I. *Symington and the Charlotte Dundas* (Falkirk Museums) 1981

Brotchie, A.W. *The Tramways of Falkirk* (NB Traction Group) 1978

Clarkson W.W. *The Post Office in Falkirk District* (Falkirk and District Philatelic Society) 1995

Dickson, J. et al. *Travelling Through Time, Transport in Falkirk District* (Falkirk Libraries) 1993

Haldane, A.R.B. *The Drove Roads of Scotland* (Nelson) 1952

Hutton, G. *Scotland's Millennium Canals* (Stenlake) 2002

Martin, D. and Maclean, A.A. *Edinburgh and Glasgow Railway Guidebook* (Strathkelvin District) 1992

Massey, A. *The Edinburgh and Glasgow Union Canal* (Falkirk Museums) 1983

Industrial Falkirk

Bailey, G. B. *Local Ceramics* (Falkirk Museums) 2002
Campbell, R.H. *Carron Company* (Oliver and Boyd) 1961
Carrongrove: 200 years of papermaking (Argyll publishing) 2000
Watters, B. *Where Iron Runs Like Water* (John Donald) 1998

Falkirk District at War

Dickson, J. *Heroes Departed: Falkirk District during the First World War* (Falkirk Libraries) 1994
Bailey, G.B. *Grangemouth: from Airlines to Air Cadets, the Story of the Drome* (GMS) 2006
Walker, J. *Target Falkirk: Falkirk and District in the Second World War* (Falkirk Council) 2001

Health

Scott, I. *Falkirk and District Royal Infirmary 1889–1989* (Forth Valley Health Board) 1990
Hutton, G. *The Royal Scottish National Hospital 140 Years* (Forth Valley NHS Trust) 2000

The Towns and Villages

Howson, A. *Camelon: Some Historical Notes* (Falkirk Museums) 1968
Jackson, A. M. *The Redding Pit Disaster* (Falkirk Libraries) 1988
Jamieson, J *Allandale Cottages: Reminiscences* (Ceejay Print) 2005
Leask, D. *Westquarter: from family estate to model village* (Falkirk Libraries) 1986
McGrail, S. *The Story of Airth 1128–1979* 1979
Porteous, R. *Grangemouth's Ancient Heritage* (Burgh of Grangemouth) 1968
Porteous, R. *Grangemouth's Modern History* (Burgh of Grangemouth) 1973
Salmon, T. *Borrowstounness and District* (Hodge) 1913
Shieldhill History Group *Shieldhill: a glimpse of the past* (Falkirk District Libraries)
Slamannan History Group *Slamannan and Limerigg: Times to Remember*
Waugh, J. *The Vale of Bonny in History and Legend* (Falkirk Libraries) 1981

Index

Abbot's Foundry 146
Abbotskerse 26, 46, 206, 277, 283
Abbotshaugh 27, 62, 102, 299
Adam, Robert provost 125
Adam's Gote Burn 158
Agricola, Julius 3, 4, 8
Airth 50, 97, 235, 268–273, 277
Airth Castle 29, 268, 269
Airth Parish Church 270
Airth royal dockyard 269
Aitchison, Revd James 137, 143
Aitken, James lawyer 88
Aitken's Brewery 79, 121, 146, 148, 149, 196
Alexander, Walter and Sons 182, 188, 196
Allandale 253
Allied Ironfounders 181
Almond (*Haining*) Castle 85, 292
Almond Ironworks 293
Ambrose, Thomas teacher 53
Anchor Brickworks, Denny 238
Anchor Mill 237
Anderson, James 199, 287
Anderson, John 229
Anderson, Sir Robert R. architect 136
Anglo-American Oil Company 215
Antonine Wall 4–17, 106, 219, 242, 249, 256, 300
Antoninus Pius 4, 10
Arnothill, Falkirk 6,150
Arran, Earl of 39, 220
Arthur, King 13,14,15, 242
Arthur's O'on 13–16, 91, 92, 258
Arts and Civic Council 205
Assembly Rooms, Falkirk 135, 144, 151, 157
Atholl, Duke of 79
Augustinian Canons 23, 268
Avon aqueduct 109
Avon, River 1, 24, 294, 297

Back Row (Manor Street) Falkirk 61, 125, 138, 139, 159
Bailey, Geoff 9, 11, 73, 77
Bainsford 27, 93, 105, 121, 123, 126, 136, 142, 146, 149, 196
Bainsford Bridge 156
Bainsford School 141
Baird, Hugh engineer 109

Ballantine's Foundry, Bo'ness 227
Bank Street, Falkirk 47
Bankier 254, 255
Bankier Distillery 255
Banknock 1, 254, 255
Bannockburn House 74, 79
Bantaskine 61, 97
Bantaskine Tunnel 109, 110
Baptist Church, Falkirk 137
Barr, Robert and Sons 149, 196
Battle of Falkirk 1298 30–35
Battle of Falkirk 1746 75–77
Baxters Wynd, Falkirk 61,156
Baynes, Cornet 64
Bean Row, Falkirk 61
Beaton, Cardinal 39
Beaton, Mary 39
Beeby, John 160
Beechmount, Larbert 266
Begg, Revd William 134, 137, 247
Bell's Meadow 189
Bellenden family 82
Bellenden Sir John 47
Bellenden, Revd Adam 67
Bellenden, Sir James 49
Bells Meadow, Falkirk 158
Bells Wynd, Falkirk 197
Bellsdyke Hospital 265–266
Bennetstown 278
Birkhill Clay Mine 231
Black, Alexander architect 122
Black, William architect 152, 153, 161, 162
Blackbraes 292
Blackness 199
Blackness Castle 223–224
Blairlodge Academy 280–281
Blakey, Leonard architect 179
Blakhal, Gilbert 55
Blind Harry 33, 270
Blinkbonny Home 164
Bo'ness 7, 8, 9, 69, 90, 97, 98, 107, 147, 174, 199, 208, 219–231, 222–231,
Bo'ness and Kinneil Railway 231
Bo'ness Fair 231
Bo'ness Journal 224
Bo'ness Motor Museum 231
Bo'ness Pottery 227

Bog Road, Falkirk 27, 182, 194
bomb shelters 189, 190
Bonar, Revd John 262
Bonny, River 74, 249, 254
Bonnybridge 4, 99, 103, 107,141,147, 249–256
Bonnybridge Foundry 252
Bonnybridge Power Station 167, 168
Bonnybridge Public Hall 253, 254
Bonnybridge Toll 250
Bonnymuir, Battle of (1820) 99, 251
Bonnywater 249
Booth Place, Falkirk 11
Bothkennar 50
Bothwell, Earl of 42
Boulton, Matthew engineer 102, 221
Boyd Street, Falkirk 156
Branks, Revd William 247
Bridgend, Avonbridge 297
Bridgeness 222–223
Bridgeness slab 7
Brightons 10, 277, 279
British Aluminium (*Alcan*) Company 196, 308
British Petroleum 215, 219, 308
Brocklay, George town drummer 52
Brockville Park 157, 187, 189
Brodie, Thomas Dawson 163
Broompark Church 239
Broomside Foundry 252
Broughton, Barony of 47
Brown and Peddie, architects 151
Bruce family of Airth 257, 269, 270
Bruce family of Stenhouse 269
Bruce, James the Abyssinian Traveller 92, 259
Bruce, Revd Robert of Kinnaird 258–259
Bruce, Robert I, King 220, 233
Bruce, Robert of Airth 269
Bruce, Sir Michael of Stenhouse 15, 91
Buchanan, Billy 249, 256
Burgh Buildings, Falkirk 152, 154
Burgh Charter of 1600 48, 298
Burgh Hospital, Falkirk 161
Burnbank Foundry, Falkirk 146
Burnet, John James architect 263
Burnett, Revd William 70
Burnfoot, Falkirk 149, 158
Burns Court, Falkirk 135, 137
Burns, James lawyer 146
Burns, James teacher 139
Burns, Robert 156, 225
bus companies 188
Bute Memorial 34
Bute, Marquis of 34
Bute, men of 34

Cadell, William 90, 91, 94, 282, 244
Cairneymount Church, Maddiston 293
Calatria [*Calateria, Calitar*] 24
Caledonian Railway 113, 211, 236
Calentyre, Christiane de 35
Calentyre, Patrick de 35
calico printing 235

California 291–292
Callander, Sir William of Dorrator 58
Callendar Abbot's Foundry 146, 181, 194
Callendar Centre 197
Callendar family 24–28, 35
Callendar House 24, 25, 32, 37, 40, 42, 43, 64, 65, 66, 68, 73, 75, 79, 85, 87, 109, 197, 204
Callendar Park 6, 11,158
Callendar Park College of Education 199
Callendar Riggs 12, 120, 121, 153, 182
Callendar Square 202, 203
Callendar, Court Book of 59–63
Cambuskenneth Abbey 23, 256
Camelon 2, 3, 4, 6, 9, 19, 74, 100, 105, 106, 107, 121, 141, 147, 151, 157, 196, 242–249, 256
Camelon Cemetery 157
Camelon Chemical Works 245, 248
Camelon Parish Church 247
Campfield 30, 99
Canavan, Dennis MSP 304–305
Cannerton Brickworks 255
Carmuirs 8, 85, 182, 194, 247
Carmuirs School 247
Carriden 4, 7, 12, 175, 199, 222, 223
Carriden House 175, 222
Carriden Parish Church 223
Carron 104, 113, 156
Carron Company 88, 89, 91–96, 98, 101, 104,106, 107, 111, 115, 126, 146, 147, 195, 200, 204, 244, 257, 259, 260, 262, 267, 277, 284, 293, 295
Carron Dock 211
Carron House 261
Carron Valley water scheme 182
Carron, River 1, 3, 8, 13, 15, 62, 65, 74, 83, 90, 92, 107, 208, 235, 236, 242, 260, 299
Carronades 94, 107
Carrongrove Mill 236, 237
Carronhall Pit 277
Carronshore 101, 207, 260–261, 272
Carronvale, Larbert 266
Castle Laurie Foundry, Falkirk 176
Castlecary 4, 8, 106, 253
cattle trysts 81–85, 278, 261, 292
Causewayend 112, 292
Central Electric Generating Company 168
Central Ironmoulders Association 155
Central Regional Council 199
Chapel Yard, Bonnybridge 250
Charity School, Falkirk 141, 144
Charles I, King 56, 57, 58, 63
Charles II, King 63, 65, 68
Charlotte Dundas 108, 208
Chartism 100
Chattan Stove Works 252
Cheyne, Reginald le 35
Children's and Youth Theatres 204
Christ's Church, Falkirk 135
churches:
    Airth 272
    Avonbridge 297

Bo'ness 227, 228
Bonnybridge 253
Camelon 247, 248
Denny 235, 238, 239
Grangemouth 209, 210, 213, 214
Larbert/Stenhousemuir 262, 263, 268
Laurieston 283
Redding 286
Slamannan 295
Braes area 292, 293
cinemas 186, 187, 224
Cistern Lane, Falkirk 117, 133, 134
'Cleddens', Falkirk 12, 60
Coal Heugh Brae 93, 113
coal mines, industrial unrest 101
coal mines, working conditions 97–98
coal mining:
    Airth 270, 277
    Banknock 255
    Bo'ness 225, 230
    Denny 236, 240
    Dunmore 274
    Redding 284, 285
    Slamannan 295, 296
    Braes area 292, 293
Cochrane's Academy 144
Cockburn Street, Falkirk 158
Cockburn's Foundry, Falkirk 146, 181
coin hoard 12
Coldstream Guards 64
Columbian Stove Works, Bonnybridge 252
Comely Park School, Falkirk 144
Commercial Bank, Falkirk 155
Congregational Church, Falkirk 135, 136
Corbet, Dr John 120
Corbiehall, Bo'ness 222
Corn Exchange, Falkirk 120–121, 122, 126,
    145, 152, 153, 157
Corporation Gas Act 166
County Fever Hospital, Camelon 161
County Mining Institute 140
County Trades School 164
Cow Wynd 61, 77, 93, 113, 155, 159
Cowan, David 147
Crawford, Dame Margaret 52
Cromwell, Oliver 58, 63, 64
Cross Well, Falkirk 66, 67
Crosses Chemical Works, Camelon 245
Crosskeys Inn, Falkirk 156
Cruikshanks Foundry, Bo'ness 236
Cunningham, Revd Robert 280
Custonhall Chemical Works 236

Dalderse 28
Dalderse Foundry, Falkirk 102, 146
Dalquhairn, Avonbridge 297
David I, King 25, 268
David II, King 35
Dawson family of Carron 102
Dempster, Revd John 100, 239
Denny 2, 147, 199, 231, 234–241
Denny Paper Works 237
Denny Parish Church 234

Denny Town House 239
Dennyloanhead 253–254
Denovan 235
Diageo Company 254
Dickson, John 174, 176
Dishingtoun, John teacher 53
Doak's Dance Hall 182
Dobbie Forbes Foundry, Larbert 181, 264
Dobbie, Major Robert 264, 265
Dollar Park 74, 75, 179
Dorcas Society 137
Douglas, Lady Agnes 40
Downie, Thomas teacher 139
Drummond, Lord John 77
Drummond, William teacher 54
Dryburgh 19, 233
Dumyat Drive, Falkirk 79
Dundas family 27, 212
Dundas School, Grangemouth 213
Dundas, Lord Thomas of West Kerse 108,
    131, 132
Dundas, Sir Lawrence of West Kerse 105,
    206, 282
Dundas, Thomas of Quarrol 92, 260
Dunipace 50, 231–234, 235, 237, 240, 257,
    270
Dunipace House 234
Dunipace, Hills of 29, 231, 232, 233
Dunipace, Place of 234
Dunmore 97, 268, 271, 273–275
Dunmore Moss 274
Dunmore Park 275
Dunmore Pottery 274–275
Dunmore village 276
Durham, Bishop of 30, 32
Dymock's Buildings, Bo'ness 224

Earls Burn 158
East Bridge Street, Falkirk 46, 118
East Burn, Falkirk 46, 158
East Port, Falkirk 47
East Stirlingshire Cricket Club 175
East Stirlingshire Development Association
    181
East Stirlingshire Football Club 157
Edinburgh–Glasgow Railway 113, 249, 250,
    279, 300
Edmonstone, William 79
Education:
    Airth 272–273
    Bo'ness 229
    Bonnybridge 253
    Camelon 246, 247
    Denny and Dunipace 240
    Dunmore 274
    Falkirk 138–145, 183, 198
    Grangemouth 210, 213–214, 218, 301, 302
    Larbert/Stenhousemuir 263, 266–267
    Polmont 280
    Redding 286
Edward I, King 14, 28, 29, 220
Edward VIII, King 183
electricity supply 166

Elizabeth, Princess 47
Elphinstone 269
Elphinstone family 273
Elphinstone Pans 276
Elphinstone Tower 273
Errol, Earl of 85, 115
Erskine Church, Falkirk 128, 129, 132, 143
Erskine, Revd Ebeneezer 128
de Erth family 269
'Engagement' the 58
Etna Foundry, Falkirk 194
Experiment, The 107

Fairbairn, George nailmaker 244, 245
Fairbairn's Square 244
Falkirk and District Motor Car Company 167
Falkirk and Larbert Water Trust 158
Falkirk Bus Station 182
Falkirk College 183, 198, 199, 303–304
Falkirk Corporation Act 153
Falkirk Cottage Hospital 162, 163
Falkirk Football Club 157, 187, 195, 305
Falkirk fort 10
Falkirk Free Church 124, 160
Falkirk Gas Works Company 118
Falkirk Golf Club 157
Falkirk Herald 122, 156, 162, 163, 173, 176, 249, 287
Falkirk Ice Rink 186
Falkirk (*and District Royal*) Infirmary 163–164, 175, 183, 185–186, 190, 306–308
Falkirk Iron Company 102, 176, 181, 195, 200
Falkirk Joint Stock Gas Company 165
Falkirk Lions 187
Falkirk Mail 161
Falkirk Parish Church 19, 37, 38, 46, 130, 131, 153
Falkirk Parish Churchyard 34
Falkirk Police Act (1859) 123–127
Falkirk Power Station 166
Falkirk Stadium, Westfield 305,306
Falkirk tartan 12
Falkirk Steeple 66, 72, 117
Falkirk Trades Council 155
Falkirk Wheel 110, 249, 298, 299–301
Fankerton 237
Faughlin Burn 158
Feuars of Falkirk 119–120, 122, 123, 152
Fever Hospital, Falkirk 160–70
Firs Park, Falkirk 157
Fleming, Lady Agnes 40
Fleming, Mary 39
Fleshmarket Close, Falkirk 61
Flodden, Battle of (1513) 273
Forbes family of Callendar 109, 197, 246
Forbes, William of Callendar 85–89, 115, 117, 119, 131, 132
Forbes, William (*the second*) of Callendar 233, 247
Forest, John teacher 54
Forester family of Torwood 257
Forester, Sir Alexander of Torwood 257

Forth and Clyde Canal 83, 89, 104–106, 109, 110, 111, 115, 167, 196, 206, 214, 243, 247, 249, 250, 261, 282, 299,
Forth and Clyde Ironworks 181, 194
Forth Ports Authority 218
Forth Valley College 198, 303–304
Forth, River 1, 2, 8, 9, 19, 86, 90, 269, 270, 271, 272, 275, 278, 299,
Free Church, Denny 235
Free Church, Falkirk 134, 166
Free Church, Grangemouth 209
Free Church, Larbert 263
Free Colliers 101, 284–285

Gair, John lawyer 124
Garbett, Samuel 90, 91, 93, 94, 260
Gardner, Peter, master potter 274
Garibaldi Pit 277
Garrison, Falkirk 134, 197
Gartcows, Falkirk 98,150, 158
gas supply 165, 166
Gascoigne, Charles 93–94, 95, 101, 260, 261
General Strike (1926) 181
George Square, Camelon 244
Gibson, Mrs Harriet 162
Gil Burn, Kinneil 221
Gillespie Graham, James architect 132
Gillespie, Revd Thomas 130
Girdwood, James surgeon 124, 126
Glasgow Buildings, Falkirk 150, 197
Glebe Street, Falkirk 152
Glen Burn 31
Glen, William of Forganhall 117
Glenbervie Golf Course 157
Gleneagles Hotel 238
Glengarry, 'Young' 79
Goldie, Dennis provost 201
Gordon, Andrew 147
Goshen, Stenhousemuir 2
Graeme High School, Falkirk 183, 301–302
de Graeme, John 33–34
Graham of Claverhouse 69
Graham, James of Airth 270
Graham, Walter surgeon 78
Graham's Muir 30
Grahams Road Church, Falkirk 136
Graham family of Airth 270
Grahamsdyke Road 9
Grahamston 30, 93, 121, 123, 124, 125, 146, 149, 157, 195
Grahamston Foundry 146
Grahamston Parish Church 136
Grahamston Station 113, 197
Grammar School of Falkirk 138, 140, 141, 143, 145
Grand Theatre, Falkirk186
Grandsable Cemetery, Polmont 32
Grange Burn 208
Grange Burn Mouth 207
Grange Dock 211
Grange Public School, Grangemouth 174
Grangemouth 107, 111, 141, 174, 199, 201, 206–219, 272, 299

Grangemouth Airfield 216
Grangemouth Coal Company 211
Grangepans 222, 226
Grant, John A. W. architect 290
Greenhill 251, 256
Grossart, James teacher 142, 143
Grossart's School, Grahamston 143
Guisborough, Walter of 30
Gunn's Square, Camelon 244

Hadden, Dr David 126
Haggs 254
Haggs Parish Church 254
Haining (Almond) Castle 85, 292
Hallglen 31, 204
Hamilton family 220
Hamilton, David architect 118, 262, 270
Hamilton, Duchess Anne 221, 222
Hamilton, Dukes of 82, 83, 93, 221, 277, 278, 284,
Hamilton, Gilbert 220
Hart, Alexander ship builder 108, 208
Hawley, General Henry 74, 75
Headswood, Denny 237
Henderson, Robert 123, 124
Henry VIII , King 39
Herbert, Catherine of Dunmore 276
Herbertshire Castle 233
Herbertshire Mill 236, 237
Herbertshire Pit 236
Hereford, Earl of 32
High School, Falkirk 143,144,145, 198
High Station Road, Falkirk 153
High Street, Falkirk 46, 61, 79, 93, 117
Hippodrome Theatre, Bo'ness 224
Holyrood Abbey 23, 26, 46, 269
Home Guard 191, 192
Hope Street, Falkirk 74, 132, 157
Hope, family 27
horsemarket of Falkirk120
house building 194, 203, 303
Howgate, Falkirk 155, 170, 183, 197, 200, 202
Howgate Centre 47, 202
Howgate windows 77–78
Hurlet Chemical Works, Camelon 245

ice hockey 187
industrial decline 229, 308, 248, 256,
industrial unrest 155, 180,181
Inveravon 2, 4, 5, 8
Inveresk Paper Company 237
iron foundries:
  Bo'ness 227
  Bonnybridge 252, 253
  Camelon 247
  Denny 236
  Falkirk 102, 146–147, 176–177, 181, 194–195
  Larbert/Stenhousemuir 265
  Laurieston 282
Irving Church, Camelon 247
Irving, Revd Lewis Hay 124, 125, 126, 137, 141

Jacobites 72, 73, 74, 75, 77, 78, 83, 234, 271,
James I, King 36
James II, King 37
James III, King 37
James IV, King 269
James V, King 38
James VI, King 41, 127, 298
James VII, King 69
Jenny Mair's Burn 158
Johnston, Fred 163
Johnstone, Alexander of Kirkland 71
Johnstone, Chevalier James 75, 81
Johnstoun, James 'reader' 53
Jones and Campbell, Larbert 264, 265
Jones, James of Larbert 264–265
Joss, Miss matron 162
Junction Dock, Grangemouth 208

Kalentyr [*Calentir*] 26
Kemper Avenue, Falkirk 12
Kerse Bridge 299
Kerse House, Grangemouth 215
Kerse Lane 138, 141, 157
Kerse, lands of 46
Kidd's Buildings, Falkirk 183, 184
Kier, Thomas provost 123
Kilmarnock, 4th Earl of 73, 81, 82
Kincaid, Grizel teacher 54
Kings Arms, Falkirk 156
Kinnaird 97, 261
Kinnaird House 109, 258, 266
Kinneil 4, 8, 219–222
Kinneil Church 222
Kinneil Colliery 230
Kinneil fortlet 219
Kinneil House 220, 221
Kirk Session of Falkirk 50–55, 58
Kirk Wynd, Falkirk 47, 61, 160
Kirkland, Dunipace 232
Knights Hospitaller 233
Knights Templar 26, 233
Knox, John 41

Ladysmill 46,158
Langtoft, Pierre de 30
Langlees 196
Larbert 50, 65, 83, 92, 96,113, 147, 234, 256
Larbert High School 301–302
Larbert Parish Church 118, 256, 262
Laurieston 4, 8, 9,103, 141, 147, 168, 281–283, 285
Lawson, Lewis 22
Lennox, Earls of 25
Leslie, Alexander 57
Letham 277
Levingstoun, James teacher 54
Lilbourne, Lady Alice
Lime Wharf Chemical Works, Camelon 245
Lincoln, Earl of 32
Linlithgow, Earl of 48
Lint Riggs, Falkirk 47, 160
Livingston:
  family 35, 36–49, 85, 86, 115, 128, 233, 257

family effigies 38
family of Westquarter 288, 289
Alexander, 3rd Knight of Callendar 36
Alexander, 5th Lord of Callendar 38–39, 40
Alexander, 7th Lord of Callendar 48, 49, 298
Alexander, 2nd Earl of Callendar 67, 68
Alexander, 3rd Earl of Callendar 69
James, 1st Lord of Callendar 37
James, 1st Earl of Callendar 56–59, 61, 63–69, 221
James, 4th Earl of Callendar 70, 71
John, Master of 39
Lady Ann, Countess of Kilmarnock 72, 73, 75
Lady Helenora of Bantaskine 68
William, 1st Knight of Callendar 35, 36
William, 6th Lord of Callendar 40–42, 44
Magdalen 41
Mary 39, 41, 42
Sir Alexander of Dalderse 68
Lochgreen Hospital 153
Lochiel, Cameron of 77
Lock 16 106, 107, 111, 112, 196, 243, 247
Longcroft 177, 254
Luke family, papermakers 237

Macdonald, Sir George archaeologist 9
MacGibbon, David architect 154
Macgregor Chalmers, Peter architect 223
MacLachlan, Revd Paul 134–135
MacMillianites 282
Maddiston 292–294
Magdalene, St Mary 30
Maggie Woods Loan, Falkirk 6, 75
Main, R and A, ironfounders Camelon 194
Mair, Craig 97
Malcolm III, King 20, 21, 22
Malherb family 294
Manor Street 46, 61, 128, 160
Manuel, Priory of 292
Maries, 'the four' 39–40
Mary Queen of Scots 39–45
Masonic Lodge, Falkirk 166
McCowan, Robert confectioner 265
McKell, Robert engineer 104, 106
McKillops Foundry, Laurieston 282
McNay, Charles potter 227
Mechanics Institute, Falkirk 144
Melville, General Robert 94
Mentieth family 270
Methodist Church, Falkirk 137
Methodist Church, Reddingmuirhead 288
middle schools experiment, Grangemouth 218
Middlefield, Falkirk 105
Middlemass, James 152
Midland Junction Railway 160
Millar, John railway engineer 279
Millennium Link 298–301
Miller, Patrick 94,107
Millfield, Polmont 279

Milltown of Dunipace 235
Milnquarter, Bonnybridge 256
Mitchell, Robert 16
Monck, General George 64, 65
Monteath, family 27
Montrose, Duchess of 158, 186
Montrose, Duke of 179
Montrose, Marquis of 57, 66
Moray, Earl of 39, 42
de Morham family 233
Morton, Earl of 44
Morton, James 215
mortsafes (Airth) 271
Motherwell Bridge Company 168
motte, Bonnybridge 250
motte, Slamannan 294
Muiravonside 22, 50, 189, 292
Muiravonside Church 293
Mumrills 8, 9, 10, 31
Mungal 27
Munro, Colonel Robert 79
Munro, Dr Obsdale 79
Murray family of Dunmore 273
Murray, John 4th Earl of Dunmore 273
Murray, Lord George 74, 75, 77, 79

nail making in Camelon 100, 244
nail making in Laurieston 282
Napiers of Merchiston 281–283
National Covenant 57
Neilson, James 125
Nervii 10
Nether Kinneil 1
New Merchiston 282
Newcarron Village 204
Newmarket Street, Falkirk 120, 132
Nicol, James teacher 54
Nimmo family, coalmasters 286, 289, 290
Nobel's Explosive Works 290–291
Norfolk, Earl of 32
North British Railway 113

Old Dock, Grangemouth 208
Oswald, Revd John 247

Palace Hill, Falkirk 25
Panbrae, Bo'ness 226
paper making 236, 240
Parkhill House, Polmont 280
Parkhouse Foundry, Falkirk 181
Peake, Dr Joseph 161
Peddie and Kinear architects 154
Peddie, Robert provost 216
Peoples Church, Falkirk 130
pest graves 63
Pineapple, Dunmore 275, 276
pit props, Bo'ness 227
plague 63
Pleasance 6, 11, 139, 140, 204,
Police Station Falkirk 301
Polish soldiers 192
Polmont 27, 50, 113, 189, 277–281
Polmont Bank 280

Polmont House 279
Polmont Parish Church 278
Polmont Park 279
Polmont Young Offenders Institution 281
Polmonthill 2
Pont, Timothy 21
poor relief 54, 164
Poorhouse 158, 164, 165
Port Downie, Camelon 245, 247
Post Office, Falkirk 154, 197
Prestonpans, Battle of (1745) 73, 93
Primrose family of Dunipace 234
Primrose, Sir Archibald of Dunipace 74
Princes Park, Falkirk 153
Princes Street, Falkirk 183
Prospect Hill, Falkirk 109
public humiliation 54–55

Quarrol 92, 261
Quarrolshore 260, 261
Quarter Mine 236
quoiting 156

Ragged School, Falkirk 141
railways 112 114, 211, 218, 231, 236, 250–251, 254, 264, 279, 295, 296
Randolph Hill, Denny 238
Rankine's Folly, Falkirk 123
Rashiehill 61
Raybould, John nailmaker 282
Red Lion Inn, Falkirk 151
Redding 27, 31, 82, 97,100, 101, 283–288
Redding Colliery 98
Redding Pit Disaster 286–287
Reddingmuirhead 288
Reddingrigmuir 83
refractory brick making 195, 252
Reid, John 16, 25, 120
Relief Church, Falkirk 130, 133, 136
Rennie, John engineer 109
Renny, Patrick teacher 54
Rhind, David, architect 254
Robert III, King 36
Roberts Wynd, Falkirk 77, 85, 202
Roebuck, Dr John 90, 91, 221, 223, 227
Roman bath house 12
Roman coin hoard 12
Romans 3–17, 18, 219, 242
Ronald, David 160, 164
Rosebank Distillery 146, 282
Rosebery, Lord 145
Rosehall, Falkirk 11
Roughcastle 8, 10, 73, 249
Roxy Theatre, Falkirk 129, 187
RSN Hospital, Larbert 265–266
Russel, James lawyer 8, 293

salt making 226, 270
Saltire Society 301
Salton Iron Works 162
Sauchieburn, Battle of (1488) 269, 270
Schank, John 108
schiltroms 32

School and Well Committee, Camelon 246
School of Arts, Falkirk 145
Scotland's Close, Bo'ness 224
Scott, Revd John 248
Scottish Aviation Limited 215
Scottish Central Railway 264
Scottish Dyes 215
Scottish Oils 215
Scottish Parliament 304
Scottish Railway Preservation Society 231
Scottish Tar Distillers 245
Scottish TUC 155
SCWS Soap Works, Grangemouth 215
Sea Box Society, Bo'ness 222
Seabegs 8, 249, 250
Sealock 207
Septimus Severus 16
Seton, Mary 39
Sheriff Court, Falkirk 151, 154, 156
Sherriff, George 102
Sherrifmuir, Battle of (1715) 71
Shieldhill 92,101, 285, 291–292
Silver Row, Falkirk 46, 128, 142, 154, 155, 182, 197
Simpson, James 285
Sinclairs, Earls of Orkney 233
Singer Sewing Machine Company 252
Skew Bridge, Laurieston 113
Slamannan 1, 22, 70, 285, 294–296
Slamannan Railway 112, 292
Slaughterhouse, Falkirk 157
Slirrie, Revd Andrew 69
Smeaton, John engineer 92, 104, 105
Smith and Wellstood, Bonnybridge 252
Smith of Maddiston 293
Smith, Adam lawyer 125, 126, 126
Smith, James 251
Solemn League and Covenant 57
South Bantaskine 77, 255
spitfire funds 192
St Alexanders (*Alchanters*) chapel, Dunipace 232
St Alexanders Church, Denny 240
St Andrews Episcopal Church, Dunmore 273
St Andrews Parish Church, Falkirk 134
St Fond, Faujas de 95
St Francis RC School 142
St Francis Xavier's Church, Falkirk 135
St Helens Chapel, Bonnybridge 250
St James Parish Church, Falkirk 136
St Modan 19
St Modans Parish Church 135, 204
Stainton family 102
Steele, Matthew architect 224
Stein family, brick manufacturers 238, 252, 279
Stenhouse 91, 92, 258, 259
Stenhousemuir 2, 83, 256, 257–258, 261–268
Stenhousemuir Cricket Club 267
Stenhousemuir Football Club 157, 267
Stentmasters of Falkirk 115–119, 120, 122, 123,

Stewart, Dugald philosopher 221
Stewart, Sir John of Bonkhill 34
Stirling, family 27
Stirling, William, architect 135
Stirlingshire Midland Railway 113
Stoneywood 237
Straiton, Alexander 250
Strang, William 155
Strathcarron Hospice 238
Stuart, Prince Charles Edward 73, 74, 75,
    78,79, 115
Summerford 158
Sunnyside Foundry 181
Swords Wynd , Falkirk 135, 197
Symeon of Durham 20
Symington, William engineer 107, 108, 109,
    112, 208

Tanners Brae, Falkirk 158, 197
tartan, the Falkirk 12
Tattie Kirk, Falkirk 133, 136
Taylor, Henry builder 118
Taylor, Robert ironfounder 265
Temperance Hall, Bonnybridge 253
Temperance Hotel, Falkirk 151
Temple-Denny 233
Thanes Hall 25
Thanes of Callendar 24–26
'Think Falkirk' campaign 201
Thornbridge 282
Thornhill 150, 182
Thracians 9
Tophill, Falkirk 109
Torphichen 37, 46, 233
Torwood 3, 4, 34, 56, 65, 257, 269
Torwood (*Tappoch*) Broch 3
Torwood Castle 257
Torwoodhall, Larbert 266
Towers refractory brickworks 195
Town Hall, Bo'ness 224, 225, 227
Town Hall, Falkirk 145,152, 153,
    154,157,166, 197
Town Hall, Grangemouth 212
trams 167–168, 187
Trinity Church, Camelon 247
Tryst Golf Club 157, 267
Tungrians 9,10
turnpike roads 103

UFOs in Bonnybridge 256
Union Canal 109–111, 124, 245, 279, 290,
    293, 299
Union Inn 111, 112
Ure, George ironmaster 161, 252

Vale Paper Mill, Denny 237
Victoria Park, Falkirk 30
Victoria Public Library, Grangemouth 212

Walker, John 189, 217
Wallace, William 14, 28, 29–35, 270
Wallacestone 29, 284
War Memorials 179, 193, 214–215, 229, 283
Water of Bonny 249
water supply 66, 124, 158, 182
Watling Lodge, Camelon 6, 8, 9, 242, 256
Watt, James engineer 102, 221
Watters, Brian 102
Well, St Alexander's 232
Wellstood, Stephen 252
West Bridge Street, Falkirk 153, 158
West Burn, Falkirk 158
West Church, Falkirk 130
West Church, Grangemouth 210
West Kerse 206
Westfield, Falkirk 305
Westpark Church, Denny 239
Westquarter 31, 61, 283, 285, 288–291
Westquarter Burn 31
Westquarter Chemical Works 290
Westquarter Doocot 289
Westquarter House 286, 289, 290
Westquarter Model Village 290
Westquarter Port, Falkirk 47
Westquarter School 289
whaling in Bo'ness 226
Whitesiderigmuir 83
Whitworth, Robert engineer 109
Whyteside 273
Wilkins, William architect 275
William III, King 69
Wilson, Revd Dr James 22, 88, 89, 130, 132,
    138
Wilson's Buildings 123,136, 151, 157
Wilsons of Banknock 255
Wilsons of South Bantaskine 76, 255
Woodlands High School, Falkirk 301–302
Woodside Home, Falkirk 164
Wooer Street, Falkirk 61,125, 173–179, 202,
    214
World War II 188–193, 217
Wornell, John master potter 212
Wright, Revd Edward 68

York Buildings Company 71, 72

Zetland Park, Grangemouth 212, 218
Zetland School, Grangemouth 213
Zetland, Earl of 209